# CHRONICLES
## OF
# WORLD
# WAR II

**Text**
Dr. Duncan Anderson
Dr. Stephen Badsey
David G. Chandler
Dr. Paddy Griffith
Colin McIntyre
Sean McKnight
Gary Sheffield
Michael C. Tagg

**Photography**
UPI/Bettmann
Keystone Collection
Kristall Productions
Peter Newark's Military Pictures
TRH Pictures

**Design**
Philip Clucas
Clive Dorman
Sally Strugnell

**Commissioning Editor**
Andrew Preston

**Publishing Assistants**
Edward Doling
Laura Potts

**Photo Research**
Leora Kahn
Kenneth Johnson

**Editorial**
Jane Adams
David G. Chandler
Fleur Robertson

**Production**
Ruth Arthur
David Proffit
Sally Connolly
Andrew Whitelaw

**Director of Production**
Gerald Hughes

4954 Chronicles of World War II
This edition published in 1997 by CLB
Distributed in the U.S.A. by BHB International, Inc.
30 Edison Drive, Wayne, New Jersey 07470
© 1997 CLB International, Godalming, Surrey, U.K.
Printed and bound in Singapore by KHL Printing Co Pte Ltd
All rights reserved
ISBN 1-85833-763-1

# CHRONICLES OF WORLD WAR II

**David G. Chandler**

**Colin McIntyre**

**Michael C. Tagg**

*CLB*

# Contents

# INTRODUCTION

Air supremacy was vital during World War II. RAF Hurricanes (left) were stable gun platforms, able to absorb punishment, and were an essential part of victory in the Battle of Britain.

The Second World War proved to be the bloodiest and most costly in history. Between 1939 and 1945, millions of troops and civilians were killed or injured, vast areas laid waste and once-proud cities reduced to smoking rubble. It was fought as a total war, transforming the face of the world in many unforeseen ways. It was, indeed, the defining conflict of the 20th century.

Over time, it became clear that some battles were more critical than others, and that a few of them could be considered as turning points that would help to determine the final outcome of the war. Some fighting was crucial because of the amounts of men or material destroyed, for example in the titanic engagements on the Russian front. Other battles had an effect out of all proportion to their immediate results. The destruction of the *Graf Spee* and *Bismarck*, for example, accounted for only two ships. Thereafter, however, German capital ships were only employed with caution and the U-boat service had to bear the brunt of the naval war.

Whether on land, sea or in the air, every battle had its own character and importance but, for the men fighting and dying in them, each was a particular kind of hell. For several years, the burning sands of North Africa had seen men and machines sweep back and forth until the Battle of El Alamein proved to be decisive. In the desert wastes, the men who fought also had to contend with heat, thirst and flies. Very different was the snowy desolation around Stalingrad. Here the oil froze in engines, and the troops were as likely to suffer frostbite as wounds from the enemy. In the Pacific theatre, the landscape was different again, with tropical heat rotting the clothes and sapping the strength of those who had to fight their way through jungles.

In due course, the very nature of the fighting changed. In the early struggles between Britain and Germany for control of the sea-lanes, and in the devastating *Blitzkrieg* which took German armies to victory after victory in Europe, the opening moves were ones of skill and innovation. The fighting was largely between professional soldiers, or trained reserves well prepared for combat. As Russia, Japan and the United States entered the fighting, logistics and sheer numbers began to tell. The industrial might of the combatant nations was strained to breaking point by the urgent need to arm and supply massive armies. By the time the Soviets launched Operation 'Bagration' in 1944, they were able to organise 1.2 million men in a single offensive. Military technology also changed rapidly. The light tanks of the early war years were replaced by mighty *Panzers* and the famous Soviet T-34 series in which heavy armour was combined with large-calibre guns to create powerful mobile striking forces.

This volume looks at some of the most important battles of the war. The account opens with the naval fighting which led to the sinking of the *Graf Spee*, just a few weeks after war began. Battle by battle the book moves on to the conclusion of the carnage. With a wealth of photographs, the text explains the progress of the fighting, and the impact of new weapons and tactics.

By recording many of the key battles of World War II, this book presents a wide-ranging view of the fighting which engulfed the world in destruction for almost six years.

Left: a German soldier, his combat knife tucked in the front of his jacket, shows the strain of continual fighting.

# THE BATTLE OF THE RIVER PLATE

**Right: the *Admiral Graf Spee* is launched, to a forest of Nazi salutes, at Wilhelmshaven on 30 June, 1934. She was actually completed eighteen months later, in January 1936, in time to take part in cruises through Spanish waters during the Civil War, in which Germany supported General Franco against the Republican government.**

Before the Second World War began, Germany sent out two of her three pocket battleships to act as raiders: the *Deutschland* to the North Atlantic and the *Admiral Graf Spee* to the South Atlantic.

Slipping out of Wilhelmshafen on 21 August, 1939, the *Graf Spee*, followed three days later by the *Deutschland*, sailed far north beyond the Faeroes. Neither ship was spotted either by the Royal Navy or by aircraft of RAF Coastal Command.

Hitler hoped that after his defeat of Poland, Britain and France would accept a negotiated peace. So for the first three weeks of war the two raiders were told not to attack any merchantmen.

Freed from this restriction on 26 September, 1939, the *Graf Spee* sank the 5,000-ton British steamer *Clement* off Pernambuco in Brazil, and the *Deutschland* sank the 5,000-ton *British Stonegate*.

Although the *Admiral Graf Spee*, under Captain Hans Langsdorff, went on to a very successful raiding career, the *Deutschland* did not. She next captured the U.S. merchantman *City of Flint* and then sank a Norwegian ship. Two neutral vessels out of three was extremely embarrassing, so she was ordered home, and her name was later changed to *Lutzow*. Hitler felt that, should she be sunk, the loss of a ship called the *Deutschland* would be too great a propaganda triumph for the enemy.

The *Admiral Graf Spee* was a fine ship. Supposedly restricted by naval treaties to 10,000 tons, she was in fact well over 12,000. Her main armament of six 11-inch guns, and a secondary armament of eight 6-inch guns, made her a powerful enemy for any British cruisers to tackle. Add thick armour plating and a speed of 26 knots and she was more than a match for any British ships about.

Her next successes as a raider were against

ships using the sea route from Capetown, at the southernmost tip of South Africa, en route to Britain. In fairly quick succession she accounted for four more British merchant ships, *Newton Beech*, *Ashlea*, *Huntsman* and *Trevanion*, before deciding to make for the Indian Ocean.

Here she was less successful, sinking only the small tanker *Africa Shell* in the Mozambique Channel between the African mainland and the French island of Madagascar. She returned to the Atlantic again.

By then she was fulfilling another role in addition to sinking merchantmen. Simply by existing she tied up a large number of British warships, needed elsewhere, searching for her.

As well as the main British South Atlantic squadron of two 8-inch gun cruisers and two 6-inch gun cruisers under Commodore Henry Harwood RN (Force 'G'), there was another force of cruisers based on Capetown (Force 'H'), and much stronger forces further north, including several battleships and aircraft carriers.

A few days later, the *Admiral Graf Spee* sank two more British ships, but one of them, the 10,000 ton *Doric Star* managed to get off an R-R-R 'Raider Report' before she was sunk.

Commodore Harwood commanding Force 'G' then had to guess at Captain Langsdorff's intentions. Would the *Graf Spee* head north and homewards, or would she continue raiding. If so, would she attack the rich shipping traffic off Rio de Janeiro in Brazil, or that in the River Plate estuary between Argentina and Uruguay? Furthermore, would she raid the Falkland Islands, where the German Admiral after whom the ship was named had been defeated in World War I?

Harwood decided that the River Plate was the most likely objective. He ordered three of his cruisers – the 8-inch gun HMS *Exeter*, under Captain Frederick Bell, and the two smaller 6-inch gun cruisers: his flagship HMS *Ajax*, under Captain C.H.L. Woodhouse, and the New Zealand ship HMNZS *Achilles*, under Captain

Left: a closer view of damage to the *Admiral Graf Spee*, showing where British shellfire penetrated the hull near the waterline. Not all the black marks are actual holes, however; some are simply scars from shell splinters. In all, the *Admiral Graf Spee* was hit by three 8-inch shells from HMS *Exeter* and seventeen 6-inch shells from the two other cruisers. Only one pierced her armoured decks. Thirty-six of her crew were killed and sixty injured.

A sad end to any ship - the *Admiral Graf Spee*, after leaving Montevideo, sailed into the roads outside the harbour and was scuttled and blown up (right) by the skeleton crew that had remained on board. The rest had been taken off by the supply ship *Tacoma* and ferried across the River Plate to Buenos Aires.

Edward Parry – to rendezvous 150 miles east of the River Plate on 12 December, 1939. His other 8-inch gun cruiser, HMS *Cumberland,* was being refitted in the Falkland Islands, and could stay there and defend the islands if necessary.

Next day, shortly after 0600 hours, smoke was sighted and at 0614 HMS *Exeter* reported: 'I think it is a pocket battleship'. Indeed it was. The sea was calm, with a slight swell. As dawn broke, visibility was good. It was summer in the southern hemisphere.

Captain Langsdorff seems to have decided on his tactics beforehand. These were to close with any pursuing or shadowing cruiser, and rely on his heavier guns and superior armour to stop the enemy in their tracks. He turned towards the British force, and brought both his forward turrets to bear on HMS *Exeter*.

At 0618 hours the *Graf Spee* opened fire. *Exeter* replied at 0620, *Ajax* at 0621, and *Achilles* at 0623. The range was just short of eleven miles. The first proper naval battle of the Second World War had begun.

What Captain Langsdorff does not seem to have anticipated is that Commodore Harwood might deploy his ships not as a combined force, but as two separate forces. The British cruisers were faster, and could engage the *Graf Spee* from different directions. They were also able to spot the fall of shells from different angles, and thus positioned, help each other to be more accurate.

The *Graf Spee* soon had HMS *Exeter* within range. One shell burst amidships killing the ship's starboard torpedo crew and wrecking both her aircraft; a more direct hit put 'B' turret out of action and showered those on the bridge with shell splinters. Captain Bell was among the wounded.

The *Graf Spee* herself was hit by a shell from the *Exeter*, which damaged her control tower. More worrying at this stage, was the proximity of the two 6-inch gun cruisers, HMS *Ajax* and HMNZS *Achilles*. Captain Langsdorff had to turn his main guns away from HMS *Exeter*, and use them against his two terrier-like attackers, 13,000 yards away. Next, he had to alter course to avoid torpedoes fired by the *Exeter*.

Langsdorff changed direction again, and laid smoke. He then redirected his fire towards HMS *Exeter*, scoring further hits. He put another turret out of action and caused a fire amidships.

Yet he did not go in for the kill, even though HMS *Exeter* had only one turret working by this stage. Shells from the *Ajax* and the *Achilles*, while not penetrating the *Graf Spee*'s main armour, were wrecking her superstructure and causing casualties. Captain Langsdorff apparently decided to get away from his antagonists, now less than five miles distant, and fight the battle at the longer range more suited to his bigger guns.

This decision probably marked the moment when the Germans lost their will to win and their belief in victory, and sought escape to the west. It was not much more than an hour since the battle had begun, but HMS *Exeter* was also ready to break off battle. Her last turret was out of action, she was listing and had taken water aboard, sixty-one of her crew were dead and another twenty were wounded.

The battle, however, was not yet over. Aboard the *Ajax*, Commodore Harwood saw no reason to let the *Graf Spee* choose the range at which the battle would be fought. Using their superior speed, he took his two cruisers in closer. Although HMS *Ajax* had been hit and had had two turrets put out of action, she too had hit the pocket battleship and started a fire aboard her.

HMNZS *Achilles* then fired four torpedoes, and so in return did the *Graf Spee*, but all were avoided. The pursuit continued until Harwood received a report that ammunition was running low aboard the *Ajax* and, he presumed, probably also aboard the *Achilles*. It wasn't, but the report was enough to decide him to

return to the traditional cruiser-shadowing role, some fifteen miles from his large adversary.

The *Admiral Graf Spee* needed to seek repairs. She had used a good proportion of her ammunition, had a nasty six-foot hole in her bows, and was in no condition to head into a wintery North Atlantic, where hostile heavy forces were searching for her. Although only one British shell had penetrated her armour, much of her superstructure was wrecked. All the sixty-two captured British Merchant Navy officers and men aboard were safely battened down. Thirty-six of her crew were dead; sixty were wounded, six seriously.

The *Ajax* and the *Achilles* continued to shadow the *Graf Spee* for the rest of the day. Whenever either of the British cruisers approached too closely, Langsdorff fired a salvo or two. This didn't stop them approaching. When it became clear that the German ship was heading for the Uruguayan capital of Montevideo, Commodore Harwood ordered the *Achilles* to keep following. His own ship, the *Ajax*, was positioned to the south, in case the German ship doubled back.

As it got dark, the *Achilles* twice went in closer, provoking further salvoes. Nevertheless, by midnight, the *Graf Spee* had entered Montevideo roads and dropped anchor. The Battle of the River Plate was over.

The next battle was a diplomatic one. Langsdorff wanted to spend fifteen days making his ship sea- and battleworthy. However, the Hague Convention allows a warship to stay in a neutral port for only twenty-

**HMNZS *Achilles*, together with another 6-inch gun cruiser HMS *Ajax* and the 8-inch gun cruiser HMS *Exeter*, drove the *Admiral Graf Spee* into Montevideo. The *Achilles* is entering Montevideo (left) after the German pocket battleship had been scuttled.**

Cheerful crew members point out battle scars on the funnel of HMS *Exeter* (right) on her triumphant return to Britain after the Battle of the River Plate. The 8-inch gun cruiser suffered heavily at the guns of the *Admiral Graf Spee*. Sixty-one of her crew were killed and twenty were injured. The two smaller British cruisers escaped with much less damage and a combined total of only eleven dead.

four hours. An exception applies if she needs repairs to become seaworthy. The British Minister to Uruguay, Eugene Millington-Drake, pointed out that, as the *Graf Spee* had steamed some 300 miles since the battle had been broken off, she could hardly be considered unseaworthy and should be made to leave next day.

The Uruguayans announced that they would inspect the ship and declare how long she needed for repairs. Suddenly the British attitude was reversed: Commodore Harwood had decided he wanted more reinforcements himself, besides HMS *Cumberland* which had steamed up from the Falklands.

It was then, that clever use of rumour was made. Reports were circulated in Montevideo that a large British Fleet was already waiting outside Uruguayan territorial waters. The ships were said to include the battle cruiser HMS *Renown* and the aircraft carrier HMS *Ark Royal* – both still a good 1,000 miles away in reality.

British Minister Eugene Millington-Drake, inevitably known to all by the nickname 'Fluffington-Duck', went back to the Uruguayans and pointed out that under the Hague Convention a belligerent warship was not permitted to leave port within twenty-four hours of the departure of a merchant vessel belonging to the other side. A British merchantman hastily left port, which meant the *Graf Spee* was not entitled to sail before the evening of 16 December, 1939.

These machinations were a delight to the newspaper world, providing a new lead to the *Graf Spee* story every twelve hours or so. It was all settled when the Uruguayans decreed a stay of seventy-two hours, and no more.

Captain Langsdorff consulted Berlin. He thought his ship's condition meant almost certain destruction by the forces he believed were ranged against him outside Montevideo. He also expressed doubt at having much chance of damaging his attackers. Should he accept internment in Uruguay, or destroy his ship? Hitler ruled against internment.

On 17 December, 1939, some 700 of the *Graf Spee*'s crew were taken aboard the German tanker *Tacoma*, and shortly after 6.00 p.m., with only a skeleton crew aboard, the German pocket battleship weighed anchor.

Watched by crowds, and with radio reporters giving a running commentary on the scene, the *Admiral Graf Spee* slowly pulled out of the harbour. Four miles out she stopped and

dropped anchor. Captain Langsdorff and the skeleton crew left. Then at 8.00 p.m. there was a series of six loud explosions aboard. She blew up and caught fire, and was soon nothing but a blazing hulk. The *Graf Spee* had been scuttled rather than have to fight again.

The crew of the *Graf Spee* were taken to Buenos Aires, the Argentine capital on the other side of the River Plate estuary. They would be seen for a few weeks, sad and forlorn figures, being entertained in the homes of members of the German community in Argentina, and still in uniform. Eventually they would be interned, though most of the officers and a few of the more resolute of the men soon escaped and made their way back to Germany. For the bulk of them, however, the war was over. Some settled in Argentina, the rest would be repatriated in 1946.

Captain Langsdorff was not interned. He wrote farewell letters to his wife and family, and to the German Ambassador, and then shot himself. His body was found lying on a German naval ensign in the hotel bedroom he had

**Left:** Captain Hans Langsdorff, commander of the German pocket battleship *Admiral Graf Spee*, attending the funeral in Montevideo of the thirty-six members of his crew killed in the Battle of the River Plate. Aged forty-five, he committed suicide in Buenos Aires on 19 December, 1939, six days after the battle.

**Right:** Nazi salutes figure prominently at Captain Hans Langsdorff's funeral in Buenos Aires. He was never considered a fanatical Nazi, and is said to have chosen to die on a German naval flag, which did not carry the swastika. Captain Pottinger, of the British merchantman SS *Ashlea*, one of the sixty-two captured British seamen who were aboard the *Admiral Graf Spee* throughout the battle and all of whom were unhurt, represented them at the funeral.

been allotted within the naval area in the port of Buenos Aires.

The Battle of the River Plate, and the events surrounding it, belong almost to another age – a bygone age of chivalry, of a comradeship of the sea and of a restraint far removed from 'Total War'. In ten weeks of raiding, Captain Langsdorff had sunk nine British merchant ships, totalling about 50,000 tons, without causing a single loss of life. The captured British officers and seamen aboard the *Graf Spee* all escaped the battle unscathed. Captain Pottinger of the SS *Ashlea* would represent them all at Langsdorff's funeral.

It was a battle that would prove untypical of the majority during the War: fought in good weather, with aircraft playing only a very minor spotting role. Three smaller and less heavily-armoured British cruisers had fought an almost classic battle and defeated one of Admiral Raeder's most prized ships.

The final episode of the *Graf Spee* saga belongs equally to that bygone era. The captain of the *Altmark*, the pocket battleship's supply ship, disregarded orders to land the 299 captive British seamen at a neutral port, and made a run for Germany. Intercepted in Norwegian waters, he denied that he had any prisoners aboard.

British destroyers cornered the *Altmark* in Josing Fiord, and HMS *Cossack*, under Captain P.L. Vian, prepared to board her. The *Altmark* turned on searchlights to blind those on the destroyer's bridge and did her best to ram HMS *Cossack*. The *Cossack*'s boarding party leapt onto the decks of the *Altmark*, and after a short fierce fight, in which six *Graf Spee* guards were killed, it was all over.

The boarding party opened the hatches of the *Altmark* and asked: 'Any British down there?'. There was an answering roar, and then the famous words were shouted back: 'Come on up, the Navy's here.'

It would be a long time before the British again won such a heartening victory as the Battle of the River Plate; or enjoyed such a colourful triumph as the rescue of the *Altmark*'s prisoners.

# BLITZKRIEG IN THE WEST

Heinz Guderian (front left) inspecting *Panzer* troops in training. Appointed Inspector General of *Panzer* troops by Hitler, Guderian developed the doctrine of mechanized war used with such devastating effect against France in 1940. His charismatic and aggressive leadership of XIX *Panzer Korps* ensured that they triumphed in their crossing of the River Meuse at Sedan.

In 1933, the Treaty of Versailles still limited German strength; a *Reichswehr* of 100,000 and no air force meant Germany feared Poland, never mind France. Just seven years later, French might was humbled by *Wehrmacht* superiority in strategy and resources. For the second time in seventy years France was prostrate before Germany and the name Sedan linked to defeat.

Hitler's rearmament programme gave Germany superiority in anti-tank guns, self-propelled artillery and anti-aircraft guns. Their six-to-one advantage in anti-aircraft guns included 2,600 versatile '88s', a weapon illustrating Germany's qualitative edge. The *Luftwaffe* had nearly double Allied numbers, while its Ju52 transport planes gave it greater operational mobility. Discounting the neutral forces of the Low Countries, the Allies were even at a disadvantage in terms of manpower.

To some peoples' surprise the figures show an Allied numerical lead in tanks. However, Germany had a slight lead in tanks capable of engaging other tanks. Even the best Allied tank was badly designed for tank-to-tank combat, lacking a radio and placing too many demands on the man in the turret. Allied tanks were primarily infantry-support weapons, while German strategy concentrated tanks into an integrated team with other mechanized forces.

To the punch of these *Panzerdivisions* was added range and mechanical reliability, producing a formation capable of exploiting a breakthrough in battle.

The combination of firepower and mobility in the German mechanized forces made *Blitzkrieg* a possibility. Concentrations of *Panzerdivisons* would rupture enemy lines and, supported by mechanized infantry divisions, exploit this breakthrough. The *Luftwaffe* could provide close tactical support, driving enemy planes from the sky and co-operating with ground forces as 'aerial artillery'. Speed of attack and chaos in the rear denied the enemy the chance to form a viable defence, allowing large enemy formations to be enveloped. In essence, *Blitzkrieg* paralysed both the enemy's will and their ability to find an appropriate response.

General von Manstein's persistence and Hitler's intuition and luck lead to the adoption of the *Sichelschnitt* or 'sickle cut'. It was calculated that an invasion of the Low Countries would pull in the Allied armies and 'fix' them against the German's Army Group B. Having drawn the Allies, German Army Group A, with most of the *Panzerdivisions*, would crash through the Ardennes and reap four Allied armies in an enormous 'sickle cut'. Conservative generals warned against the plan, but, like

**The Fall of Sedan, May 1940. The speed of the German *Blitzkrieg* amazed the French High Command.**

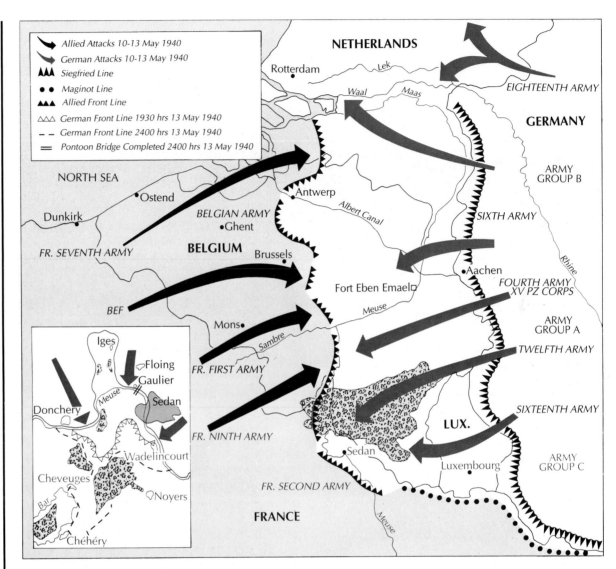

Legend:

- Allied Attacks 10-13 May 1940
- German Attacks 10-13 May 1940
- Siegfried Line
- Maginot Line
- Allied Front Line
- German Front Line 1930 hrs 13 May 1940
- German Front Line 2400 hrs 13 May 1940
- Pontoon Bridge Completed 2400 hrs 13 May 1940

NETHERLANDS
Rotterdam
Lek
Waal
Maas
EIGHTEENTH ARMY
GERMANY
NORTH SEA
Ostend
Dunkirk
BELGIAN ARMY
Ghent
Antwerp
Albert Canal
ARMY GROUP B
SIXTH ARMY
BELGIUM
Brussels
FR. SEVENTH ARMY
Aachen
Rhine
BEF
Fort Eben Emael
FOURTH ARMY
XV PZ CORPS
Mons
Meuse
ARMY GROUP A
Sambre
FR. FIRST ARMY
TWELFTH ARMY
FR. NINTH ARMY
SIXTEENTH ARMY
LUX.
Sedan
ARMY GROUP C
Luxembourg
FR. SECOND ARMY
Meuse
FRANCE

Inset:
Iges
Floing
Gaulier
Meuse
Sedan
Donchery
Wadelincourt
Cheveuges
Bar
Noyers
Chéhéry

Hitler, the man leading the sickle's cutting edge was a bold gambler. The moment had arrived for the commander of XIX *Panzer Korps*, Heinz Guderian – his aim was to cross the Meuse at Sedan.

It is easy to point to Allied inferiority in resources and strategy. The French Army prepared for trench warfare and Britain contributed minimally to ground forces. Tanks were wasted in dispersed defensive packets, fulfilling only an infantry-support role. Allied air forces lacked a policy of close support and co-operated poorly with ground forces. Allied assets should not be ignored, though: France had 11,200 artillery pieces, the Maginot Line secured Alsace-Lorraine and a rapid expansion of armoured forces had started. When Chamberlain said 'Hitler has missed the bus', he should have been right, for resources and strategy by themselves do not suffice to explain the defeat.

The single biggest contribution to the defeat of France was made by the French Supreme Commander, General Gamelin. A glance at the map illustrating the campaign plans makes the French reaction to the German invasion clear: they had offered a powerful thrust following the German invasion of the Low Countries, the Maginot Line had been held in strength, while the central 'joint' was weakly held. The 'joint' did not need greater strength because it was thought that the 'impassable' Ardennes protected it, and so, naturally, little had been done to add any defences here.

Facing page top: French General Gamelin conferring with senior commanders on an inspection tour of the Western Front. Gamelin was a peacetime soldier who proved incapable of handling the speed with which events moved in the 1940 offensive. His insistence on an overly bold advance into the Low Countries and his inept response to the German breakthrough were major factors in the Allied defeat.

Facing page bottom: Allied officers examining part of the Maginot line. Locked into this impressive line of fortifications was a significant portion of the French Army that would have been better employed further north. These major fortifications ended at Longwy, so at Sedan the Germans encountered weak, incomplete defences.

Below: a German howitzer in action in Belgium. The advancing German forces brushed aside Belgian and French units in their advance through the Ardennes. Traffic jams caused the main delays - not Allied resistance.

At dawn on 10th May an early morning call by the *Luftwaffe* ended the smug neutrality of the Low Countries. Ignoring intelligence warnings, General Gamelin ordered forty divisions into Belgium. Behind them, unseen, seven *Panzerdivisions* moved into the Ardennes – the cutting edge of the 'sickle' was about to fall on ten French infantry divisions holding a hundred-mile front in the 'impassable' Ardennes.

Guderian's XIX *Panzer Korps* had the crucial task of breaking through at Sedan. Under his command were 1st, 2nd and 10th *Panzerdivisions*, plus the *Grossdeutschland* Regiment. Following to support the breakthrough was Wietersheim's XIV Motorized Corps. Boldly lead, these elite troops were confident and highly motivated. The same cannot be said for the three French divisions defending the Meuse around Sedan; all three were under-equipped, 'B' class divisions composed almost entirely of reluctant conscripts.

Much to Guderian's relief, the enemy presented few problems during the advance to the Meuse. His vehicles, snarled in an enormous traffic jam, were not bombed, and at *Wehrmacht* High Command (O.K.H.) Halder

commented 'Enemy air force astonishingly restrained'. The Belgian *Chasseurs Ardennais* performed some limited demolitions and withdrew northwards. Stiffer resistance was offered by the French light cavalry, but lacking in anti-tank guns and equipped with the under-gunned Hotchkiss 35 tank, these units could hardly even slow a *Panzerdivision*. Even the important town of Bouillon fell in a matter of hours. At last, on 12th May, the Allies made a major effort in the air, but bombing the Bouillon 'salient' failed to prevent the Germans from moving rapidly over the Semois – the last natural barrier before the Meuse. Sufficient man-made fortifications to delay the Germans had not been built – in fact, not even the simple measure of tree-felling to block roads had been tried. By the evening of 12th May the French were blowing the bridges over the Meuse. The *Wehrmacht* had arrived in half the time the French had thought possible.

Heights like La Marfée dominated the Meuse near Sedan and to this natural strength the French had added pillboxes. However, Laffontaine's 'B' class 55th Division was spread thinly over twelve miles and many of the pillboxes were incomplete. Its artillery was well placed to inflict casualties, but on the day was

rationed to fifty rounds per gun because Corps Commander Grandsard believed at least four days would pass before an assault. *Blitzkrieg* attacks don't pause for breath – the Germans planned to cross on 13th May.

Guderian selected 1st *Panzer* to make the main assault, while 2nd and 10th *Panzer* attempted crossings on either side. Heavy artillery from the rest of the corps and the *Grossdeutschland* stiffened 1st *Panzer*. The all-arms nature of the *Panzerdivision* is illustrated by the crossing; artillery, anti-aircraft guns, assault engineers (*Sturmpionieren*), engineers and rifle regiments all played important roles. Throughout the day the courage and leadership qualities of these men was seen at all levels.

The *Luftwaffe* put 1,500 planes into the air above Sedan and it is difficult to envisage how a crossing could have succeeded without such aerial support. From 7am to 3pm continuous *Luftwaffe* assault supplemented the artillery effort. With no Allied aerial riposte 55th's morale fell and Stuka dive bombers spread panic, especially in the badly protected French artillery positions. The bombardment suppressed French fire and made it possible to cross a big river in rubber dinghies.

Leading 1st *Panzer's* assault, *Grossdeutschland* crossed near Gaulier just after 3pm. Flak guns at the water's edge kept the pillboxes busy and several were hit through their unprotected weapons slits. Reaching the west bank, small groups of infantry pressed into the gaps between pillboxes, discovering few French interval troops. The more stubborn pillboxes were destroyed by *Sturmpionieren* attacking them from the rear with explosives. Following *Grossdeutschland*, Balck's 1st Rifle Regiment crossed and swung west, and then south towards La Marfée. By midnight Balck's men had overrun most of the hill, depriving the French of the best artillery positions to shell the bridge newly erected at Gaulier. At midnight on 13th May the bridge was complete and the tanks started trundling over the Meuse.

The day had gone well for the other crossings attempted by XIX Corps, despite their being short of artillery. Crossing at Donchery, 2nd *Panzer* had used Pzkpfw IV tanks at the water's edge to provide covering fire and once again *Sturmpionieren* had proved their worth. The audacious courage and initiative displayed by the assault troops enabled them to penetrate to their objectives, linking with 1st *Panzers* advance at about 8pm. To the north, both General Reinhardt's and General Hoth's corps had elements on the west bank of the Meuse. The 'sickle cut' was poised to thrust into the backs of the Allied armies in Belgium.

**A heavy French artillery piece in action. The artillery, the pride of the French Army, was was expected to play the same dominant role as it did in the First World War. Unfortunately, very few self-propelled guns were in service, and at Sedan the French artillery performed poorly.**

The Ju 87 Stuka was used to fearsome effect when Guderian's men crossed the Meuse. Functioning as 'aerial artillery' it created panic in the French artillery, while providing the Germans with the suppressive firepower they needed to cross the river. In reality it was a limited plane that owed its early success in the war to the panic it inspired.

Below: the town of Sedan immediately after the campaign. Sedan was unfortunate enough to be bombed by both sides.

Every hour that passed strengthened the German bridgehead, but an early attack could have caught XIX Corps with its tanks still on the east bank. The fate of French counterattacks on 14th and 15th May illustrates basic deficiencies in the French Army, contrasting starkly with the bold initiatives of the German campaign. Grandsard placed two tank battalions and two infantry regiments under Laffontaine's command for a counterattack. The chaos in French lines and direct disobedience to orders only exacerbated the slowness of response of an army reacting at the speed of trench warfare. The counterattack went in five-and-a-half hours late, with only half its allocated forces; the alarm it caused among the Germans suggests an earlier, stronger attack by the French could have had a dramatic effect. The French were slow to exploit an initial advantage and at 8.30 were struck by 1st *Panzer,* which destroyed half 7th Tank Battalion's obsolete tanks retaking Chémery. This failure meant the dissolution of 55th and 71st divisions, which by noon were panic-stricken mobs.

Similarly Allied air forces made their efforts late – throughout May 14th, pilots fought with great courage to destroy the pontoon bridge at Gaulier. Their delay had allowed XIX *Panzer Korps* to erect 200 flak guns and the *Luftwaffe*

German engineers built sturdy pontoon bridges (facing page) with great rapidity over the Meuse. Their efficiency ensured that major German forces joined their surviving assault units on the western bank of the Meuse before the French were able to organise a counterattack.

Right: German infantry assaulting a French village on the west bank of the Meuse. The Germans showed great flexibility in their infantry tactics and small groups often took hair-raising initiatives. Much of the credit for crossing the Meuse goes to the NCOs who led small groups in daring assaults.

was able to bring about 800 machines into the air. The Allies launched twenty-seven piecemeal attacks and lost ninety planes, but to no avail. The bridge remained intact.

The best opportunity the French had for reversing the situation was General Flavigny's newly formed XXI Corps, made up of newly arriving 3rd Armoured and 3rd Mechanized divisions. Unlike previous units, these divisions had tanks capable of engaging German tanks in combat. The familiar French pattern of delay meant no attack was ready till 3.30pm when the Germans already had 500 tanks over the Meuse. Flavigny cancelled the attack and dispersed the tanks over a twelve-mile front. It was not until the afternoon of 15th May that the XXI Corps attacked in three separate actions. *Grossdeutschland* provoked the first

attack by taking the hilltop village of Stonne and only just held off French tanks with their self-propelled anti-tank guns. The second attack, at 5.30pm, was based around a battalion of 'Char B' tanks that thrust towards Chémery, raising alarm at Guderian's HQ. The final action – an attempt of two companies of 'Char Bs' to take Stonne – got into the village, but were driven out by the arrival of riflemen from 10th *Panzer*. French attacks displayed individual courage, but lacked co-ordination, both between the tanks themselves and between the tanks and the infantry.

In combat the French lacked the initiative to exploit initial advantages and, perhaps most basically, they had yet to learn the folly of using tanks in 'penny packets'. The arrival of 29th Motorized Division on the morning of 16th May settled the matter – the southern flank of the bridgehead was secured and the movement westward of Guderian's *Panzerdivisions* could continue.

The battle of Sedan was, in effect, over. As early as May 14th Guderian had gambled that *Grossdeutschland*, reinforced by 10th *Panzer*, would hold, and had ordered 1st *Panzer* to turn west. The French in front of XIX *Panzer Korps* were in chaos; heroic defiance, such as 3rd *Spahi's* at La Horgne, was to no avail as, at the same time as they were being annihilated, 2nd *Panzer* was outflanking them with ease. On 16th May Guderian made contact with 6th *Panzer* and the three separate bridgeheads became one front. With whole divisions dissolving in panic, the *Luftwaffe* dominating the sky and the roads crammed with refugees, it would have taken better men than the French High Command possessed to retrieve the situation. Guderian's *Panzer Korps* were not to receive an attack as threatening as General Flavigny's recent failure all the way to the

Channel – in fact, the German victory was more threatened by German High Command than by the French, as later even Hitler lost his nerve and tried to hold the *Panzerdivisions* back.

The qualities displayed by the men of XIX *Panzer Korps* had been extraordinary throughout the battle of Sedan. Commanders such as Guderian and Balck had inspired their troops by leading from the front. Small groups of ordinary soldiers displayed similar qualities; men like Feldwebel Rubarth who, with ten men, broke through a 300-metre stretch of bunkers at Wadelincourt, knocking out three of them and winning the *Ritterkreuz*. To this reckless taking of initiatives and quality of leadership, *Wehrmacht* training had added great skill in all arms co-operation. Yet, unfortunately for them, all the *Panzer Korps'* combat virtuosity was soon to be of no avail as their 'invincible' Fuhrer burst the bounds of restraint and summoned up enemies even their skills were unable to defeat.

**Advancing German motorized forces. Despite the misgivings of his superiors, Guderian pushed his men hard to exploit their initial breakthrough. The *Panzer* forces advanced with such speed they denied the Allies the breathing space they needed to respond. In their advance to the Channel they took prisoner thousands of dazed Allied soldiers.**

While the battle for the perimeter rages inland, British troop stolidly wait to be picked up near Dunkirk. Excellent discipline prevailed, even though some troops would have to wait three days before they could leave the beaches.

On 10th May, 1940, the storm that had already engulfed Poland, Denmark and Norway abruptly burst against western Europe. Just nine days later, German armoured units reached the Channel coast.

On the same day that the Germans attacked in the west, Winston Churchill succeeded Neville Chamberlain as British Prime Minister of a coalition government. What happened by 18th May on the central sector around Sedan and Dinant has been described in the first chapter. In the northern area, meanwhile, after four days of fighting, Holland surrendered. As the Germans of General von Bock's Army Group B attacked Belgium – serving, in Sir Basil Liddell Hart's phrase, as 'the matador's cloak' – General Lord Gort's British Expeditionary Force, almost ten divisions strong, swung forward into central Belgium, accompanied on either flank by the crack French armies – 7th and 1st – to meet what was thought to be the enemy's major offensive. They were soon made aware of their great error. 'The news from France is very bad' Churchill warned first Parliament and then the British people at 9pm on 19th May.

It was rapidly to get much worse. Changes in the Allied High Command on 18th May (General Weygand replacing the discredited Gamelin as the Allied supremo) did nothing to stop the rot. Attempts to contain the deep enemy salient failed – there was no such thing as a strategic reserve available to plug the huge gap so rapidly torn in the Allied front. German exploitation of their success was boldly and brilliantly executed; by 21st May the Allied armies were effectively sundered in two. This was *Blitzkrieg* on a scale and at a speed no-one had envisaged – including the Germans. Indeed, many *Wehrmacht* generals feared that von Rundstedt's Army Group A's armoured thrust would become exposed to a telling counterattack (as the small British action by 'Frankforce' at Arras on 21st May seemed to demonstrate), but at this stage Hitler and Commander in Chief General von Brauchitsch backed their armour specialist General Guderian's intuition to the hilt.

Meanwhile, General von Bock's Army Group B, with Holland already out of the war was thrusting deep into Belgium. By 27th May the Belgian government was considering surrender in its turn. A week earlier, Lord Gort, apprehensive that such a dire event would indeed soon occur, thus severing the BEF's links to the Channel ports, and being already dubious of

France's sustained fighting power, had secretly requested the War Office to plan an evacuation. This would mean taking his forces out of French supreme command, and, if need be, heading for the coast.

As a preliminary move, hospitals and other rear installations were already heading for Dunkirk, where the first fighting troops were embarked for England on 26th May. Next day, Gort received the British government's definitive order to regard the evacuation of as many as possible of the BEF to safety in England as his overriding priority. The scene was now set for one of the great dramas of the Second World War.

Operation 'Dynamo', as the evacuation was codenamed, was entrusted to Vice Admiral Bertram Ramsay, responsible for the logistical support of the BEF, who set up his headquarters in Dover Castle. The speed of the German advance and the intensity of enemy air activity greatly increased the problems he and Lord

Gort faced. Hopes that both Boulogne and Calais would be able to supplement Dunkirk were dashed when the former fell on 24th May, to be followed by the latter two days later after a heroic defence by 1st Battalion the Rifle Brigade, which literally fought to the last round

**Below: as a Lockheed Hudson of Coastal Command overflies the scene, dense clouds of oily smoke rise from the blazing oil tanks of Dunkirk's port complex, set alight by _Luftwaffe_ bombing. This picture gives a clear impression of the gradually shelving beaches that made approach difficult for rescue vessels.**

**Left: a closer view of the blazing oil tank from adjoining Dunkirk. Although the myth of Dunkirk attributes the 'miracle' of the evacuation to the famous 'little ships', in fact the vast majority of soldiers were taken off from the moles of Dunkirk harbour by a succession of destroyers.**

*Blitzkrieg* leaves the BEF trapped at Dunkirk at the mercy of a brilliant strategic manoeuvre by the Germans called the 'sickle cut'. On 25th May, Hitler called a halt to the advance, thereby allowing the Allies to evacuate to England. The decision to halt was a critical one which had far-reaching consequences. It was, arguably, the first German mistake of the war.

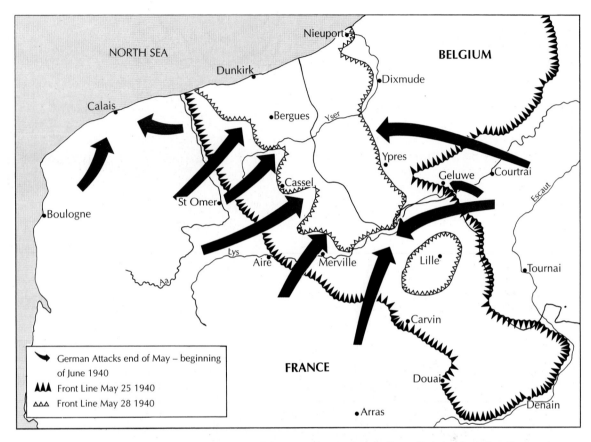

German Attacks end of May – beginning of June 1940
▲▲▲ Front Line May 25 1940
△△△ Front Line May 28 1940

under Brigadier C.N. Nicholson before succumbing.

The main lift from Dunkirk would inevitably be the responsibility of the Royal Navy, but to supplement its capacity an appeal was issued for owners of 'little ships' – ranging from ferries and fishing boats to weekend holiday craft – to collect their craft in the Thames Estuary and south coast ports. But grim estimates claiming that at best only some 45,000 troops might be saved showed how pessimistically the situation was regarded in London.

But then Fate took a hand in the unlikely guise of Hitler himself. Remembering his own days in the muddy trenches of Flanders a quarter of a century earlier, the Fuehrer suddenly became obsessed with the need to preserve his jubilant but nigh-exhausted *Panzer* spearhead for the conquest of the greater part of France that lay south of the Somme. The savage British riposte at Arras – however small in scale – further reinforced the need for caution, while the assurances of Hermann Goering that the *Luftwaffe* alone could complete the destruction of the Allied forces in the pocket

were also influential factors in decreeing a pause in land operations. Accordingly, von Rundstedt ordered his 4th Army to halt on 24th May to rest, resupply, and repair. A two-day partial lull ensued that was to prove of critical importance for the Allies.

Two further developments also helped the embattled and seemingly hopelessly trapped BEF to survive. From 24th May Lord Gort was receiving decrypted German messages from Bletchley Park, where the 'Enigma' coding machine had revealed some of its secrets. Secondly, the next day a captured document revealed von Bock's plan to exploit a wedge his troops had driven between the Belgian and British troops between Menin and Ypres. Lord Gort at once cancelled orders for two British divisions to break out south to the Somme, and diverted them in the nick of time to plug the developing gap that could have proved fatal to any evacuation. Thus, when full-scale German pressure was resumed on 27th May, the Allied defensive perimeter around Dunkirk was complete.

The third largest port in France today, in

As the lines of men on the beaches thin out, the crew of a destroyer's anti-aircraft gun maintain a ceaseless watch for the next raid by Stuka dive-bombers or Heinkel IIIs. Their beached vessel was highly exposed, and the strain upon the gunners clearly shows in their expressions. Six destroyers were sunk and nineteen damaged.

1940 Dunkirk already possessed a hundred acres of dockland and was a thriving town with a population of some 65,000. By 4th June, over eighty per cent of the town would be laid in smouldering ruins, and in 1945 it would be designated a 'Ville Héroique'. On either side of the town lay miles of soft sand dunes running northeast towards La Panne and Nieuport and southwest towards Gravelines and Calais, with hardly any cliffs of any height dividing the hinterland from the beaches. Two important canals ran roughly parallel to the coast, linking Dunkirk with Bergues and Furnes, where both joined the Loo Canal.

On 27th May Lord Gort ordered four British divisions and neighbouring units making up about one third of French 1st Army to abandon the Lille pocket and head for Dunkirk through the Furnes gap. This move came at the last practicable moment, for the very next day Belgium surrendered, just as Lieutenant General Alan Brooke's II Corps closed the gap in the line near Nieuport. Lille was surrounded on 29th May, and a day later the Dunkirk perimeter

was finally isolated. The French were made responsible for the western sector, the British for the eastern. BEF Headquarters were established at La Panne amidst the dunes. To its east, behind the Loo Canal, 4th Division held the sector nearest to Nieuport, with Major General Bernard Montgomery's 3rd Division as its neighbour around Furnes and the canal junctions. Moving westwards, the perimeter followed the line of the Bergues-Furnes Canal, 50th (Northumbrian) Division completing Brooke's II Corps. Beyond this boundary Lieutenant General 'Bubbles' Barker's I Corps' 1st Division took up defensive positions, with 46th Division taking post on its right flank as far as Bergues and its canal, running northwards parallel with Route 16A towards Dunkirk, some four miles away. The westernmost flank beyond this canal was entrusted to the French 68th Division. This completed the front line of the perimeter as on 30th May.

Closer to the sea, the remnants of six more divisions, three French and three British, stood in reserve. In a line from west to east in the rear

En route for England and safety, exhausted and sodden British, French and Belgian troops watch the dense lines of shipping of all shapes and sizes steam out of Dunkirk harbour for the short, perilous voyage across the Channel. Some ships made several such journeys.

of I Corps were the French 32nd and 60th and the British 12th divisions. Over the inter-corps boundary stood the British 5th and 23rd Divisions. Both 12th and 23rd Divisions had been badly mauled on 18th May and, apart from their 68th Division, the French were in little better state. A considerable number of Belgian troops and many refugees, both Belgian and French, were also within the defended zone. Many thousands of vehicles – tanks, trucks and artillery towers in addition to civilian transport – packed the area. In terms of men, a total of some 360,000 troops and perhaps as many more civilians were placed with their backs to the sea within a quadrangular perimeter measuring approximately twenty-four miles in length with a depth varying between five miles in the west and two in the east – an area of about a hundred square miles. Every road within this area could be commanded by German artillery fire. As III Corps began to embark the outlook for the BEF seemed bleak indeed.

The first factor that allowed the 'miracle' of Dunkirk to take place was the slowness of the Germans to test these defences. Only on the southwestern section, where General Guderian commanded 9th *Panzer* and 20th Motorized divisions of German 4th Army, and rapidly approached the River Aa, was much energy displayed at first. Remarkably, 18th and 14th Divisions of German 6th Army (part of Army Group A) did little against the centre of the Allied line, and the same was true of the formations of German 18th Army (part of Army Group B), including 265th Division facing the Furnes and Nieuport sectors on 27th and 28th May. Perhaps the meeting of the army group boundaries partly accounts for this rather than any theory that Hitler deliberately allowed the British to escape in the hope of making a quick peace.

So the evacuation got under way. The town and port of Dunkirk were heavily bombed and ablaze – particularly the oil-storage installations – from 26th May onwards, but many troops were nevertheless taken off the moles of Dunkirk and Malo-les-Bains ports for safe transport aboard naval shipping. Many vessels were hit (including eventually six destroyers sunk and nineteen more damaged, including a hospital ship), particularly from 29th May as the *Luftwaffe* attack intensified. Overhead and in

the far distance the RAF fought valiantly against overwhelming numbers, displaying its skill by losing, on average, only one plane for every three of the enemy's shot down.

Fighting around the perimeter sharpened from 30th May, but most ground was held except in the east; Lord Gort was recalled to England next day, and Force Headquarters had to leave La Panne late on 1st June. Meanwhile, the armada of 'little ships' from England had made its appearance. Not only did these vessels carry much of the shore-to-ship traffic, thus permitting men to be taken off the beaches around Gravelines, despite constant dive-bombing, aerial machine-gunning and artillery fire, they also carried some 30,000 of the 53,823 soldiers taken off on 30th May (the best day) back to England. Losses to these craft were inevitably severe. Of the thousand or so ships of all sorts and sizes taking part in Operation 'Dynamo', 243 had been sunk by the end of the evacuation on 4th June.

Despite all the problems, the total of men saved rose higher and higher. Brooke handed over command of the rearguard to Major General Harold Alexander, and by late on 1st June only 46th, 1st and 50th divisions of the BEF remained ashore. By now it was only possible to use the harbour moles at night, forcing ships to sail when packed to dangerous levels above and below decks. At last, at 11pm on 2nd June,

Captain Tennant RN could signal to England 'BEF evacuated'.

By this time, the rapidly shrinking perimeter was manned by the French. On 3rd June the Royal Navy returned to take off 30,000 French troops, but many more than planned for appeared, and some confusion ensued. Despite Herculean efforts, some 40,000 Frenchmen had to be abandoned as German tanks entered the streets of Dunkirk. At 3.40am on 4th June the last British destroyer – HMS *Shikari* – set sail. The evacuation was over. At 9am the French garrison surrendered.

A brief wave of euphoria swept Great Britain, and Churchill had to warn the nation that '.. wars are not won by evacuations.' Although a total of 338,226 Allied troops (French and Belgians accounting for a third) had been brought safely to English ports, there was no concealing the fact that the BEF had lost all its tanks, transport, stores and equipment. Only a single Royal Artillery battery managed to save its guns. All the rest had to be put out of action or destroyed to prevent their use by the enemy. The wrecks of 2,472 guns, 68,879 vehicles, 20,548 motorcycles and half a million tons of ammunition and stores fell into German hands. It had indeed been a 'splendid deliverance', but it was also a potentially crippling defeat, for England now stood open to invasion.

Naturally the French government – which had moved to Bordeaux on 12th June and asked for an armistice on 21st June – did not support the British action. Vichy propagandists seized upon the fact that a total of 368,491 British troops had returned to British shores before the Franco-German armistice to insinuate that 'perfidious Albion' had saved its menfolk at the expense of its allies. In fact, British shipping had taken off 139,911 French and Belgian troops from Dunkirk, the balance of 144,171 British troops having been evacuated from other French ports – notably Le Havre and Cherbourg. These soldiers included reinforcements shipped to France after Dunkirk, lines of communication troops and representative units sent to help man the Maginot Line. Major General Bruce Fortune and the 8,000 men of 51st (Highland) Division were not so lucky, being compelled to surrender on 12th June after being trapped by Major General Erwin Rommel, commanding 7th 'Ghost' *Panzerdivision*, at St. Valry-en-Caux, west of Dieppe. Meanwhile, on 10th June, thinking it safe, Italy had joined Germany, and soon the war would spread to Egypt, Libya and East Africa.

Churchill did what he could for France in the few remaining days of the Campaign of France. Against all advice by colleagues anxious for our ability to wage the forthcoming 'Battle of Britain', he sent RAF reinforcements over the Channel. The generous offer of joint Anglo-French citizenship was cold-shouldered by Reynaud, Petain and Laval, even in the hour of their country's extremity. The hard British decision to sink the French fleet at Mers-el-Kebir in North Africa on 3rd July to prevent Vichy from allowing it to fall under German control, killed over 1,250 French sailors. This justifiable but ruthless deed did nothing to lessen French Anglophobia, and has left its scar to the present day. Such was the 'cruel necessity' forced upon Great Britain by twentieth-century total war.

Britain now stood alone, and braced itself for an all-out *Luftwaffe* attack to be followed by the seemingly inevitable German invasion of our shores. In fact, the 'Battle of Britain' would be won in the skies over southern England by 'the Few' of the RAF, and the German Operation 'Sealion' would never be implemented as Hitler's attention turned eastwards towards the Balkans and Russia. But none of this was known in late June, 1940. Winston Churchill remained the typification of British 'bulldog' defiance, enjoining the British people to so comport themselves during the toils and perils lying ahead that future generations would declare: 'This was their finest hour'. And so it was to prove. The sacrifices of Dunkirk and Mers-el-Kebir were not in vain.

'The harder they fall, the higher they bounce.' Distinctly cheerful 'Tommies' wait at Waterloo Station, London, for trains to disperse them throughout England. Despite the threat of imminent invasion, many were sent on 'survivor's leave'.

A group of 'little ships' on their way up the Thames for minor repairs after the evacuation of Dunkirk was over. Pleasure cruisers, yachts and fishing boats had all taken part, proving to be invaluable for transferring troops from the beaches to the larger vessels waiting offshore. Some small craft made the Channel crossing several times.

# THE MEDITERRANEAN

Mussolini proclaimed the Mediterranean to be *Mare Nostrum*, Our Sea. The Royal Navy would ensure that it was anything but that.

The Mediterranean in World War II was the scene of fierce fighting and some desperate convoy battles, but more than anything else the battles there served as a pointer to things to come in the war at sea. For the first time it became clear that future sea warfare would depend as much on air power as on the big guns of the navies.

Until France surrendered in June 1940, the Mediterranean was dominated by the British and French navies. The British had bases in Gibraltar at the Mediterranean's Atlantic end, at Alexandria in Egypt, and on Malta in the centre. The French controlled the western Mediterranean from their North African bases at Oran, Mers-el-Kebir and Bizerta, and from the great French naval port of Toulon.

With the fall of France, and Italy's entry into the War, the situation changed radically, and would do so again more a year or so later when Hitler moved powerful German air groups southwards.

Sadly, the British Navy had the unenviable task of ensuring that Admiral Darlan's French naval forces did not fall into Axis hands. This led to British attacks on the ships of their former allies at Oran, Mers-el-Kebir, and around in west Africa, on Dakar. The distress aroused by these attacks would have an impact on the North African landings of Operation Torch two years later.

Apart from invading Albania in April 1940, Italy had sat on the fence while Germany smashed the British and French armies in France. Four days before the Germans entered Paris, Mussolini declared war on Hitler's side. In September 1940, Italian troops invaded Egypt and started the fighting in the Western Desert that would go on for nearly three years. In October 1940 Italian troops invaded Greece. The Mediterranean had become an active theatre of war.

The British naval commander in the Mediterranean, Admiral Andrew B. Cunningham, with a force of five battleships, two aircraft carriers and ten 6-inch gun cruisers, faced what seemed to be a formidable enemy. Italy's four battleships, seven 8-inch and fourteen 6-inch gun cruisers included some of the newest and fastest warships in the world. More importantly, they were backed by a strong air force, many of whose pilots had undergone combat service in the Spanish Civil War.

At that time, British aircraft carriers did not carry fighters to help defend their fleet, only reconnaisance planes and torpedo bombers. In the first few months of confrontation there were a number of engagements between British and Italian forces, but none of great significance. In the main, the Italians stayed in port and made only occasional sallies to protect their convoys to Libya.

The first important clash came on 9 July, 1940, when a British submarine reported that two Italian battleships, the *Conte di Cavour* and the *Guilio Cesare*, were supporting a convoy bound for Libya. Admiral Cunningham, with three battleships, an aircraft carrier, five cruisers and seventeen destroyers headed to intercept.

Despite Italian air attacks, which damaged the British cruiser HMS *Gloucester*, and unsuccessful attempts by torpedo-carrying

Left: a Fairey Swordfish torpedo bomber takes off from HMS *Illustrious*. In November 1940, less than two dozen of these old-fashioned biplanes attacked the Italian fleet, which was anchored at Taranto in the heel of Italy. The battleship *Littorio* was sunk and two other battleships hit. It was an early lesson in the importance of air power which the Japanese did not fail to observe.

The Royal Air Force was used in a much more tactical way in the Western Desert than was the practice elsewhere at that stage in the War. Many of the lessons learned in North Africa about air support for the army would be applied in Europe after D-day. In early 1941, the RAF hit and set on fire the Italian cruiser *San Giorgio* (top right), leaving her settled on the bottom in Tobruk harbour.

Bottom right: British cruisers on convoy escort in the Mediterranean get up speed prior to facing an air attack. Air power would prove a key factor in many Mediterranean naval battles and in the British evacuations from Greece and Crete.

aircraft from HMS *Eagle* to slow the Italians down, the gunfight was soon over. The Italian heavy cruiser *Bolzano* was damaged, and a single fifteen-inch shell from Cunningham's flagship HMS *Warspite* hit the battleship *Giulio Cesare* at long range.

The Italian fleet departed behind a smoke screen and, although pursued to within twenty-five miles of the Italian coast, escaped.

Ten days later, five British destroyers encountered two Italian cruisers, and retired, closely pursued, in the direction of their supporting cruiser, the Australian 6-inch gun HMAS *Sydney*. The *Sydney* shattered and sank one of the pursuers, the *Bartolomeo Colleoni*, and seriously damaged the other, the *Giovanni delle Bande Nere*.

After these two clashes the Italians made no further attempts to get in the way of British operations for over two months. The British navy

The direction in which her guns are pointing, shows where the British cruiser (left) thinks the danger lies. She is prepared to face an air attack, whilst on convoy duty in the Mediterranean.

Right: a pom-pom gun crew, aboard a British destroyer, closed up and ready for action whilst on patrol in the Eastern Mediterranean, in May 1942.

The Mediterranean saw a good deal of underwater warfare, with submarines from all the belligerents attacking each other's convoys and warships. Top left: HMS *Barham* listing after being torpedoed on 25 November, 1941. The only British battleship to be sunk at sea by a U-boat during World War II, she blew up a few minutes later with the loss of 859 officers and men. Built in 1915, the twenty-five-year old vessel was hit at close range by torpedoes from U-331. A year later, U-331 was herself sunk in the Mediterranean by planes from HMS *Formidable*.

The end of the confrontation between the Italian and British navies came when Italy sued for peace, and an armistice was signed on 3 September, 1943. British sailors on HMS *Warspite* watch the arrival of a Littorio-class battleship in Malta (bottom left), where the Italian fleet had been ordered.

was kept busy escorting troops to Malta and flying in aircraft reinforcements, as well as bombarding the Libyan coast in support of the army.

Then, in November 1940, Cunningham decided to take the initiative. He launched an air attack on the Italian battle fleet in harbour at Taranto, its main base in the south of Italy.

Compared to later aircraft carrier attacks it was all on a pitiably small scale. Cunningham's force had been strengthened by the arrival of HMS *Illustrious* with her twelve fighters and twenty-two torpedo bombers and reconnaisance aircraft. On the other hand, HMS *Eagle* had been damaged by a fire in a hangar and could not take part. Five of the *Eagle*'s torpedo bombers and their crews transferred to the *Illustrious*.

Cunningham sailed from Egypt with four battleships, supporting cruisers and destroyers, and the *Illustrious*. On 11 November, 1940, two strike forces left the aircraft carrier roughly one hour apart, the first force consisting of twelve torpedo bombers, the second of nine.

The Italian fleet was taken by surprise. Despite anti-aircraft fire, the Fairey Swordfish made their approaches. With three torpedoes they sank the battleship *Littorio*, and then hit the 69 *Conte di Cavour* and the *Caio Duilio* with a single torpedo each. Half Italy's battleships had been put out of action, for the loss of two ancient biplanes and five torpedoes.

The Swordfish are supposed to have escaped destruction because nobody on the ground or in the ships believed that any aircraft would fly so slowly. With an absolute maximum speed of 160 m.p.h. the anti-aircraft gunners were all aiming hopelessly far in front.

Four and a half months later Admiral Cunningham would win the biggest naval battle of the War up to that point. It was fought off Cape Matapan in Greece, in that part of the Ionian Sea to the west of a line drawn between the Greek mainland and the island of Crete. Although the result was not as decisive as it might have been, its influence went beyond the statistics for ships sunk or damaged.

Italy's Eastern Fleet set out on a foray on 27 March, 1941, to attack British troop transports and supply ships going to Greece. Their secondary aim was to attack the British naval base established at Suda Bay in Crete. They relied on land-based aircraft for their protection, but failed to carry out some very necessary air reconnaissance.

The British, on the other hand, thanks to radio intelligence and aircraft reports, knew exactly what was happening. Cunningham, flying his flag in HMS *Warspite* under Captain D.B. Fisher, left Alexandria and headed straight towards the Italians. By then the enemy had split their forces, one group going towards the north of Crete, the other sailing south of Crete to find the convoys. The battleship *Vittorio Veneto*, under Captain Sparzani and flying the flag of Vice-Admiral Iachino, was in the rear, in support of both squadrons.

All day and through the night the Italian and British fleets steamed on a collision course. At 0745 hours on 28 March, 1941, the British light cruiser HMS *Orion*, scouting ahead of Cunningham's force, encountered the *Vittorio Veneto*, which opened fire on her. The Italian battleship pursued the *Orion* – straight towards the British battleships *Warspite*, *Valiant* and *Barham*.

It was then that an air strike from the aircraft carrier HMS *Formidable*, some one hundred miles behind the battle fleet, once again proved what air power was for. In three attacks, at 11.30 a.m., 3.30 p.m. and dusk, its torpedo bombers successfully attacked the *Vittorio Veneto* and one of the groups of Italian cruisers.

The *Vittorio Veneto* having narrowly escaped several times and only too aware by now of the presence of three British battleships, turned away after the first air attack. She was hit by HMS *Formidable*'s second strike, a torpedo hitting her above her port propellor. She shipped a lot of water, but was able to keep going. The Italian cruiser *Pola* was not so lucky, being badly damaged in the third strike. With her steering gone she was soon stopped and vulnerable.

The climax of this battle came at about 10.00 p.m. The British fleet descended upon the stricken *Pola*, and two other Italian heavy cruisers and four destroyers that had returned to help her. The British took these ships by surprise, their guns still trained fore and aft, and most of the crews abed.

The destroyer HMS *Greyhound* used her searchlight to illuminate the enemy whilst HMS *Warspite*, at a range of about 4,000 yards, wrecked the 8-inch gun *Fiume*. The same fate met the *Zara* and two Italian destroyers, the *Alfieri* and the *Carducci*. British destroyers later used torpedoes to finish off all three cruisers.

At one stage HMS *Jervis* went alongside the *Pola* and took off twenty-two Italian officers and 236 men who were still on board. There was even some thought of trying to tow the cruiser back to Alexandria as a prize of war, but the danger from Axis aircraft was too great.

Nevertheless it was a singular victory. The British picked up some 1,000 Italian seamen as prisoners before they were forced to leave their rescue operations by the advent of dawn, and the threat of land-based air attacks.

They wirelessed the position of the remaining survivors, and more would be picked up by an Italian hospital ship and other vessels, but Italian losses were still high at around 3,000. The British lost two aircraft, but not a single man aboard their warships.

The victory had been an incomplete one, however, for the damaged *Vittorio Veneto*, which at first was even thought to have sunk, managed to reach her home base. Incredibly, when eight British destroyers led by HMS *Jervis*, under Captain Philip Mack, were sent after her, they missed her. The *Vittorio Veneto* had worked up a speed of 20 knots – 5 knots faster than her estimated maximum. The destroyers missed the damaged battleship by thirty miles.

There were several cases of mistaken identity during that confused night of battle. Separate squadrons sailed past in the darkness without identifying each other. At one stage the Italian cruisers returning to support the *Pola* were thought to be the British cruisers, and ignored. At another, both the British cruisers and destroyers spotted a red rocket signal, but each thought the other force was dealing with it.

Finally, there was a controversial signal given by Admiral Cunningham – the kind of signal best interpreted with hindsight in naval memoirs. In the midst of a fierce melee between destroyers, in which everyone was firing torpedoes, Cunningham signalled: 'All ships not engaged in sinking the enemy steer to the northeastward.' He meant it to refer only to those destroyers milling around the British

battleships. It was not intended for the eight destroyers pursuing the *Vittorio Veneto*, which Cunningham thought were engaged in action with the enemy. They were not, and obediently steered northeast.

Even if the Battle of Cape Matapan was not as decisive as Cunningham and all naval strategists would have liked it to be, it *was* influential. Thereafter the Italian fleet would never again attempt to intervene in this same way. Had they done so, the British evacuations from both Greece and Crete might have been even more hard-pressed than they actually were.

Nor did the Italians attempt any major sorties as a battle fleet against the Malta convoys, which they might well have done had they been successful at Cape Matapan. Malta was able to hold out for three years against constant attacks. Despite being so close to Sicily and the heel of Italy, she never contemplated surrender. Malta fully earned the George Cross which King George VI awarded to the island and its people.

Nine months later the Axis powers had their revenge when German U-boat U-331 sank the battleship HMS *Barham*. Her captain and 861 of her crew were lost, but 450 were saved. She was to be the only Allied battleship sunk at sea in European waters by a submarine, although HMS *Royal Oak* had, of course, been sunk in 1939 while at anchor in the supposedly safe harbour of Scapa Flow in Scotland's Orkney Isles.

Further revenge followed a month later, on the night of 18 December, 1941. Three manned 'chariots' from the Italian submarine *Scire* penetrated Alexandria harbour and fixed explosive charges to the battleships *Queen Elizabeth* and *Valiant*.

Nonetheless, the man who dominated sea warfare in the Mediterranean in those early years of the War was undoubtedly Admiral A.B. Cunningham. He would go on to become an admiral of the fleet and would ultimately be ennobled as Viscount Cunningham of Hyndhope.

**In a scene reminiscent of the surrender of the German High Seas Fleet at Scapa Flow in 1919, the Italian Navy lies off Malta following the armistice signed in September 1943. Plans to incorporate the Italian battle squadron into the British Fleet going to the Pacific were abandoned when it proved impossible to ensure a supply of spares and equipment for them from Allied sources.**

British Prime Minister, Mr. Winston Churchill. 'I expect the Battle of Britain is about to begin,' he said after the fall of France, coining the name by which the world's first great battle to be fought entirely in the air was to become known.

# THE BATTLE OF BRITAIN

The Battle of Britain was to be the prelude to 'Operation Sealion', the invasion of Britain. The Local Defence Volunteers, soon to be renamed The Home Guard, began training to support the full-time army. Anti-aircraft fire was part of their training - but it was carried out without using any ammunition.

The rescue of over 300,000 men from the beaches of Dunkirk was a tremendous achievement. Without it World War Two might have been over there and then. On 1 June 1940 *The New York Times* declared, 'So long as the English tongue survives, the word Dunkirk will be spoken with reverence. In that harbour – such a hell as never blazed on earth before – at the end of a lost battle, the rags and blemishes that had hidden the soul of democracy fell away. There, beaten but unconquered, she (England) faced the enemy, this shining thing in the souls of free men which Hitler cannot command. It is the great tradition of democracy. It is the future. It is victory.'

But British Prime Minister Winston Churchill,

with one of his most outstanding speeches, drove home to his people that this had not been a victory, only a spark of triumph at the end of a crushing defeat. ' ... the Battle of France is over. I expect that the Battle of Britain is about to begin.', he warned, coining the term which was to become a milestone in the history of air warfare.

The battle of France had been a land battle, although air supremacy had played a vital part in its outcome. Churchill's assurance that 'we shall fight on the beaches, we shall fight on the landing grounds, in the fields, in the streets, and in the hills', suggests he expected that the Battle of Britain would be mainly a land battle also. How could he know that it would be an air

battle? At that time there had never been a battle fought entirely in the air.

Germany was riding on the crest of a wave. Everything had gone according to plan – or even better. In a little over two months the whole of mainland Western Europe had been overrun. All that stood between them and the total domination of the area was Great Britain. The best part of three months remained before the autumn gales would make the narrow sea crossing difficult, and cause the invasion of Britain to be delayed until 1941.

Germany would adopt the usual plan. The total annihilation of the opposing air force, followed by a rapid advance on the ground, with close air support to break up local pockets of resistance. The English Channel would be treated as just another river, and so far the Wehrmacht had taken rivers in their stride. Admittedly it was a bit wider than the others.

Bridges were out of the question, and everyone would have to go by boat or by air. So there was also going to be the possibility of a hostile navy taking a hand in proceedings. The German Combined Staffs admitted that they did not have total command of the sea, but they decreed that this would not matter once they had established supremacy in the air. So, at least in the opening stages, this was going to be an air battle.

After Dunkirk a number of German aircraft were retained on airfields in northern France to harry the sea ports in the south of England, and the shipping in the English Channel, disrupting the delivery of much needed supplies to Britain. However, the majority of Luftwaffe units were withdrawn to Germany to rest and re-equip.

Meanwhile, Britain prepared to repel an invasion. The army had brought back large numbers of men from France, but the bulk of

**The Luftwaffe's long-range fighter, the Messerschmitt Bf.110, was the only fighter with the ability to escort the bombers throughout their sorties over England. They were unable to match either the Spitfire or the Hurricane in combat, and had to rely upon the tactic of forming a defensive circle to fight a rearguard action whilst the bombers made their escape.**

The Heinkel He.111, the mainstay of the Luftwaffe's bombing effort during the Battle of Britain, was another German combat aircraft that had cut its teeth during the Spanish Civil War.

their equipment had been left behind. A great deal of re-equipping and retraining had to be done before they would be ready to face an invader. To help out, a 'citizens army' was formed. The 'Local Defence Volunteers', soon renamed the 'Home Guard', consisted of those who were too young, too old, or those considered unfit to serve in the regular forces. Members of the Home Guard were equipped with few modern or automatic weapons, often with no ammunition, and even with some obsolete arms from World War One or earlier, and often nothing more than farm implements or wooden replica rifles with which to carry out their drills. For many years they were the butt of music hall humour.

The air defence of Great Britain was to be the responsibility of the Royal Air Force's Fighter Command, led by Air Chief Marshal Sir Hugh Dowding. Dowding was an elderly ex-soldier who had seen operational flying in France during World War One, and who had already been warned that his retirement date was approaching. Perhaps this knowledge had helped his determination when, during the days before Dunkirk, he had confronted Churchill and the War Cabinet, resolutely refusing to allow any more of his single-engine fighter squadrons, the vital Spitfires and Hurricanes, to be sent to almost certain doom in France. What had he to lose except, perhaps, the war? 'I would remind you', he said, 'that the last estimate as to the forces necessary to defend this country was 52 Squadrons, and my strength has now been reduced to the equivalent of 36 Squadrons.'

Air Chief Marshal Sir Hugh Dowding, commander in chief of RAF Fighter Command. Dowding, a veteran of World War I, was due to leave the RAF in 1940. His retirement date was progressively deferred until the Battle of Britain had been won. He was then sent to the United States on a liaison mission.

Fighter Command was not alone in being commanded by a World War I veteran. Reichmarshal Herman Goering (right) had already had a distinguished career as a fighter pilot on the Western Front.

The pilots of 601 'County of London' Squadron (below right) play cricket whilst 'at readiness', waiting for the order to 'scramble'. The fitters sit in the Hurricanes, ready to start the engines as soon as the bell rings.

His command was divided geographically into Groups. Number 11 Group, under Air Vice-Marshal Keith Park, guarded London and the south east counties. They would bear the brunt of the attacks. The immediate support would be provided by Air Vice-Marshal Trafford Leigh-Mallory's Number 12 Group, based in the midland counties, to their north.

The respite before the onslaught, whilst Hitler waited to see if Britain would take fright and sue for peace, provided valuable breathing space for the RAF to lick its wounds from France, and to prepare for what was to come. The aircraft factories worked furiously to supply aircraft. After Dunkirk Dowding's operational squadrons could muster no more than 330 Hurricanes and Spitfires. Only 36 more were available in storage for issue as replacements. Eight weeks later, when the Battle began, the squadrons had over 600 aircraft, and almost 300 more were in reserve.

Pilots were a different matter. France had seen the loss of 300 fighter pilots, and these had been the cream. The front line was made up to strength by bringing young men early from the training schools. They were going to polish their craft the hard way. The Royal Navy loaned 58 pilots from the Fleet Air Arm, one squadron was manned by the Royal Canadian Air Force, and four squadrons by men who had escaped to Britain from the decimated air forces of Poland and Czechoslovakia. The Air Staff now estimated that Dowding would need 120 squadrons for his task. He still had no more than 60, and there was no chance of making up the difference. To make matters worse there was a shortage of anti-aircraft guns. Before the war the Chiefs of Staff had specified a requirement of 4,000 guns. A more recent review had doubled this. There were only 2,000, and the factories could turn out no more than 40 each month.

The one redeeming feature was radar, or 'RDF', – radio direction finding – as it was called at that time. Germany was aware of its existence, and had been keeping an eye upon

A team of four armourers could rearm a Spitfire in under ten minutes. This entailed replacing the empty ammunition boxes with full ones, feeding the belts of ammunition through, cleaning out the barrels, and cocking the guns. This particular Spitfire belonged to 610 'County of Chester' Squadron.

The Junkers Ju.87 (right) had been a star performer in Spain, Poland and Western Europe. However, it was found to be vulnerable over Britain, where the Luftwaffe did not have air superiority, and its use there was limited.

Two Hurricanes (overleaf) of 501 'County of Gloucester' Squadron take off to join in the fighting of Sunday, September 15, 1940. This was the day on which the battle reached its climax; the day which, ever since, has been commemorated as 'Battle of Britain Day'.

The Dornier Do.17, nicknamed the 'Flying Pencil' because of its long, slender fuselage, was the third of the Luftwaffe's long-range bombers to be employed during the Battle of Britain.

its progress since before the beginning of the war. Fortunately for Britain they did not fully appreciate its potential, nor fully realise how it was to be employed. By the standards of fifty years later it was ludicrously crude. In 1940 it was a principle that had been discovered only a few years earlier. It bore no resemblance to the 'plan position indicator' so familiar today, with a screen showing a map of the area covered, and a speck of light indicating each aircraft within range. This was no more than a trace on an oscilloscope. From a peak in the trace the operator had to estimate the direction and range of the target, and decide whether it represented a single aircraft or a formation. It was already possible to identify which traces were created by friendly aircraft, but the equipment looked in one direction only – out to sea. Once a raider, or a defender, had crossed the coast and was flying over the land, its progress could be tracked only by visual observation, or, at night, by its sound.

The stage was set.

By mid-July the Luftwaffe had returned from Germany. Lined up on the airfields in France and Belgium were 2,600 aircraft. Of these, 1,200 were long range bombers, with 1,000 escort fighters. Their task, within the general orders for

the invasion of Britain, issued at that time, was twofold. They were to eliminate the RAF in the air, and disrupt its ground organisation, and they were to strangle the flow of supplies to Britain by stepping up the attacks on its ports and shipping. This latter effort was to begin at once. The onslaught upon the RAF would begin early in August, on a date to be decided, and was to be code named 'Eagle Day'. In its previous campaigns the Luftwaffe had taken between 12 and 48 hours to dispose of any air force which had confronted it. In acknowledgement of the fact that the RAF was the most powerful opponent yet, three to four weeks were allowed for its destruction, so the invasion, code named 'Sea Lion', would begin during the first two weeks of September.

The size and frequency of raids against ports and shipping built up, with occasional attacks against the airfields and the radar stations in the coastal area, and the Germans began to probe Britain's air defences. Large formations of fighters carried out sweeps over southern England, and small formations of bombers, with heavy fighter escorts, raided targets just inland from the coast. The object was to bring the RAF into combat, and to begin the attrition which would destroy Fighter Command.

There was more than one way of bringing down the enemy. There were a number of instances of pilots who were out of ammunition intentionally colliding with their adversary. A leading aircraftman of the ground crew examines the wing tip of a Hurricane which has been clipped in a collision with an enemy aircraft.

The original wartime caption to this July 1940 photograph identifies the pilot as Sergeant Corfe, seen here at the controls of his Spitfire, ready to return to the battle above.

A Spitfire breaks away to pass beneath a 'Flying Pencil'. It was usually the Hurricanes which were directed to attack the bombers, whilst the faster and more agile Spitfires provided top cover to fend off the Messerschmitt Bf.109s.

With the attacks taking place only over the coast, the RAF received insufficient early warning to gain a height advantage, and were always entering combat from below their opponents. And they quickly discovered that the tight formations of their 1930s air show manoeuvres were not ideal when the opposition meant business. They quickly learned to fly much looser formations, what became the classic 'finger four', giving better mutual protection – a lesson which had been learned by the Germans in the Kondor Legion in Spain.

The Luftwaffe found that they were not gaining the upper hand they had anticipated, and they began to probe deeper into British territory, in order to extend the time during which they could engage the defending fighters. But this only gave the fighters more time to gain height, and the results did not significantly improve.

The long-range escort fighter, the twin-engine Messerschmitt Bf.110, proved to be short of speed and manoeuvrability, and they were unhappy when confronted by Hurricanes and Spitfires. The Luftwaffe single-engine fighters found that they had to escort them, as well as the bombers. Not only that, but the RAF retaliated with unexpected aggression and pursued the bombers far out to sea, so that the Germans had to keep fighters in reserve to escort them home. The German fighter pilots were finding things more difficult than they had in the past.

But it was not just the Luftwaffe that was finding life hard. Fighter Command's pilots were under severe strain. Three or four sorties a day was the usual demand, six or seven was not

uncommon, and on most occasions they found themselves at a grave disadvantage. Not only were they attacking an enemy who usually had the advantage of height, but a mere handful of Hurricanes or Spitfires frequently found themselves engaged in mortal combat with formations of a hundred or more German aircraft. Leigh-Mallory, of 12 Group, supported the tactic of getting his aircraft into the air and forming them into 'big wings' before entering combat, but this took time. Park, with his 11 Group in the front line, could not afford the luxury of getting his squadrons airborne and into wings in anticipation of an attack, in case

they were in the wrong place, or beginning to run short of fuel when the attack developed. By the time he had warning of a raid, there was just no time.

In the period from 10 July until 10 August around 100 of Fighter Commands aircraft were shot down, but they had accounted for well over twice that number of Germans. This advantage was enhanced because the RAF was fighting over its home territory. If a pilot was shot down, and survived uninjured, he was soon back in the fray. A well-respected summary of the battle, published thirty years later, records a Hurricane pilot, shot down by a Bf.109 and

The people of southern England were able to watch the Battle of Britain being fought above their heads. When the aircraft were too high to be seen by the naked eye, their movements could be discerned in the tracery of vapour trails left in the sky.

Another Luftwaffe victim of the battle. This Messerschmitt Bf.109 has crash-landed, but is relatively undamaged, embedded in the shingle, somewhere on the coast of England.

An astonishing number of soldiers have turned out to escort these Luftwaffe aircrew into captivity on September 11, 1940. Most of the airmen captured during the Battle of Britain were transferred to Canada until the war was over.

The turning point in the battle came when the Luftwaffe's attention was transferred from the RAF, its airfields and installations to the city of London. The skyline of London (overleaf), with the 300-year-old St. Paul's Cathedral in the background, was shrouded in smoke throughout the first half of September.

slightly wounded, himself shooting down a Bf.109 just three-and-a-half-hours later.

Meanwhile, the Luftwaffe was beginning to build up night bombing, in addition to the daylight raids. Their main night targets were the British aircraft industry, to disrupt the supply of replacements to Fighter Command, and the airfields of RAF Bomber Command. As well as delivering probing attacks into Germany itself, and beginning to seek out and attack the build-up of troop-carrying barges in the Channel ports, Bomber Command's aircraft were attacking the German front line airfields, and interfering with their conduct of the battle. The night activity did not particularly affect the RAF's day fighters, but it did put extra strain on the raid reporting and fighter control organisation, and on the thinly spread anti-aircraft guns.

And the concentrated attack on the RAF had yet to begin.

'Eagle Day' had been provisionally set for 10 August, but, because of unfavourable weather forecasts, this had been put back to 13 August. However, the RAF must have been aware of a change of tactics on the 12th. Early in the morning the Germans launched fierce attacks against the radar stations in the southeast corner of England, so that by 9 o'clock there was a gap in the early-warning system stretching from Dover to beyond the Isle of Wight. Undetected now, a series of further raids were assembled over France, including one of over 200 aircraft, briefed to attack targets throughout the southeast area, including three of the RAF's airfields in the coastal area.

By an enormous effort, all but one of the radar stations were operating again by the evening, so that, when 'Eagle Day' dawned, the defenders could again see what was happening.

From then on, the pressure on Fighter Command was unremitting. The Luftwaffe no longer waited to draw the fighters into combat. They attacked them on their own airfields, or, if they were already in the air, their fields were attacked behind their backs, so that they had nowhere to land. At Tangmere, near Chichester, a pilot returning from a sortie in his Hurricane found the airfield under attack. He was obviously having great difficulty in finding a path for his landing, but he managed to touch down safely, and the aircraft rolled to a halt. Immediately it was set upon by a swarm of

enemy aircraft, guns blazing, and within seconds the Hurricane was an inferno. The ground crews made superhuman efforts to extract the pilot from his cockpit, and he was carried to hospital with severe burns. The next day he died of his injuries, and Pilot Officer William Fiske became the first American volunteer to die flying with the RAF in the defence of Great Britain.

It was on the same day that the Victoria Cross – Britains highest award for gallantry in combat – was awarded to Flight Lieutenant James Nicolson. Nicolson was leading a flight of three Hurricanes into an attack on a formation of Bf.110s, when the Hurricanes themselves were attacked by Bf.109s diving out of the sun. Immediately all three Hurricanes were hit, two of them bursting into flames. As his wing man abandoned his blazing aircraft, Nicolson, wounded by cannon shells which had struck his aircraft, and sitting in a cockpit full of flames from a ruptured fuel tank, realised that his Bf.110 was still in his sights. He remained in his aircraft to press home the attack, before he himself bailed out, suffering serious burns to his face and hands, and with his clothing alight. It was the only time that the Victoria Cross was awarded to a Fighter Command pilot in the whole of World War Two. Sadly, Nicolson was never credited with the Messerschmitt which he destroyed, and he died later in the war when an aircraft in which he was travelling as a passenger crashed.

Day after day the battle continued. Day after day the Royal Air Force destroyed two enemy aircraft for each one they lost. But their fighter pilots were under continuous strain, attacked on the ground as well as in the air, and the Luftwaffe had had more than twice as many aircraft to begin with. By the end of August Fighter Command was virtually on its knees. New pilots were coming from the training schools with less than ten hours training on front-line fighters. Bomber pilots were being transferred to fill the gaps. At this crucial moment the Luftwaffe changed its tactics.

On 24 August German bombs fell on London. It is now believed that this was accidental. A bomber, uncertain of its position and in difficulties, jettisoned its load to help make good its escape. The RAF retaliated. Over a succession of evenings Bomber Command despatched 80 aircraft or more to attack targets in Berlin. This Hitler could not tolerate. On

September 2 the Luftwaffe received orders that from now on the main target was to be London.

Five days later the new strategy was put into effect. September 7 started quietly, then towards the end of the afternoon the defenders became aware that a raid, which looked like the biggest so far, was building up. Almost a thousand enemy aircraft flew towards the Thames estuary. As they had done on previous days, the fighters fell back inland to defend their airfields, so that when the raiders turned west to follow the River Thames, they had an unopposed approach to the city of London. The fighters rushed in to protect their capital, but they were too late. The Germans lost 40 aircraft as they fought their way home, but by that time the docklands, and the residential areas of London's East End which surrounded them, were ablaze. The sky was hidden by thick, black smoke. As darkness fell it was the turn of the night bombers. Some 250 aircraft, their target illuminated by the fires which blazed under the pall of smoke, marked as no target

had ever been marked before, dropped their bombs into the inferno. Even more bombs than had fallen during the daylight raid.

London's loss was Fighter Command's gain. Now that their airfields were left alone, they were able to operate with renewed confidence and vigour, even though their resources were saturated by the concentrations of raiders thrown against them.

The climax came on September 15. Wave upon wave of raiders assembled over the French coast, watched by the far-seeing eye of the RAF's radar. A mass of aircraft which took so long to assemble that 17 of 11 Group's squadrons were able to get airborne and climb to a favourable height over the south of England while waiting for the attack to come. There was even time for five of 12 Group's squadrons to form up into their 'big wing', to back them up. Even so, it was impossible to deflect such an armada. Large numbers of the raiders reached London. Harassed by the fighters it was impossible for them to aim at specific targets.

**The Home Guard, on duty again, watch over a Junkers Ju.88.**

German aircraft shot down over England were a valuable source of technical intelligence, and were guarded to prevent pilfering by souvenir hunters. Home Guard soldiers, in full field order, pass the time by studying the victory symbols on the fin of a Messerschmitt Bf.110.

Haphazardly their bomb-loads rained down across London and its suburbs, before they turned for home, severely mauled. Then, as the fighters landed to refuel and rearm, more raiders approached. Air Vice-Marshal Park called for more support from his neighbours in 12 Group. Prime Minister Winston Churchill was visiting 11 Group's Headquarters at Uxbridge, and was watching the activity in the Operations Room from the gallery above. The state boards seemed to indicate that all the available squadrons in 11 Group were either engaged, or on the ground being refuelled and rearmed. 'What reserves have we?', he asked. 'There are none, sir.' replied Park. But with this last gasp the enemy was repulsed.

'185 Victories!', cried the newspapers next morning. When the claims had been checked, and duplicates had been eliminated, the true tally was nearer 60. Even so, the Luftwaffe was defeated.

The German daylight attacks on England, their attempt to overthrow the Royal Air Force and pave the way for the invasion of Britain; showed a sharp downturn. At German War Headquarters, the War Diary recorded, 'The enemy air force is still by no means defeated. On the contrary, it shows increasing activity. The weather situation does not permit us to expect a period of calm. The Fuhrer therefore decides to postpone Operation "Sealion" indefinitely.'

The Battle of Britain had been won. The tide had been turned by 3,080 young men of 14 different nationalities, serving with the Royal Air Force. More than one in five of them died during the Battle, and less than half of them would survive to celebrate the final victory in 1945. In the words of Churchill, that great orator who, on September 15 had looked in vain for reserves: 'Never was so much owed by so many to so few.'

# SINKING THE BISMARCK

Germany's mightiest battleship, the *Bismarck*, was launched on 14 February, 1939, in Hamburg. She was christened by the Countess Dorothy von Lowenfeld, a granddaughter of the Iron Chancellor, Prince Otto Eduard Leopold von Bismarck (1815-1895), after whom the battleship was named.

In May 1941 a running battle in the North Atlantic resulted in the loss of HMS *Hood* and the sinking of Germany's mightiest battleship, the *Bismarck*. It was to be one of the last encounters of its kind.

Between them, both sides made almost every mistake in the book; victory was nevertheless achieved because at the same time the Royal Navy also obeyed most of the rules for success in war. If that sounds contradictory, that is the way of battle at sea.

After the loss of the *Admiral Graf Spee* in the River Plate in December 1939, Hitler was fairly cautious with his use of warships. The *Admiral Scheer* was out raiding for nearly six months in the winter of 1940-1941. She sank 100,000 tons of shipping and the armed merchant cruiser HMS *Jervis Bay*, whilst the latter was protecting her convoy.

The heavy cruiser *Admiral Hipper* made two raids in late 1940 and early 1941, one more successful than the other. The battleships *Scharnhorst* and *Gneisenau* were also out in early 1941, under Admiral Lutjens. Though they were deterred by battleships from attacking two big convoys, they still sank over 100,000 tons of shipping.

As a reward, Admiral Lutjens was appointed to command Hitler's next major naval sortie, flying his flag in the *Bismarck*, under Captain Lindemann. The cruiser *Prinz Eugen*, under Captain Brinkmann, was to provide support. Plans to involve the *Scharnhorst* and the *Gneisenau* were shelved; they had both suffered RAF bomb damage in Brest.

The *Bismarck* and the *Prinz Eugen* were in the Baltic, facing a difficult passage to the North Sea and the Atlantic. They had to pass through the narrow Kattegat between Denmark and Sweden and the almost equally narrow Skaggerak between Denmark and Norway.

They were spotted by a Swedish warship. Learning of this, the British naval attaché in Stockholm, alerted the Admiralty in London. Strike one to intelligence. An RAF Coastal Command attempt to bomb them while they lay in a Norwegian fjord failed.

The commander in chief of the British Home Fleet, Admiral Tovey, began moving ships into place as soon as he knew there was a possibility that the *Bismarck* might come out. He already had a force of cruisers patrolling the wide stretch between Iceland and the Faeroes. There was also a regular cruiser patrol in the narrower passage of the Denmark Strait between Iceland and Greenland – the route the *Bismarck* would choose.

In the Denmark Strait, the cruiser *Suffolk* was about to be relieved by another 8-inch gun cruiser, the *Norfolk*. Flying the flag of Rear-Admiral Wake-Walker, she would play a key role in the battle. Admiral Tovey despatched the battlecruiser HMS *Hood*, together with the battleship HMS *Prince of Wales*, to Iceland, to support the waiting and watching cruisers.

The decision to send the *Prince of Wales* was a brave one, for she was so new that contractors were still working on some of her 14-inch guns, and she had not completed her working-up period.

Tovey's main Home Fleet force at Scapa Flow included his own flagship, the battleship HMS *King George V*, under Captain Patterson; a dozen or so cruisers and destroyers; the battlecruiser HMS *Repulse* and an aircraft carrier, the HMS *Illustrious*, the latter two detached from convoy escort duties.

That important element in all battles in northern waters, bad weather, soon began to play its part. The two German ships had slipped out to sea while visibility was low, hence their absence was not noted till a single Fleet Air Arm aircraft flew in to look at the fjord and the Norwegian port of Bergen on the evening of 22 May. Admiral Tovey and his main force left Scapa Flow at once; this time it was the *Luftwaffe* who were prevented by the weather from observing the British movements and the ships' departures.

Despite rain and snow squalls, the *Bismarck* and her consort did not pass round Iceland and through the Denmark Strait unobserved. At 1922 hours on 22 May HMS *Suffolk* saw them steaming between her and the ice in the Strait, heading south-west towards the open Atlantic.

HMS *Suffolk*, under Captain Ellis, then began one of the most intense shadowing operations of all time. She was joined about an hour later by the cruiser that had been due to relieve her on patrol, HMS *Norfolk*, under Captain Phillips. Although briefly under fire from the German ship, the cruisers were able to send out a Sighting Report, and keep tracking, using smoke or the poor visibility to keep out of trouble. Meanwhile, HMS *Hood* and HMS *Prince of Wales* headed across from south of Iceland to intercept.

Then, everything began to go wrong. The shadowing cruisers lost the *Bismarck*, and Vice Admiral Holland in HMS *Hood* guessed wrongly about the direction in which to head for an encounter. When this encounter finally came about, he did not recognize it to be with the *Prinz Eugen*, which had taken the lead, whilst the *Bismarck* had dropped behind to deal with any shadowing cruiser that came too close.

The *Norfolk* and the *Suffolk* were actually a good fifteen miles behind when battle began. The role allotted them, which was to take out the *Prinz Eugen* while the two big British ships concentrated on the *Bismarck*, was thus way beyond their reach.

Worse errors were yet to come. When the British ships came under fire the much more vulnerable *Hood* was in the lead. What's more, neither the *Hood* nor the *Prince of Wales* were on a bearing that allowed them to use both their fore and aft sets of guns together. The *Hood* began firing at the *Prinz Eugen*, thinking it was the *Bismarck* because of its leading position – the German silhouettes were admittedly similar. Meanwhile the *Prince of Wales* engaged the *Bismarck* with her forward turrets only. From the start, both German ships concentrated their full sets of eight 15-inch guns and eight 8-inch guns on HMS *Hood*.

They immediately scored hits on HMS *Hood*, and started a fire. At 0600 hours, just as the two British ships altered course so as to bring all their turrets into action, the *Hood* blew up. Shells from the *Bismarck* had gone through her decks and hit a magazine. HMS *Hood* simply disintegrated. Only three men were rescued; Admiral Holland, Captain Kerr and all the other 1,419 officers and ratings were killed.

With hindsight it is clear that HMS *Prince of Wales* should have been in the lead. In the same way that three battlecruisers had been sunk at Jutland in World War I, so went the *Hood*, with shells crashing down on her decks. Speed was no substitute for armour.

**Left: the *Bismarck* in all her glory. Not completed until August 1940, she displaced 42,000 tons and carried eight 15-inch guns, with a secondary armament of twelve 5.9-inch guns. She could steam at 30 knots, and had a range of well over 10,000 miles.**

**Top right: the British battlecruiser HMS *Hood*, pre-war flagship of the Royal Navy and, at the start of the War in 1939, one of the finest warships afloat. Built in 1920, she displaced 42,000 tons. Her armament was eight 15-inch guns, with a secondary armament of fourteen 4-inch guns. Despite her designation as a battle cruiser, she was really more of a fast battleship; though events would prove her to be too lightly armoured for that role. Bottom right: HMS *Hood* engaged in pre-war manoeuvres with the British Home Fleet in the English Channel. Most pre-war German battle-planning and naval exercises were held with the Hood as the enemy centrepiece that had to be defeated.**

Top left: the *Bismarck* photographed at sea from her accompanying cruiser the *Prinz Eugen*. The latter was a heavy cruiser of some 15,000 tons with eight 8-inch guns, twelve 4-inch and 12 torpedo tubes.

Another photograph taken from the *Prinz Eugen* shows the *Bismarck* (bottom left) in action against HMS *Hood* and HMS *Prince of Wales*. The *Prinz Eugen* would soon leave her consort and head out into the Atlantic by herself.

Right: the British battleship HMS *King George V*, flagship of Admiral Tovey, commander in chief of the British Home Fleet. She led the hunt for the *Bismarck* and helped reduce her to a shattered hulk. Completed in 1940, the *King George V* carried ten 14-inch guns and sixteen 5.25-inch guns. Her heavily armoured decks and speed of 30 knots made her a fine fighting ship.

Both the *Bismarck* and the *Prince of Wales* had scored hits on each other. Neither knew the extent of the damage they had inflicted. Had the *Bismarck* known her only opponent had half her main guns out of action, she might have closed to finish her off. However, the *Prince of Wales* made smoke and turned away to await reinforcements.

As it happened these were heading for the scene at full speed. Admiral Tovey's force was some 300 miles to the southeast; Force 'H' from Gibraltar had left its convoy to head north, as had at least two other battleships and another aircraft carrier.

*Bismarck* had her 'shadows' with her again, and they reported she was heading south towards France or the Atlantic, rather than returning to go around Iceland and back to Germany. Aircraft launched from HMS *Victorious*, after being put off by coming unexpectedly across a neutral U.S. coastguard vessel in the area, did score one innefective torpedo hit on the *Bismarck*.

The *Prinz Eugen* was detached to continue on into the Atlantic alone. She did so, but a few days later developed engine trouble and had to sail to France. She need concern our story here no more.

Then the British lost the *Bismarck* again, mainly because they thought she was heading west into the Atlantic. She had actually turned for St. Nazaire, the only French port with repair yards big enough to handle a vessel of her size.

The net was tightening, but still the *Bismarck's* luck held. The British Admiralty made a mistake in its analysis of the direction from which the German battleship's signals were coming. It seemed she might be heading for the Iceland-Faeroes passage.

By the time it became clear that the *Bismarck* was heading for France, Admiral Tovey had already come to the same conclusion and set course accordingly. Bad weather prevented RAF Coastal Command from finding the German ship again till the morning of 26 May, 1942, – over three days since she was first sighted. Bismarck was less than 700 miles from Brest and the full protection of German aircraft and U-boats.

But Admiral Somerville's Force 'H' was closing. Although his World War I vintage battlecruiser HMS *Renown* had been ordered not to tangle with the *Bismarck*, there were still the planes from the *Ark Royal*.

Survivors of the *Bismarck* come ashore in a British port after being rescued from the cold waters of the Atlantic by British warships. Only 119 from the 2,400 men on board the *Bismarck* survived. Admiral Lutyens and the ship's commander, Captain Lindeman, were not among them. Only three survivors were picked up from HMS *Hood's* crew of over 1,400. They did not include Admiral Holland or Captain Kerr.

The *Bismarck*'s survivors under armed guard in a British port before being taken away to spend the rest of the war as POWs. One officer survivor, Baron Burkard von Mullenheim-Rechberg wrote a book about his experience, *Battleship Bismarck: A Survivor's Story*.

Torpedoes might just reduce the *Bismarck*'s speed, and allow Admiral Tovey and his two Home Fleet battleships to catch up. Sixteen aircraft from HMS *Ark Royal* took off in vile weather and, by mistake, launched their attack on the British cruiser HMS *Sheffield*. Luckily, drastic evasive action and a fault in the torpedoes' magnetic firing mechanism saved the *Sheffield*.

The torpedoes on the next flight of fifteen planes from the Ark Royal were equipped with contact charges. They were directed to their target by the *Sheffield*. In dreadful weather, high wind and poor visibility the aircraft attacked, despite heavy anti-aircraft fire.

It was a brave and magnificently uncoordinated attack. Thirteen torpedoes were dropped, two of which hit the *Bismarck*. One of them, like the torpedo hit scored from the *Illustrious* a day earlier, did little damage as it crashed into the ship's heavily-armoured side. However the other hit near the stern, wrecking the steering gear and jamming the rudder. The *Bismarck*'s luck had at last run out. Admiral Lutjens signalled Germany: 'Can no longer manoeuvre. We fight to the last shell. Long live the Führer'.

British destroyers, led by Admiral Vian of Altmark fame, raced in and fired more torpedoes, further slowing the crippled battleship. Admiral Tovey now knew that the *Bismarck* could not escape. There was no need to risk a night action. At dawn next day his two battleships, HMS *Rodney* and HMS *King George V*, bore down on the *Bismarck* with their nine 16-inch guns and ten 14-inch guns.

The *Bismarck* fired her forward guns but soon these were hit, as were her control positions, both forward and aft. The *Bismarck* fought on, now using her aft guns singly. By 1000 hours even these were hit; the pride of the German Fleet was a burning wreck.

Two cruisers, HMS *Norfolk* and HMS *Dorsetshire*, closed, and fired torpedoes. It is not clear whether these, or scuttling charges placed by the German battleship's crew, did the trick, but shortly afterwards the *Bismarck*'s bows rose up and she sank, stern first.

The *Bismarck* had put up a gallant fight, and went down with her colours still flying. With her went Admiral Lutjens, Captain Lindemann and all but 119 men out of the some 2,400 on board. In addition to Admiral Lutjen's staff, there were a number of prize crews on board.

New Yorkers read the news about the sinking of the Bismarck on a bulletin board in Times Square. The follow-up story suggesting that the *Prinz Eugen* would also be taken care of was not fulfilled at the time. The cruiser developed engine trouble, however, and could not continue her Atlantic raid, seeking safety in a French port.

Their job would have been to bring the *Bismarck's* captures home. There was also a posse of war correspondents there to describe her exploits to the world.

What lessons can be learned from this particular battle? First, that there is always going to be an element of luck involved. Luck as to where shells strike, as in the case of the *Hood*, or as to where a single torpedo hits, as in the case of the *Bismarck's* steering gear. Secondly, that the weather will always be a great influence, for good and for ill. It stopped aircraft from finding the *Bismarck* at first, but played a key role in the attacks later. Finally, despite two lapses, the 'shadowing' tactics employed by the cruisers were textbook examples of this procedure.

Perhaps the best aspect from the British point of view was the way in which the British Admiralty trusted the man on the spot, and did not override his decisions from headquarters. Admiral Tovey also let his flag officers take decisions – though he always greatly regretted not ordering HMS *Prince of Wales* to lead, and HMS *Hood* to follow.

There was courage too. From the slow-moving torpedo planes of HMS *Ark Royal* to the terrier-like attacks of Admiral Vian's destroyers, which could have been blown to smithereens even by the *Bismarck's* secondary armament. Nor must the courage of the men of the *Bismarck* herself be forgotten.

Though no-one knew it at the time, the loss of the *Bismarck* marked the end of German warship raids against convoys in the Atlantic. Her remaining warships would be used against the Russian convoys. British battleships were now free to travel to the Pacific.

# BARBAROSSA - THE DRIVE EAST

A tracked vehicle pulls a wheeled trailer loaded with bicycles along one of the better Russian roads. Often termed a mechanized army, the Germans in fact suffered from a severe shortage of tracked vehicles. The much vaunted 'modern' army took 625,000 horses into Russia.

On Sunday 22nd June, 1941, during the small hours of the morning, elements from 148 divisions – totalling 3,300,000 German soldiers – were mobilized. With them were nineteen *Panzerdivisions* (excluding *Schutzstaffel* forces); 3,350 tanks; 7,184 artillery pieces; 600,000 vehicles; 625,000 horses and 2,000 aircraft – all ready to begin Operation 'Barbarossa'. They were supported by the German Navy, the Finnish Army, Rumanian armies and Italian, Hungarian, Slovak, Croatian and Spanish units. This campaign was intended to destroy the Soviet Union.

The German strategy for the invasion of Russia was indecisive: contradictory edicts from Army High Command (OKH), Armed Forces High Command (OKW) and, occasionally, direct interventions by Adolf Hitler himself combined to produce a number of unresolved aims and objectives. The campaign was launched with the hope that the bulk of Soviet strength could be trapped and destroyed by the time the Dneiper River had been reached. Further goals were to be determined in

accordance with later circumstances.

Order Number 21, which established Operation 'Barbarossa' in December, 1940, gave mention to the Donets Basin and Moscow in just a single paragraph.

The forces of the Soviet Union already mobilized in the west before the implementation of Operation 'Barbarossa' were scattered through lines of first and second echelons to a depth of over 250 miles in some places. They were organized under Special Military Districts which converted to fronts (Army Groups) in time of war. To the south of the Pripet Marshes, covering a front of 540 miles, the Russian Southwestern Front and South Front defended the Ukraine. The Southwestern Front consisted of 5th, 6th, 12th and 26th armies; whilst the South Front consisted only of 9th Army and some independent units of corps' size. The best estimates break these forces down into between sixty and seventy infantry divisions, eleven cavalry divisions and twenty-eight armoured brigades. Few of the extant infantry divisions were at more than half wartime

strength and the mechanized units were, for the most part, still in the process of formation. The tank strength of the units deployed over the whole front before June, 1941, averaged fifty-three per cent of their potential force.

Moreover, Soviet forces were under dual command: on the Southwestern Front, for example, Colonel General M.P. Kirponos was the military commander and Nikita S. Khrushchev was the political commander.

Attached to the Southwestern Front was Army Group South, under Field Marshal Gerd von Rundstedt. Separated from the rest of the Front by a gap of about sixty miles because of the Pripet Marshes, its initial goal was to take the Ukraine. For this task there were two armies, consisting of thirty infantry divisions: 1st *Panzergruppe* commanded by Colonel General Ewald von Kleist and 4th Air Fleet. Italian, Hungarian, Slovak and Croation troops, equivalent to about eight or nine divisions,

were also under this command. To the south, along the Soviet-Roumanian border, were one joint German-Roumanian and two Roumanian armies.

In 1941, full-strength divisional numbers were as follows: German forces incorporated an infantry of 17,734 men; a *Panzerdivision* of 15,600 men; 165 tanks, and a motorized infantry of 16,400 men. Russian military might incorporated infantry divisions across three levels of strength – their full wartime divisional complement amounted to 14,483 men. Armoured divisions incorporated about 12,000 men and 375 tanks; motorized divisions incorporated about 12,000 men and 275 tanks.

The Russian Southwestern Front put up a far more organized opposition to the German advance than was mounted against them elsewhere. Despite having 277 Russian aircraft destroyed by noon on the first day of Operation 'Barbarossa's' implementation – and having,

German infantry storming a railway station. The lack of good roads - only three percent were metalled in Russia - increased the importance of the railways for supply. As they retreated, the Russians destroyed as much line and rolling stock as they could. The Germans also had to convert the Russian gauge to suit their trains.

July, 1941: a Russian aircraft is loaded with bombs. Unfortunately, on the Southwestern Front 277 Russian aircraft had been destroyed on June 22nd; and virtually the entire air arm had been put out of action within the first two weeks of the conflict.

A Russian T-34 moves past an abandoned German anti-tank gun. The process of re-equipping the Red Army with the T-34 as its standard battle tank was in its early stages. Too few of these excellent tanks were available, while those in use were too thinly distributed to be effective in 1941.

by the end of June, virtually no air cover at all (through combat losses and simple lack of high-octane fuel and spare parts), Kirponos nonetheless managed to extricate the bulk of his forces from the line of attack by sacrificing most of his available armour in an effort to impede the advance of von Kleist.

He also managed to avoid the hammer of 6th and 17th armies in their attempt to crush his troops against the anvil of 11th Army which, with the Roumanian 3rd and 4th armies, had moved onto the offensive across the Prut River on 1st July. By 9th July, Kirponos had managed to establish a new line. The following day, Soviet Supreme Command reorganized all their southern forces and channelled them into the Southwestern Front. Marshal Budenny and Khrushchev were given command with Kirponos and General Tyulenev acting as field commanders.

Von Rundstedt's schedule had given him four weeks in which to destroy the enemy forces in the western Ukraine and take Kiev.

Although this sector was regarded as the best tank country on the Russian front, summer rainstorms could quickly turn the black earth into a quagmire and the countryside would be littered with vehicles waiting for the ground to dry out – only three per cent of roads and tracks in the Soviet Union were surfaced.

Despite the German armies' slower than expected progress, by early August the Russian 6th and 12th armies had been trapped and were being destroyed in the Uman pocket, where the Germans claimed 103,000 prisoners. On 8th August, Odessa was cut off and besieged, and on 18th August General Zhukov uttered his famous warning to Joseph Stalin about the impending danger of complete destruction of the Southwestern Front as Budenny's forces were pushed back onto the Dneiper River. The danger which Zhukov foresaw was building to a crescendo, but not so much from Army Group South as from the north.

The success of German Army Group Centre

Two German NCOs examine a disabled Russian T28 heavy tank. Such obsolescent machines were used as defensive strongpoints by the Russians, as they were far too slow, and therefore vulnerable, to be effective in an attacking role.

was producing worries for German High Command. Its advance to Smolensk had left flanks dangerously exposed. One third of its lorries were out of action and ammunition was not being sufficiently replenished, which brought stocks to worryingly low levels. The supply of POL (petrol, oil and lubricants) was insufficient, and subsistence supplies were

Facing page: Colonel General Franz Halder, the Chief of General Staff, OKH, stands over Colonel General Heinz Guderian, commander of the Second *Panzer* Group. As one of Hitler's favourites, Guderian was permitted to defy OKH policy and keep his entire Group together during the drive south.

The German Army's use of concentrated tank formations (below) was a major factor in their success during the first months of the war. Despite this, the 'tank lobby' continued to be in periodic conflict with traditionalists, including Hitler, who wanted as large a number of Russian prisoners as possible.

frequently nonexistent. Moreover, ferocious Russian resistance in the Smolensk pocket until 5th August and an unsuccessful battle to hold the Yel'nya salient ate into German attempts at stockpiling. By the end of July, elements of 9th Army had relieved most of 2nd *Panzergruppe* at the Front, and Colonel General Heinz Guderian could repair and replenish his units. On 1st August, XXVI *Panzer Korps* moved southwards toward Roslavl'. Its aim was to secure the Gomel-Bryansk area as the base for a 'right hook' on Moscow.

Within German High Command the lack of clear strategy with which Operation 'Barbarossa' had been launched was once more under discussion, with arguments also rising about the target priority of Leningrad, Moscow or the Ukraine. There were arguments too about the tactics of armour and infantry: should armoured divisions attack well in advance of infantry, or should the two forces stay closer to each other?

After nearly a month of disagreements a compromise was formed by Colonel General Franz Halder, the Chief of General Staff OKH,

and Colonel General Alfred Jodl, Chief of Operations Department OKW. They felt that campaigns against Moscow and the Ukraine could be launched simultaneously if 2nd *Panzergruppe* was divided and the proposed formation of the Leningrad Front delayed. Their plan collapsed when Guderian visited Hitler on 23rd August and persuaded him that his own *Panzergruppe* should not be split. As a result it was determined that the Ukraine was to be taken first and Moscow would be the subsequent target.

On 18th August, Zhukov sent a telegram to Stalin warning him of the imminent threat of forty-four Russian divisions on the Southwestern Front being encircled by the enemy. He proposed that a force of army size be composed from troops taken from the Far East and the Moscow defence lines to be deployed along the Desna River. Stalin was convinced that the attack would be on Moscow and that Guderian's move south was a prelude to his turning northeastwards towards the city. On 18th August this surmise was correct. There was little possibility that Stalin could know of the

indecisive and changeable German target strategy. Only on 23rd August did he become suddenly terribly wrong.

The following day Marshal Shaposhnikov, who had replaced Zhukov as Chief of General Staff, informed Lieutenant General Eremenko on the Bryansk Front that he was to attack Guderian's forces as they swung to the north. That day, 24th August, 17th *Panzerdivision* was in Pochep and 3rd *Panzerdivision* had reached Starodub. The Russian 13th Army was splintering.

On 25th August, Colonel General von Weichs' 2nd Army began to push down between the Dneiper and Desna rivers, advancing on 5th Army of Major General Potapov, who had failed to turn his northern flank to defend Chernigov. On 26th August, 10th Motorized Division established a bridgehead over the Desna River, between Novgorod Seversky and Korop. Colonel General

Kuznetsov, the commander of 21st Army, began to withdraw across the river but did not inform 40th Army, commanded by Major General Podlas, of his decision. As 40th Army shifted southeastwards, an gap developed. On 31st August, the last day of the month, a single 5th Army corps, 15th Rifle Corps, was the only force there to delay von Weichs. On 2nd September, an attack was launched at last from the Bryansk Front against Guderian's flank towards Roslavl'. The bulk of 2nd *Panzergruppe* was already over one hundred miles to the south, crossing the Desna River.

The northern flank of the Southwestern Front disintegrated. On 8th September, Zhukov met Stalin to warn him that Guderian would drive through it and create a pocket with von Kleist's 1st *Panzergruppe*, breaking out from the Kremenchug bridgehead. Again he urged the abandonment of Kiev. In fact it was probably already too late to get Russian forces out intact. The day before Guderian crossed the Seym River, Chernigov fell to 2nd Army, which had started across the Desna River. By 10th September, as 40th Army collapsed around Konotop, 3rd *Panzerdivision* took Romny on the Sula River. Kirponos sent a desperate request for reserves. There were none. The gap in Russian defences was now over forty-miles wide.

On 11th September, a telegram arrived at Supreme Command in Moscow, pleading for permission to attempt a withdrawal. Permission was refused. Marshal Timoshenko would replace Budenny. A suggested rescue bid with forces from the Bryansk Front was put in perspective when Eremenko revealed that he had only twenty available tanks still in battle condition. The Southwestern Front's role now was to stand its ground and fight simply in order to soak up German men, materials and time.

On 12th September, 1st *Panzergruppe* smashed through 297th Rifle Division of 38th Army. Southwestern Chief of Staff, Major General V.I. Tupikov, informed Shaposhnikov: 'The catastrophe has begun'.

The trap closed on 16th September when 1st and 2nd *Panzergruppen* met north of Lubny. Two days later, permission was given at last for Russian forces to fight their way out. Kirponos and his staff were all killed in a fire fight on 20th September, and the Russian pocket had been eliminated by 26th September.

**Left: German infantrymen cross the Dneiper River in a rubber boat. The advance of von Kleist's 1st *Panzer* Group from the Kremenchug bridgehead over the Dneiper met up with Guderian's drive south to close the trap that eliminated the Soviet's Southwestern Front. Rivers generally proved ineffectual as defence lines on the Eastern Front. The German infantry, slogging along days behind the glamour units in the *Panzer Korps*, had the task of mopping up the vast pockets of Red Army troops. Such cut-off units had often been left still capable of fierce resistance.**

German troops move past huge quantities of Russian equipment. As well as claiming over 600,000 prisoners, the German forces took the vehicles, guns and equipment of four complete Russian armies in the Kiev pocket.

The Germans claimed the destruction of four Russian armies: 5th, 21st, 26th and 37th, and the terrible mauling of three others: 13th, 38th and 40th. They claimed 665,212 prisoners and enormous quantities of equipment either destroyed or captured. Soviet figures give 677,085 as the number of soldiers on the Front, of whom 150,541 were outside the encirclement or escaped. German casualties in the Battle for the Ukraine numbered around 160,000.

Whichever figures are closest to the truth, the Battle of Kiev was a massive disaster for the Russians. Over half a million were dead or prisoners of war with, it transpired, a ten per cent survival rate to the war's end. The fall of the Ukraine opened up the Donets Basin and Crimea to Germany. These three areas produced over half of the Soviet grain harvest. Industrial production figures were plummetting by the end of 1941: compared to summer production figures, for example, steel production levels fell to thirty-three per cent, artillery shells to sixty per cent and aircraft to twenty-seven of their previous totals. Moreover, the black-earth region was the most important area for Russian production of coal, iron, steel, power, aluminium, chemicals and heavy engineering.

Guderian judged Kiev to be a tactical but not a strategic victory. The standard argument is that the diversion of 2nd *Panzergruppe* and 2nd Army to the south delayed the launch of Operation 'Typhoon' against Moscow by a crucial six weeks. That meant continuation of the operation into a second year, and Germany's chance of victory through *Blitzkrieg* was lost. Thereafter the contest became one of attrition.

The Battle of Kiev raises several important points. Only a maximum of fourteen to seventeen armoured and infantry divisions could have been launched on Moscow in September. This would have been insufficient. A drive by armoured divisions alone into the Moscow Zone of Defence would have been risky and unlikely to secure such a large urban area. Thus, even allowing for the consumption of resources entailed in the drive south, this campaign only contributed a couple of weeks to the delay of Operation 'Typhoon'.

Zhukov's analysis was that to leave a Southwestern Front capable of striking the flank of an advancing centre would have been courting disaster. The major industrial base of the country would also have been allowed a winter of production. Finally, would even a successful attack on Moscow have been a strategic victory? That great tactical victories may counteract a fundamental disproportion of strength between protagonists is not unknown in history, but is sufficiently rare. Even rarer would be a situation in which achieving such a victory was itself the cause of the lesser power being beaten by the greater.

# INFAMY AT PEARL HARBOR

Fifty years after the event it is easier to take an objective view as to what Japan's attack on Pearl Harbor meant to the Allies. Although 7 December, 1941, has gone down in history as a day of infamy and of treachery of the basest kind, it is now seen almost as a 'blessing in disguise' in terms of World War II.

War in the Pacific was inevitable in view of Japan's aggressive and expansionist policies in Southeast Asia. The manner and method of that war's beginning polarised public opinion in the U.S.A and in the rest of the Free World against the Axis powers.

Hitler and Mussolini, who were as surprised as anybody when the attack at Pearl Harbor took place, decided quite needlessly to declare war on the U.S.A. This left Congress, which had great doubts about fighting a two-ocean war, no choice but to accept that America must fight in Europe as well as in the Pacific.

In terms of the battle at sea, it marked the real moment of changeover from battles fought with guns to battles fought with aircraft. Against Pearl Harbor Japan launched the biggest force of carrier-borne aircraft ever to take part in a war at sea. Compared with the British attack on Taranto, which the Japanese had assiduously studied and in which twenty-one planes were used, Japan employed over 350 in her attack on America's great naval base in Hawaii.

The political manoeuvres that preceded 7 December are now all known. How, even as her envoys were negotiating peace in Washington, Japan's war fleet had sailed from the Kuriles. Led at sea by Vice Admiral Chuichi Nagumo, the fleet's centrepiece was two aircraft-carrier forces. These totalled six of the largest and fastest vessels of their kind – the *Akagi*, the *Kaga*, the *Hiryu*, the *Soryu*, the *Shokaku* and the *Zuikaku*. Between them, they housed some 430 bombers, torpedo-bombers and fighters. Their crews were fully-trained professionals, many of them already having had combat experience in China. The carriers were protected by two battleships, the *Hiyei* and the *Kirishima*, two heavy cruisers and a destroyer flotilla of ten ships.

The aircrews trained for this operation for months, and knew the model of Pearl Harbor and its defences intimately. It is said that so

fierce and realistic was their training that they actually lost more aircraft during the rehearsals than they did on the day.

Anchored in Pearl Harbor was the great bulk of the American Pacific Fleet: eight out of nine battleships, and over eighty other vessels. The battleships were mainly tied up in pairs along the quayside. It was a Sunday in peacetime. Most of the crews were ashore, and most people were asleep, when the attack began.

There will probably always be some controversy about how much the highest echelons in Washington knew of Japanese intentions. They knew an attack was likely but probably not where or when.

In the north of the island of Oahu (Pearl Harbor is on its southern coast) a couple of army men finishing their night shift at a radar

Almost exactly a year before the Japanese attack on Pearl Harbor, a series of publicity pictures were issued by the military authorities to present the base as the U.S.A.'s Hawaiian stronghold. The sentry in the still (left) was described as typical of the thousands of men guarding what was described as America's Gibraltar. The series also included a picture of the searchlights of the U.S. battlefleet lighting up the peacetime night sky over Pearl Harbor (top right); a picture that the events of 7 December, 1941, would render unfortunate.

While the Americans were enjoying their last few months of peace, the Japanese were planning their attack on Pearl Harbor. The Japanese air crews used a model mock-up (bottom far right) to familiarize themselves with 'Battleship Row' at Ford Island. It is said that the Japanese rehearsals for the attack were so fierce and realistic that they lost more aircraft in practices than the twenty-nine they lost on the day itself.

Bottom right: a Japanese view of the attack on Pearl Harbor on 7 December, 1941, taken from one of the aircraft actually involved in it.

station detected a large 'blip' on their screens. They were not particularly alarmed, thinking it was probably a naval exercise they had not been told about; inter-service rivalry had a habit of complicating communications in Hawaii. When they eventually found an officer to report to, he was similarly unconcerned, as he was expecting a flight of B-17s to arrive that day.

The first strike wave of 184 Japanese aircraft went into the attack a few minutes before 8.00 a.m. local time, 7 December, 1941. Drilled on exactly which targets to attack, they swung across the harbour and launched their bombs and torpedoes. They did so unopposed, for it was not till the bombing was well under way that there was any response from the watch on duty in the ships below.

None of the battleships escaped unscathed, though the USS *Maryland* and USS *Pennsylvania* were damaged to a lesser extent. The USS *Arizona* was hit first, and badly; her forward magazine exploded and she split in two. Forty-seven officers and 1,056 men died, including her captain and Rear Admiral Isaac C. Kidd.

The ancient World War I USS *Oklahoma* was the next most serious victim. She was hit by five torpedoes and capsized, taking twenty officers and 395 men with her. Several bombs and a torpedo hit the USS *Nevada* while the USS *West Virginia* was also torpedoed. The USS *California* and the USS *Tennessee* were also damaged. Three cruisers and three destroyers were disabled, and the former battleship *Utah*, downgraded to a target ship, was also hit.

One hour after the first attack, a second strike wave of 170 Japanese aircraft arrived over Pearl Harbor. They continued attacking the warships and also the airfields, which proved to be in a similar state of unreadiness. Most of the aircraft were undispersed, lined up wing tip to wing tip, and forming sitting targets. Nearly

**Left:** a view of burning buildings and ships after the surprise attack on Pearl Harbor by 350 carrier-borne Japanese aircraft.

**Right:** an often reproduced but nonetheless most spectacular photograph taken during the bombing of Pearl Harbor.

Bottom left: the smoking hulk of the battleship USS *Arizona*, which was the first ship to be badly hit and which was split in two by an explosion. Forty-seven officers and 1,056 men died on board, including her captain and Rear Admiral Isaac C. Kidd.

Top left: two further battleships that were bombed at Pearl Harbor - the USS *West Virginia* and the USS *69 Tennessee*. Though disabled to varying degrees by the attack, they were amongst those ships worth repairing and were eventually sent back into action.

Right: blasted by bombs and torpedoes, the battleship USS *California* settles slowly into the mud. Of the eight battleships hit, two, the *Arizona* and the *Oklahoma*, would never sail again, but the others would all return to service eventually.

200 U.S. aircraft were destroyed or damaged on the ground.

It was a brilliantly planned and executed attack and represented a victory for the aircraft carrier over the battleship. The Japanese lost twenty-nine aircraft, fifty-five crew members, and five midget submarines. Admiral Yamamoto, whose overall plan it was, had knocked out his enemy's capital ships in one fell swoop.

However his men had not hit any American aircraft carriers. By a lucky chance, the USS *Enterprise* and USS *Lexington*, which would otherwise have been with the battleships, were engaged in delivering aircraft to Midway and Wake. The third aircraft carrier, the USS *Saratoga*, and the ninth and last battleship of the Pacific Fleet, the USS *Colorado*, were on the west coast of the U.S.A.

Another misfortune for the Japanese was that their plans had neglected to include the destruction of the oil terminals and storage-tanks. Had these gone up too, the American Fleet would have been even more severely handicapped. As things stood, the American Navy had lost two battleships forever: the *Arizona* would be left at the bottom of the harbour, and the *Oklahoma* would prove not to be worth repairing. The other six, though disabled to varying degrees, would all return to service. There were twenty cruisers and sixty-five destroyers still battleworthy.

The Japanese Fleet turned away, leaving the Americans to bury their dead and succour their wounded, many of whom had ghastly burns from flaming fuel. 2,400 had died: 1,763 men on the ships and another 700 people or more on shore.

With hindsight we can say that the aforementioned 'blessing in disguise' took several forms. Because the battle occurred in a harbour, most of the ships could be reclaimed. Had the same devastation taken place on the high seas, the battleships would have gone to the bottom, taking far more of their crews with them. The aircraft carriers were spared to fight another day, as were nearly all the cruisers and destroyers, together with their crews. Lessons were learned, and 'avenge Pearl Harbor' became a rallying cry and a cause for a whole nation.

Although the Japanese put their major effort into attacking Pearl Harbor, they simultaneously attacked other American and Allied targets. Guam, which was surrounded by Japanese islands, surrendered within three days; Wake fought back but was captured on 23 December.

In fact, the Japanese, most of whose forces were still fighting in China, launched five separate new campaigns: Hong Kong; the Philippines; Burma; Malaya and Singapore; and the Dutch East Indies. Hong Kong held out only until Christmas.

If further proof of battleship vulnerability were needed, it came only a few days later, when Japanese land-based aircraft sank both the British battleship HMS *Prince of Wales* and the battlecruiser HMS *Renown* off Malaya.

Admiral Tom Phillips had taken his two capital ships up from Singapore to try and interrupt a Japanese landing. At 11.00 a.m. on 10 December, 1941, some 250 miles north of Singapore, and with no air cover, the two capital ships were attacked. Nearly one hundred Japanese aircraft were employed from airfields near Saigon, in Vietnam. It was over almost as quickly as Pearl Harbor. Both ships went down, taking 840 of those onboard with them, including Admiral Phillips.

On both land and sea the Japanese could hardly be checked anywhere. General MacArthur in the Philippines probably delayed them most, retreating by way of the fortress peninsula of Bataan. The capture of Malaya and Singapore, which Japan expected to take one hundred days, was over in considerably less. Singapore fell on 15 February, 1942, with the capture of 130,000 British and Commonwealth prisoners.

Japanese ships later swept into the Indian Ocean, as far as Ceylon, which was now the British naval headquarters. They did not, however, find the British Far East Fleet, which had left harbour to face the enemy on the open seas. After attacks on bases at both ends of Ceylon, the Japanese withdrew to Singapore. Meanwhile their army colleagues were finding rich pickings in the Dutch East Indies and in the island archipelagos beyond.

**Although battleships were the main targets, other ships were sunk or damaged, amongst them the destroyers USS *Downes* and USS *Cassin* (left). The battleship USS *Pennsylvania*, which was only lightly damaged, can be seen in the background.**

**Nearly 200 U.S. aircraft were destroyed or damaged in the Japanese attack on the airfields around Pearl Harbor (right). Hangars suffered badly too. Most of the aircraft were stacked wing tip to wing tip, and the American air forces were as unprepared as the fleet for the attack.**

# THE RISING SUN

While the carrier-borne aircraft of the Japanese Navy were changing the course of history at Pearl Harbor on 7th December, 1941, their land-based counterparts were far from inactive elsewhere in the Far East.

The Japanese launched a seaborne assault on the British territory of Malaya at Kota Bharu, in the northeast corner of the peninsula. All the available aircraft of the Royal Air Force and the Royal Australian Air Force were employed in an attempt to hurl the attackers back into the sea. Many sorties were flown, and significant impact was made on the landings, but it turned out that this invasion was, at the outset, more in the way of a diversion. Everything appeared to be happening at Kota Bharu, with the result that all the available defending aircraft were lured to the area. Meanwhile, the bulk of the invasion

fleet was making unopposed landings fifty miles further north, at Patani and Singora in Thailand. This was discovered by a Beaufort of the Royal Air Force, which returned, badly damaged, from a reconnaissance of the area. The pilot reported a large concentration of Japanese vessels in the area, but, more ominously, the film from his cameras revealed that sixty or more Japanese aircraft, mostly fighters, had occupied the airfield at Singora.

The next day, the Allied air strength in the area began to wilt. The Japanese landings had carried them to the boundary of the RAF's airfield at Kota Bharu, and the ground crews were obliged to engage in hand-to-hand fighting to gain time for the aircraft – American-built Hudsons of the Australians, and obsolescent Wildebeest biplanes – to withdraw

Whilst the Japanese carrier-based aircraft were acting with such devastating effect at Pearl Harbor, their land-based counterparts of the Army Air Force were having an almost comparable influence around the Malay Peninsular. The workhorse of their fleet was the Mitsubishi Ki-21 'Sally'. Over 2,000 'Sallys' were built, and they took part in every one of Japan's major land operations.

The American-built Lockheed Hudson (right) of the Royal Australian Air Force, based at Kota Bharu, was one of the more up-to-date aircraft available to the Allies at the time of the outbreak of war in the Far East.

There was only one Bristol Beaufort (below right) operating in Malaya in December 1941. It was badly damaged on the first day of the war with Japan, as its crew obtained the vital information that Japanese troops had made a virtually unopposed landing at Singora, just one hundred miles north of the Siam/Malay border.

Practically touching the wave tops, Mitsubishi G4M 'Betty' torpedo bombers (overleaf) head for their target through a hail of anti-aircraft fire.

to Kuantan, further south. The airmen themselves were able to withdraw under cover of darkness, and escaped by train to Singapore.

While this was happening, the Japanese aircraft from Singora made heavy and continuous attacks on all the airfields in northern Malaya. It was noticed that the heaviest raids seemed to be made as the defending aircraft were landing, or being refuelled, and evidence was obtained that information on aircraft movements was being passed to the enemy. It was a disastrous day for the Allied air forces. By the evening, out of 110 aircraft available for operations in the morning, only 50 remained serviceable in the evening.

The implications of this loss of air power in northern Malaya was to be far reaching. The Royal Navy had two capital ships in the area, the latest of Britain's battleships, HMS *Prince of Wales*, accompanied by an older battlecruiser, HMS *Repulse*. With their escort of four destroyers, they had sailed from Singapore to interfere with the Japanese invasion ships at Singora. Admiral Sir Tom Phillips' little fleet had reached the area abeam Kota Bharu when he received a signal telling him that, because of the enemy air action in the area, he could no longer expect to pick up fighter cover from the local airfields. Without this fighter cover his operation at Singora would have been suicide, so he

**This picture may have been taken for propaganda purposes, but there was indeed every reason for the morale of the Japanese Army Air Force pilots to be high during December 1941.**

HMS *Repulse* was the older of two capital ships sent to join the Royal Navy's Far East Fleet. Commanded by Admiral Sir Tom Phillips, from HMS *Prince of Wales*, the fleet set out to harry the Japanese invasion fleets. With the loss of the RAF's airfields in northern Malaya, the fleet was soon beyond the range of effective air cover.

turned south again. On his way south he intercepted a message saying that Japanese landings were now taking place at Kuantan, and he turned to assist. The fleet was maintaining radio silence, but the Admiral assumed that his intentions would be guessed by those ashore, who would despatch air cover for him from Kuantan. In this he was wrong. His air cover never appeared, and, arriving at Kuantan to find no sign of a Japanese landing, he turned again for Singapore. Unfortunately, the delay caused by his diversion resulted in the fleet being intercepted by a force of almost 80 Japanese Navy aircraft, carrying bombs and torpedoes, who were on their way back to

their base at Saigon.

The Japanese high-level bombers achieved several near misses on the two capital ships, and then *Repulse* received a direct hit amidships. Meanwhile, the torpedo aircraft were running in, attacking in massed formation, and from either side at the same time, to make adequate defence impossible. Admiral Phillips had always maintained that a ship such as *Prince of Wales* could put up 'such a hail of steel' that no aircraft could get through. *Prince of Wales* put up a hail of steel, but to no effect. By the time the Brewster Buffalo fighters could get to the scene from Singapore, in response to a desperate signal that the fleet was under air

As HMS *Repulse* closed to help the *Prince of Wales*, she was attacked simultaneously from either side by the torpedo bombers. The use of her main armament might have been impressive, but the rate of fire of the massive fifteen-inch guns could have done little more than provide something of a smoke screen to impede the 'Bettys'. Struck by at least five torpedoes, the *Repulse* listed heavily, and sank within six minutes.

With a complete lack of air support, any success by the British gunners could provide no more than a spectacular interlude before they were overwhelmed (right) by the attacking aircraft.

The crew of the *Prince of Wales* were luckier than their colleagues in the *Repulse*. The former's more modern construction enabled her to stay afloat for almost an hour after taking three torpedoes. 1,285 officers and men (below right) were taken aboard the destroyers of the escort screen, before the *Prince of Wales* turned over and sank.

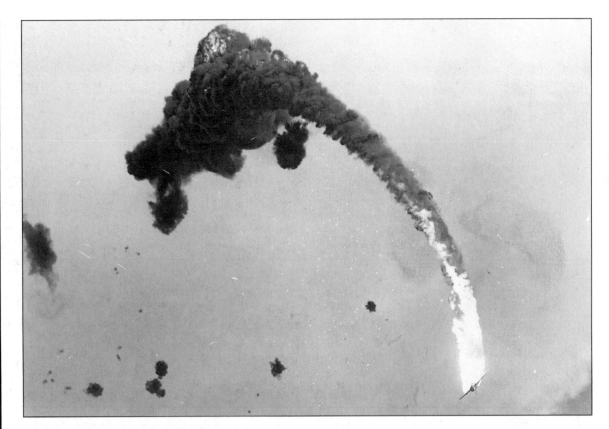

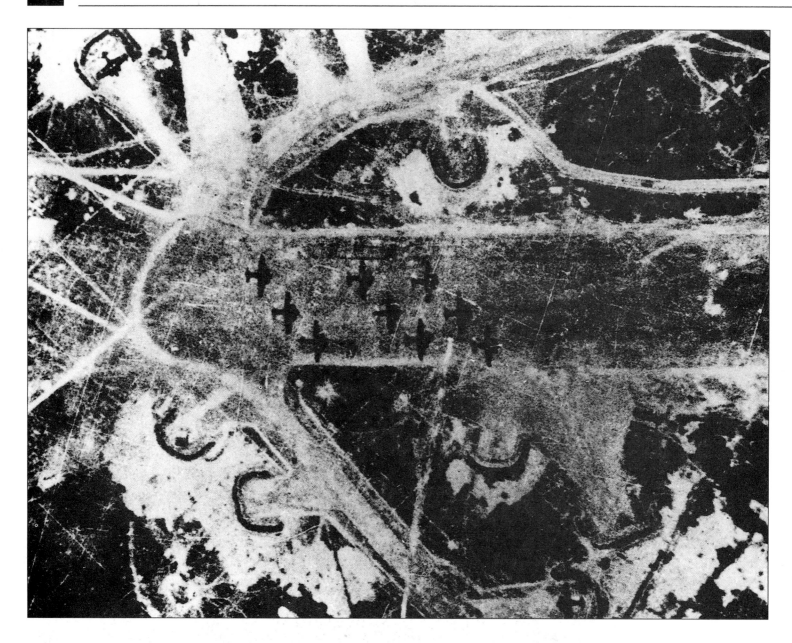

attack, it was too late. When they arrived all that was to be seen was a vast area covered with fuel oil and debris, with the destroyers moving slowly through it to pick up survivors.

This was the first time that capital ships, at sea, had been lost to air attack. From the two ships 840 officers and men were lost, including the Admiral.

After the fall of Singapore, the remains of the British Eastern Fleet was moved to Ceylon, so that, principally as a result of two tremendously successful aircraft-versus-ship actions – at Pearl Harbor and off the coast of Malaya – the Allies had, for the time being, no significant presence in the Pacific, the China Sea or the Indian Ocean. Between December 1941 and May 1942, Japan had gained control of one third of the earth's surface; an area which included the oilfields of Borneo and Indonesia, and almost 90 per cent of the world's rubber production. From the shores of Japan itself, in the north, to Australia in the south – from the Philippines in the east, to India in the west.

The conquest had taken little over four months – it would take the Allies four years to win it back.

Mitsubishi Ki-21 'Sallys' took off from their bases in Cochin, China, and ranged the South China Sea to find and bomb the British fleet. Initial bombing attacks disabled HMS *Prince of Wales*, preventing her from taking action to avoid subsequent attacks by torpedo-carrying aircraft.

# THE SIEGE OF LENINGRAD

**From 22nd June Army Group North advanced at a rapid pace towards Leningrad. Most of the huge losses of Soviet vehicles were a consequence of their abandonment due to lack of fuel and spare parts rather than their loss during combat. The swift overrunning of supply depots and the lack of Soviet logistical organization was disastrous for the Soviets.**

Founded in 1700 to replace Moscow as Russia's capital, St. Petersburg had its name changed to Petrograd, to commemorate the birthplace of the Revolution in 1917, and Leningrad, in memory of the Bolshevik leader, in 1924. Located at the mouth of the River Neva, which links Lake Ladoga with the Gulf of Finland across the Karelian Isthmus, Leningrad was the symbolic and practical manifestation of a meeting between Western and Slavic traditions in Russia. A base for Russia's northern fleet and a major industrial centre containing almost three million inhabitants, Leningrad resented Moscow's displacement of it as Russia's premier city. Yet it was true that the advantage of its access to the Baltic Sea was undermined by its exposed position less than twenty miles from the border with Finland, albeit that the Russo-Finnish War of 1939-40 had mitigated this weakness by pushing the frontier beyond Vyborg.

Leningrad featured prominently in 'Barbarossa', the German plan for the attack on the Soviet Union; its name seems to have drawn Hitler's ire in the same way that Stalingrad was to do in 1942. More practically, the aims were as follows: to secure a northern bastion for a line running south to the Ukraine from which the second phase attack could be launched; to linkup with Germany's Finnish allies; and to knock out the Russian Baltic Fleet at Kronstadt. As Directive 21 stated: 'Only after the fulfilment of this first essential task .. (including) the occupation of Leningrad and Kronstadt, will the attack be continued with the intention of occupying Moscow'. The task was given to Army Group North.

Positioned in East Prussia under Field Marshal Wilhelm Ritter von Leeb were twenty infantry divisions, three motorized divisions, three *Panzerdivisions* and 430 front-line fighters and bombers. With other forces, this amounted to half a million men divided into two armies (16th and 18th armies, commanded by colonel generals Ernst Busch and Georg von Küchler respectively), Colonel General Erich Höpner's Fourth *Panzergruppe* and Colonel General Alfred Keller's First Air Fleet. Four German divisions

On 30th June the authorities in Leningrad began to form militias for the defence of the city. The lack of officers, uniforms, weapons and ammunition meant these units were of dubious effectiveness, particularly in open battle. In street fighting in the suburbs, however, such considerations were less important.

Zhukov, the Russian hero of the Great Patriotic War – as the Second World War was known in the Soviet Union – commanded the defences of Leningrad until they were stabilized. On 6th October he was personally ordered by Stalin to return to the Moscow front to face Operation 'Typhoon'.

had been sent to Finland to support Finland's Marshal Baron Gustaf Mannerheim, who intended to reverse the result of the Russo-Finnish 1939-40 War.

Facing von Leeb on the Northwestern Front was the Russian Colonel General F.I. Kuznetsov, his 8th, 11th and 27th armies scattered across the Baltic States. Only 105 of his 1,150 tanks were new models, seventy-five per cent needed repair or servicing, while all but five of his divisions were between fifteen and thirty per cent below requirement in personnel and equipment. On the Northern Front, 14th, 7th and 23rd armies covered the frontier from Murmansk to Vyborg and here Lieutenant General Markian M. Popov was in command.

Von Leeb predicted he would be in Leningrad by 21st July. The River Dvina was reached in four days, from whence the main advance continued towards Pskov, which was entered on 8th July. A hundred miles further on, the Russians were desperately constructing the Luga Line for the shattered remnants of Northwestern Front to fall back on. Two thirds of Kuznetsov's divisions had sustained losses of over fifty per cent, few vehicles were operative and ammunition was almost exhausted. Troops were stripped from the Northern Front and thrown into the battle. Between 30th June and 7th July, 160,000 citizens of Leningrad signed up for a militia; recruitment was especially high amongst the Young Communists. With no training, inexperienced officers and little equipment, three divisions (later a fourth) were formed and sent to the River Luga. There they joined 60,000 civilians working eighteen-hour shifts to build defences. Having advanced nearly four hundred miles in three weeks, von Leeb needed to rest and replenish his forces, and his deadline passed as the Luga Line held.

Full-scale attack was relaunched by the Germans on 8th August. The arrival of 39th *Panzer Korps* from Army Group Centre secured von Leeb's southeastern flank against the Valdai Hills and allowed him to force the Line. North of Leningrad, the Finns had begun their attack on 11th July, but their major offensive wasn't launched until the last day of the month. Bled of troops, the Russians faced a two-to-one disadvantage in men, the Vyborg Line was abandoned and the front began to crumble. The enemy was closing on Leningrad from the south and north.

Leningrad was bulging at the seams. In the chaos of the first months of the war, evacuation had been ill organized. The rail network had been jammed with trucks loaded with industrial plant, while refugees had crowded in from the west. Dmitri V. Pavlov, Commissar of Trade and executive of the main administration of food supplies of the Defence Commissariat, who was sent from Moscow to take charge of food, estimated there were 2,887,000 civilians and half a million soldiers and sailors. The city had done its best to prepare for attack. Its citizens had built 18,000 miles of trenches, 450 miles of anti-tank ditches, twenty-two miles of barricades and 15,000 pillboxes.

The Germans reached Chudovo on 21st August, cutting the main rail line to Moscow; but more important was their capture of the town of Mga on 30th August. This last rail link with the outside world remained in German hands until 1944. Two days later, the shelling of Leningrad began. On the same day, the Finns reached their pre-1939 border. It was the city's good fortune that, despite great pressure from Berlin, the Finnish government adopted a policy of not advancing beyond its former frontiers. The battle in this sector became a series of skirmishes for minor strong points until the main

A camouflaged Russian machine-gun team wait for the *Luftwaffe*. The destruction of the bulk of the Soviet Union's initial air capability in the first few weeks of the war placed a great burden on its anti-aircraft ground defence until the losses could be replaced. Goering's boast that Leningrad would be destroyed by the *Luftwaffe* led to a sustained bombing campaign.

Although the main weapon used was the incendiary bomb, high explosives were also dropped (below left). The raids caused distress, but were much more strategically threatening when used against the vital supply line into the city across Lake Ladoga.

The shelling of Leningrad by German heavy artillery (facing page) was heavy and virtually continuous. Before the end of 1941 over thirty thousand shells had landed on the city, and in 1943 the Germans could still achieve a rate of over ten thousand a month.

German troops, dressed in winter white, move along a communication trench through woodland. As the battle stagnated into a siege, the fighting settled down into a static war for over two years. It was fought around buildings, thousands of bunkers and strongpoints, and hundreds of miles of trenches.

Russian advance of 1944.

When Schlüsselburg fell to the Germans in hand-to-hand fighting on 8th September, Leningrad's last land link with the rest of the Soviet Union was closed. There is strong evidence that the Soviet government considered scuttling the fleet and blowing up and abandoning the city. The airlift of specialists

Spotters for Soviet artillery keep watch in a lookout post on the outskirts of Leningrad. By 1944 the Red Army had gathered 21,600 guns, 1,500 Karyusha rocket batteries, 1,475 tanks and self-propelled guns, and 1,500 planes on the Leningrad and Volkhov fronts for the final relief of the city.

and weapons was out, not in! Only lack of pontoons stopped the Germans crossing the Neva that day. As the disaster in the Ukraine moved to its climax and Stalin's thoughts concentrated on the battle he was convinced was soon to begin for Moscow, Leningrad was left to survive on its own resources. He was prepared to loan one asset though: Marshal Georgi K. Zhukov.

Von Leeb concentrated eleven divisions, including two *Panzerdivisions*, for the assault. They fought their way through the final defence line outside the city, taking Pushkin on 16th September. The Leningrad edition of *Pravda* carried an editorial beginning: 'The enemy is at the gates ..' The following two days saw fighting in Ligovo on the edge of the city. The Russians held one last building there, Klinovsky House, and rooms changed hands several times. Zhukov seemed everywhere, ordering continuous attack and threatening execution for any retreat.

Although the Russians did not know it, the assault was about to end. Operation 'Typhoon' was a higher priority for the Germans and the withdrawal of the *Panzers* could wait no longer. On 21st September, Army Group North began to dig in. Leningrad was to be reduced by siege; the ever optimistic Goering claiming

that he could level the city with his *Luftwaffe*.

A city of Leningrad's size could be expected to consume around 3,000 tons of food a day. When Pavlov arrived, his first two actions were to tighten up rationing and to take stock of all the food available. On the new ration limits, it was estimated that there were sufficient stocks of grain, flour, cereals and meat to last a month and enough sugar to suffice for two months. The only way to bring in supplies was from the Volkhov railhead downriver to Novaya Ladoga, across Lake Ladoga to Osinovets, and by truck or narrow-gauge railway to Leningrad. The trip took sixteen hours (without allowing for loading or unloading) and so could not be completed under cover of darkness. It was subject to shelling at both ends, and air attack on the lake. By 15th November, when ice stopped the boats, twenty days worth of food had been brought in since Leningrad's isolation. This wasn't replenishing consumption, and stocks had diminished to a fortnight's supply of basic food commodities. Private use of coal and kerosene had already been halted and, tragically, the winter ahead was due to be the coldest in living memory.

Worse still, though the German advance into Leningrad had been halted, their drive east had not. On 9th November, Tikhvin fell,

which meant that the closest railhead was then Zaborie, which lay over one hundred miles from Lake Ladoga as the crow flies, and much further through the forest and swamps. The food ration for troops and manual workers was cut to 1,000 calories a day. Other groups got less. Five men, a horse and a sled were sent out from the city on still-thin ice to see if there was a route across Lake Lagoda. They made it after sixty hours in a continual blizzard. On 24th November, ten light trucks set out on the trail they had blazed. Two fell through the ice and the other eight brought a meagre thirty-three tons of food. The people of Leningrad were starving to death.

On 9th December, the Soviet 4th Army recaptured Tikhvin. As a result, the six-day journey on the track cut from Zaborie was redundant, but the twenty-seven-hour ice road across the lake was still horrific. Throughout the month, little food came into the city, despite heroic efforts on the ice that cost thousands of lives. When the cats, dogs and rats had been eaten, evergreen leaves, glue from bookbindings, leather, industrial cellulose and, it was whispered, human flesh came onto the menu. In January, the last power station closed, and as a result so did the last water pumping station supplying the crucial bakeries. Volunteers were called for to meet the bakeries' needs by bucket. The destruction of all wooden houses in the city to provide fuel was ordered. The death rate reached 4,000 a day from starvation, hypothermia and diseases brought on by malnutrition. Mass graves were dynamited out of the frozen earth.

The winter grew harsher, and this was a turning point, for Lake Lagoda froze to a great depth. New, solid ice roads were constructed, and by January's end a daily average of 1,708 tons of food was being brought in. This was raised to 3,072 tons in February and 3,660 tons in March. The lorries took 539,400 people out of the city. The death toll remained high, reaching a peak in April, for starvation is a slow but, beyond a certain limit, irrevocable death. In all probability at least 800,000 died from hunger and resultant causes, and another 200,000 troops and civilians were killed in the fighting and bombardment. After a further 448,694 people were evacuated across Lake Ladoga in the summer of 1942, only 600,000 of the original population remained in Leningrad.

Although the Germans had plans to renew their attack on the city in 1942, these were forestalled by greater events elsewhere on the Eastern Front. The Soviet Union, likewise, was content simply to break the blockade, when Schlüsselberg was recaptured, with Operation 'Iskra' at the beginning of 1943. That year was spent building up 1,250,000 men to overwhelm Army Group North, commanded since June 1942 by von Küchler. When the attack came in 1944, it was part of the process of total German collapse that led the Red Army to Berlin. The official ending of the siege of Leningrad on 27th January was but a footnote, but the initial battle for Leningrad had had significance. If the city had fallen in 1941, much more of Army Group North would have been freed to sweep south towards Moscow, as the original planning of Barbarossa outlined. The loss of the Russian Baltic Fleet would have allowed the Germans to ship to a forward supply base, and use the Leningrad rail network from there. The psychological effect on both sides can only be guessed at, but it must be presumed that it would have been considerable. The Murmansk supply line to the west, quantitively limited but psychologically important, would most probably have been cut. However, the siege of Leningrad continued because of its increasing unimportance to both sides, which meant that neither committed sufficient forces to break the deadlock until the Soviet Union was advancing on all fronts in 1944. Finnish caution meant the ring was never tight enough. Other battles, at Moscow, Stalingrad and Kursk, would decide the outcome of the war: Leningrad received the Order of its namesake.

Field Marshal von Küchler's Army Group North (below), divided into 16th and 18th Armies, could muster only 385 tanks in 1944. His 741,000 men were substantially outnumbered by the 1,241,000 officers and men of the Red Army facing them. The Russian offensive that began on 14th January did not halt until the Germans unconditionally surrendered.

Right: men of the Imperial Japanese Navy marching in the annual New Year Review at Japan's huge Yokosuka naval base. It was these men, together with the men of the Japanese Army, who swept through southeast Asia and the Pacific after Pearl Harbor, and who were poised to invade Java by mid-February 1942. The Allied attempt to oppose their relentless progress resulted in the disastrous Battle of the Java Sea on 26/27 February, 1942.

The Battle of the Java Sea on 26/27 February, 1942, was a disaster. If nothing else, it proved that heroism and seamanship are not always enough, and that victory generally goes to those who can produce the largest concentration of big guns, torpedoes and aircraft. This time, air power was not a major factor, though, as was usual at this stage of the War, the Allies were operating with virtually no direct air support.

It was a very mixed Allied force too, with ships ranging from useful 8-inch gun cruisers to destroyers that dated back to World War I. In its very multinationality lay additional reasons for the defeat.

Lead by Dutch Rear Admiral Karel Doorman, this ABDA (Australian British Dutch American) force consisted of two heavy cruisers, HMS *Exeter* and USS *Houston*, three light cruisers with 6-inch guns, the Australian HMAS *Perth* and the Dutch cruisers, the *De Ruyter*, which was Doorman's flagship, and the *Java*.

Additionally there were nine destroyers: four American, three British and two Dutch. The problems arose because the fleet had never worked together before, but had merely been assembled from the very few ships available in the area. Each nationality relied on very different communication practices and procedures. Inevitably they all had trouble understanding each other's signals throughout the action.

The Japanese plans to create an empire in Southeast Asia are aptly described by Richard Hough in his book, *The Longest Battle*, as 'outrageous in scale, brilliant in conception, and so far successful in execution'. These plans included seizing the wealth of the Dutch East Indies by moving southwards from Singapore, by land through Sumatra and by sea to Java. The eventual target was Australia.

By mid-February 1941 Sumatra was theirs, and they were poised to invade the next large island in the chain, Java. Here some 30,000 Dutch and other troops faced the Japanese 16th Army. In a last desperate attempt to meet this threat, Rear Admiral Doorman's fleet headed out of its base at Sourabaya to try and stop any landings.

There was only one possible outcome. Before the ABDA force had much of a chance of reaching the transports, they were engaged by a more powerful Japanese force. This outnumbered the Allies about two to one in 8-

The British heavy cruiser HMS *Exeter* (top left), which had distinguished herself at the Battle of the River Plate in December 1939, was one of the casualties of the Battle of the Java Sea. Outnumbered two to one, the *Exeter* and the USS *Houston* took the brunt of the Japanese attack, and the *Exeter* had to pull out of the battle and try to reach Australia for repairs. She would be sunk on 1 March, 1942, as she tried to make her way southwards.

Right: the *Exeter*'s crew in happier days, being addressed by Winston Churchill, then First Lord of the Admiralty.

Although she survived the actual Battle of the Java Sea, the USS *Houston* (bottom left) would be sunk a day later after sinking two Japanese transports. An Augusta-class cruiser of 9,200 tons she carried nine 8-inch guns and twelve 5-inch guns.

inch guns, a superiority the Japanese would exploit.

Standing off and shooting from a range of about thirteen miles, they concentrated their fire on HMS *Exeter* and USS *Houston* – the only two ships that could respond at that range. The *Exeter* was hit in the engine room, and had to pull out. The victor of the Battle of the River Plate would be sunk a couple of days later, on 1 March. She went down together with her

escort, the U.S. destroyer *Pope*, as she tried to make her way to Australia through the Sunda Strait.

The British destroyer *Electra* was another early casualty. Set ablaze by big shells, she was finished off, still fighting gallantly, by the more modern, more powerful Japanese destroyers. The Dutch destroyer *Kortenaer* was torpedoed and sunk, and her consort damaged when one of her own depth charges exploded under

The Battle of the Java Sea saw the destruction of most of the Netherlands East Indies fleet. A mixed Allied force, commanded by the Dutch Admiral Karel Doorman, had sailed out to try and attack the Japanese landing forces bound for Java. Encountering superior forces, Admiral Doorman went down with his flagship, the *De Ruyter*; another Dutch cruiser, the *Java*, and a Dutch destroyer were also lost. The Dutch would fight on mainly with their submarines, five of which can be seen refuelling from a mother ship (left).

her stern. The British destroyer HMS *Jupiter* was lost when she ran into a Dutch minefield.

By this stage, the Japanese had closed and both Dutch cruisers had been sunk, Rear Admiral Doorman going down with the *De Ruyter*. Of the cruisers, only the USS *Houston* and HMAS *Perth* still survived, and they made their way to the island's capital of Batavia, now Jakarta.

A few days later they managed to sink two Japanese transports and two other ships, but as they moved through the Sunda Strait towards Australia they too were attacked, and sunk.

On 5 March, Batavia had been declared an 'open city'. A few days later all Java surrendered. A gallant and sacrificial effort by the small Allied force had probably not even delayed the irrepressible Japanese.

Two other lessons were learned at the Battle of the Java Sea. The first was the way in which the Japanese compensated for their lack of radar by using seaplanes for reconnaissance. While the Allies were failing to communicate even with one another, Japanese seaplanes were out and about everywhere reporting back to their big-gun cruisers the whereabouts of all their opponents.

The second was the noteworthy success of the Japanese in the deadly use of their 'Long Lance' 24-inch torpedoes. These were oxygen powered, effective within a range of up to 22,000 yards and travelled at speeds of well over 40 knots.

As mentioned before, other navies had experimented with these oxygen-powered torpedoes, but most had rejected their use as too dangerous. The Japanese had persevered, accepting a rate of casualties in their handling that probably no other navy would tolerate, and this paid off in the Java Sea.

# THE DOOLITTLE RAID

Lieutenant Colonel 'Jimmy' Doolittle - air racer, barnstormer, and master aviator - was selected by Lieutenant General H. H. Arnold, commanding general of the United States Army Air Force, to carry out the imaginative and daring plan suggested to him by the naval aviators.

The people of the United States of America were, understandably, keen for some form of retaliation for the 'day of infamy' at Pearl Harbor in December 1941. The President, Franklin D. Roosevelt, missed no opportunity to raise the matter when in conference with his chiefs of staff.

An air strike against the Japanese mainland seemed the most appropriate form of action, but how was this to be achieved? No bases for land planes were available within reach of the target, and the Navy's planes had a maximum range of 600 miles. To sail the carriers to within 300 miles of enemy coastline was to put them into unacceptable hazard. It seemed, within the department of Admiral Ernest J. King, Chief of Naval Operations, that the answer lay somewhere between the two. Less than a month after Pearl Harbor an idea was already taking shape that perhaps it would be possible to launch army medium bombers against

Japan from aircraft carriers, a safe distance from the target. One thing was certain; it might be possible to launch medium bombers from an aircraft carrier, but there was no way that they would be able to return to it. Aeroplanes of that size were not equipped with arrester hooks, and they needed a much longer landing run than a carrier could offer.

The officers on Admiral King's staff who had dreamed up the idea were sent to discuss it with Lieutenant General H. H. Arnold, Commanding General of the Army Air Forces. General Arnold had the ideal man to evaluate the suggestion. He called in Lieutenant Colonel Jimmy Doolittle, a veteran airman with a world-wide reputation, who had won international air races, and broken world air speed records Doolittle suggested that the only medium bombers which might be able to take off, fully loaded, with a run of no more than 500 feet, were the Douglas B-23, or the the Mitchell, the

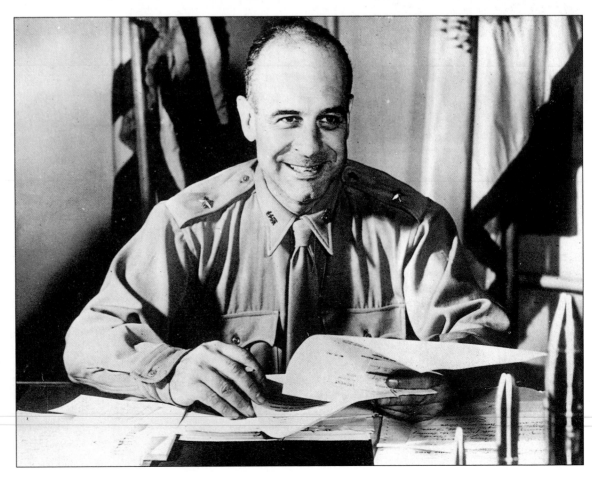

Far left: Admiral Ernest J. King, chief of naval operations, United States Navy, in January 1942. Officers on Admiral King's staff were the first to come up with a viable proposal that would satisfy the American population's lust for an attack upon the Japanese mainland to appease their anger at the onslaught on Pearl Harbor.

William F. Halsey (left), himself a qualified aviator, was appointed by Admiral Chester Nimitz, commander in chief of the Pacific Fleet, to command the Task Force that was to carry the B-25s of the Doolittle Raid to within striking distance of Tokyo. The photograph shows Halsey two years later, commanding the United States Third Fleet.

The USS *Hornet* (below left) put to sea carrying two USAAF B-25 Mitchell bombers, simply to show that it was possible for these to take off from an aircraft carrier. That being proved, the two army pilots flew back to their base with no idea why they had been asked to risk their lives in this eccentric experiment.

The B-25s of the 'Special Air Project' are tethered to the deck of USS *Hornet*, en route for the launching point. The aircraft had been fitted with new propellers, painted to prevent corrosion whilst exposed to the sea air and spray, and had extra fuel tanks in the fuselage.

North American B-25. When told that the maximum width available would be seventy-five feet, the choice was made automatically. The B-23 had a wing-span of ninety three feet, the Mitchell only sixty-seven.

Admiral King's men arranged for two B-25s to be hoisted onto the carrier USS *Hornet* at San Francisco, and they put to sea to prove that it could be done. It could. The two army pilots dragged their aircraft off the end of *Hornet's* deck, and disappeared over the horizon, back to their base, wondering what on earth they had done it for.

Meanwhile, Doolittle was arranging for modifications to be made to 24 Mitchells. Turrets were removed, leaving only the top turret with its two 0.5 inch machine guns, and one 0.3 inch gun in the nose, and extra fuel tanks were built into the space saved. The heavy radio equipment was also removed. Radio silence would be observed, and even more fuel tanks would be useful.

Early in March, volunteer crews were called together at Eglin Field, Florida, to begin training, although it would be another month before they would learn what it was that they had

The North American B-25 Mitchell was destined to take part in many famous operations during World War II, but none would eclipse the raid that Lieutenant Colonel James H. Doolittle led on Tokyo on April 18, 1942.

One of Doolittle's B-25s claws its way into the air (below left) as it leaves Shangri La, the mythical departure point in President Roosevelt's announcement to the American people of a token reprisal against Japan for the attack on Pearl Harbor.

Lieutenant Colonel Doolittle, at the controls of his Mitchell (right), aligns the aircraft with the white lines painted on the *Hornet's* deck to ensure that his wing tip clears the carrier's island, and races his engines as he prepares to head for Tokyo.

volunteered for. They were already trained on the Mitchell, but until now they had been using a mile of runway for their take-offs. Now they were being asked to do it in one tenth of the distance. Doolittle trained with them, although he had not yet obtained permission to lead the operation. He flew to Washington to play off General Arnold against his Chief of Staff, getting each to leave the decision to the other, and returned to Eglin ready to go.

On April 1 the Mitchells flew to Alameda Air Station, Sacramento, to be loaded onto the *Hornet*, Captain Marc A. Mitscher commanding. The aircraft were lashed to the deck, and covered up, and in the middle of the morning next day they sailed, in company with two cruisers, four destroyers and a tanker. Five days later Vice-Admiral William Halsey, flying his flag in the carrier *Enterprise*, was due to leave Hawaii with a similar force, to join up and form Task Force 16 to carry out the 'Special Air Project'.

Shortly after they had passed under the Golden Gate Bridge, everyone found out, at last, what the 'special project' was to be. 'Now

hear this,' boomed Mitscher's voice over the ship's loudspeakers, 'We are bound for Tokyo.' Now the target folders were handed out, and the aircrews could begin to discuss flight plans, and bomb loads. None of them had seen a B-25 take off from a carrier, let alone tried it for themselves. And if they made it, none of them would be landing back. If not on the carrier, where? Russia? China? Russia said no. They were not at war with Japan, and were not anxious to jeopardise the fragile peace. Chiang Kai-shek, in China, had at first been supportive, but was having second thoughts, fearing reprisals from the Japs. So when Doolittle put to sea he had had no confirmation. As he was now subject to radio silence he would have to assume that by the time they took off, diplomatic channels would have everything fixed up.

Take off was planned for April 19, but early on 18th they ran into the Japanese seaborne early warning. The Japanese radar cover was not good, and to warn of impending attack they had a cordon of small look-out vessels, 650 miles from the coast. The fleet spotted Patrol

Boat Number 23, the *Nitto Maru*, and at the same time they intercepted her radio message, 'Three enemy aircraft carriers in sight.' In the murk, her look-outs had presumably mistaken one of the cruisers for a third carrier. They had not intended to take off until late afternoon the next the next day, and to make a night raid on Tokyo, but Admiral Halsey decided that, as the cat was out of the bag, the wisest move would be to get the Mitchells into the air. He gave the order to 'Launch planes', and Doolittle and his crews came dashing from their quarters below decks.

During the cruise from San Francisco the aircraft had been tested, and tested again. All that was required, while the crews received their final briefing, was to drag the covers off, load the four 500 pound bombs into each one, and top up the fuel tanks to replace any that might have leaked or evaporated. In the briefing room Doolittle reminded his men to look for targets of military significance – ports and shipping, railways and heavy industry – and to remember that the Emperor's palace was strictly off limits.

Up on deck the Mitchells were ranged in the order in which they were to take off. Because of the aircraft behind him, Doolittle had the shortest space to get into the air. To give him the best possible chance, the last in the line was balanced precariously on the end of the flight deck, its tail and half of its fuselage hanging out over the water. It would not be possible to finish loading it until they could roll it forward a little.

At 8.20 a.m., with *Hornet* charging into a 27-knot gale, Doolittle roared down the deck, keeping his nose and port wheels on the white lines painted on the deck to make sure his starboard wing tip missed the superstructure, and trying to time his run so that the pitching carrier would toss him into the air with the rise of its bows. He made it, and circled the ship to watch number two's attempt. This time the timing was not so good. The bows rose too early, and the pilot found himself struggling uphill. Staggering over the bows, he was practically brushing the crests of the waves before he gained safe flying speed, and climbed away to join his leader. Eventually they were all safely airborne. The whole operation had taken an hour, by which time

The Japanese declared that any of the Raiders who fell into their hands, either immediately after the raid or subsequently, would be punished by death. Eight of the survivors were captured, three of whom were then executed. It is unlikely that this airman, pictured in 1943, had taken part in the raid - his fate is unknown.

Barrack blocks at Yokosuka Naval Base (right), photographed by the copilot of crew No. 13, Lieutenant Richard Nobloch, as the crew climbed away from their attack on the base's technical buildings.

As the war progressed, and the USAAF were able to operate their heavy bombers against the Japanese mainland from captured land bases, damage was caused to enemy factories (below right), which made the Doolittle Raid more than just a token reprisal.

Doolittle was well on his way to the Japanese coast.

As soon as the last aircraft was off, Halsey spun his fleet around and headed out into the Pacific to get as much space as possible between Task Force 16 and the enemy.

The message from the *Nitto Maru* had indeed got through, and a strike force had taken off from Kisarazu, near Tokyo, to look for the fleet. They returned to base, not having found anything, although a plane on a routine patrol reported having seen a twin-engined bomber heading for Japan. This was considered extremely unlikely, and, just as at Pearl Harbor, the warning was disregarded.

Five hours after takeoff, Doolittle was bombing Tokyo. On the run in he had met many Jap aircraft, mostly training types, but some fighters. Flying as low as possible, none seemed to interfere with him, and he was not attacked except by anti-aircraft fire after he had dropped his bombs.

All of the crews reached their targets, and, with one exception, carried on into China to look for landing grounds. They had been hoping to pick up Chinese radio beacons, but none of them succeeded in doing so. The odd man out, having used more fuel than expected en route from the *Hornet*, decided that he would not make China. Instead, disregarding

The majority of Doolittle's Raiders made it safely to China, and from there back home. Another photograph from the camera of Lieutenant Nobloch, of crew No. 13, shows the rest of the crew with some of the Chinese who escorted them to safety. The incensed Japanese murdered thousands of Chinese in reprisal for the help given to the Raiders.

After thirteen hours in the air, Doolittle left his aircraft on automatic pilot and he and his crew baled out over China. The following afternoon, with all of his crew accounted for, Doolittle and his crew chief, Paul Leonard, climbed the mountainside on which their aircraft had crashed.

instructions, he headed for Russia, and found an airfield in the vicinity of Vladivostok, where the aircraft was confiscated and the crew interned.

This was the only one of the raiders to make a safe landing. Doolittle was one of eleven who, unable to find an airfield, ordered his crew to bail out. The others made forced landings, from which, in general, the crews fared less well, most being killed or injured in the process.

Doolittle and his crew had bailed out after thirteen hours in the air. They quickly regrouped on the ground, and by the morning of the 20th had got together with four other crews. Through the Embassy in Chungking, Doolittle passed a message to General Arnold of the success of the raid.

Quickly the news was announced to the delighted American public. President Roosevelt enigmatically declared that the raid had 'taken off from Shangri-la.' The nation and the press discussed where Shangri-la really was. The idea of an aircraft carrier was suggested, but was, by and large, discounted. It was over a year before the truth was revealed, but the truth was of no great significance. What was important was that the United States of America had begun to avenge Pearl Harbor, and the nation could think about holding up its head once again.

# BATAAN AND CORREGIDOR

A pre-war practise of firing one of Corregidor's ten ton 12' breech-loading mortars. A good crew could fire a 1,000lb shell once every two minutes. The Japanese concentrated their massed artillery fire on the mortars' open casements and, on 5th May – the day the Japanese landed – only two were still in action.

During the summer of 1940, the Japanese Imperial General Staff started to draw up large-scale plans to destroy Western control of Southeast Asia. There were major disagreements about what to do with the Philippines. Many senior army officers were keen to by-pass the archipelago altogether and focus attacks on the British in Malaya and the Dutch in the East Indies. What could be gained, they argued, from capturing the Philippines? The islands, while still technically an American protectorate, were due to achieve complete political independence in 1945. Invading Japanese troops could scarcely pretend to be liberating an oppressed colonial people: their reception might be hostile rather than friendly. The Philippines had few of the rich natural resources which made the Dutch and British colonies such attractive targets for those who dreamed of a self-sufficient Japanese 'New Order', and an attack on the Philippines meant war with the United States – something to be avoided at all costs.

Admiral Yamamoto, commander of Japan's Combined Fleet, offered equally powerful counter-arguments for Japan's invasion of the Philippines. It was argued that it was simply too dangerous to leave the Philippines alone. Any southward move would mean war with America, a war which Japan would certainly lose unless it eliminated American naval and air power in the Pacific at the outset. At Yamamoto's insistence, the Japanese government agreed to begin their expansion with an attack on the American Fleet in Hawaii, an operation coordinated with simultaneous strikes against American bases in the Philippines. In the autumn of 1941, Masaharu Homma, one of Japan's most flamboyant generals, was appointed to command the Philippines invasion force, Formosa-based 14th Army (veteran 16th and 48th divisions) supported by an air fleet of some 500 front-line war planes.

The Americans were aware of the Philippines' vulnerability to Japanese attack ever since they had seized them from the Spanish in 1898. Exercises conducted throughout the 1920s and

Their flag of the rising sun streaming in the breeze, Japanese infantry trudge south from Lingayen Gulf on 22nd December, 1941. Japanese march discipline was poor. They straggled along, often strapping their rifles and equipment to bicycles, and that evening were ambushed by the 26th Cavalry outside Rosario.

1930s had shown that the Philippines' 7,000 islands were virtually impossible to defend. War Plan Orange (WPO-3), formulated over a number of decades, supplied a feasible strategy to ward off the Japanese. The Americans would concentrate on holding the neck of the Bataan Peninsula and the island fortresses of Corregidor and Fort Drum, denying the Japanese access to the vital Manila Bay area until the U.S. Pacific Fleet came to the rescue. It was a stop-gap measure: from 1935 onwards, Washington accelerated the plans for full Philippine independence by 1946, after which all U.S. defence obligations would cease. In the autumn of 1935, General Douglas MacArthur, recently retired army Chief of Staff, was sent to the islands to create a native army for the new, independent Philippines. MacArthur's emotional commitment to the islands – where he had served at the start of his military career in 1904 – led him to view this assignment as the fitting culmination of his life's work. He was determined to bequeath to the Philippines a large, Swiss-style citizen's army, capable of defending the entire archipelago. MacArthur was soon heavily involved in local politics. Financially dependent on the Philippine administration for the success of his cherished, embryonic Philippine army, he inevitably began to exaggerate its capability and efficiency. He tried to convince Washington to scrap WPO-3 and to authorise him to defend

all the islands with his army. Initially a political ploy to gain funds and attention, by 1940 MacArthur had been convinced by his own propaganda. Some of his aides (Major Dwight D. Eisenhower among them) questioned his judgement and mental stability. Admiral Hart, commander of the United State's small Asiatic fleet, confided to his wife: 'Douglas is not completely sane, and may not have been for some considerable time'.

On 26th July, 1941, Washington abandoned WPO-3 in favour of MacArthur's strategy of defending the entire archipelago; a move which was less an affirmation of faith in MacArthur than a warning to Japan – who had recently moved into southern Indo-China – that further expansion southward would lead to conflict with the United States. The Roosevelt government made the message clear by sending reinforcements to the Philippines and promoting MacArthur from the local Filipino rank of Field Marshal to Commander American Army Forces Far East. By December 1941, MacArthur commanded 100,000 Filipino and some 30,000 U.S. regulars, including the redoubtable American-Filipino Philippine Scouts. In addition, he had 277 aircraft, including thirty-six B-17 heavy bombers and a hundred modern Warhawk fighters (the most powerful concentration of U.S. air power outside Hawaii) and Admiral Hart's Asiatic Fleet of three cruisers, thirteen destroyers, several

squadrons of torpedo boats and twenty eight submarines. MacArthur organised his forces into four commands which covered the entire archipelago; the vulnerable north Luzon region was to be commanded by Major General Jonathan Wainwright, who was allocated four divisions, about half the available manpower.

Wainwright's four divisions were responsible for the defence of about 300 miles, but both he and MacArthur knew that, apart from heavily defended Manila Bay, there was only one other place in northern Luzon where a large-scale landing could take place – Lingayen Gulf on the western coast of the Philippines, halfway between Manila and the northern city of Aparri. It was on the shores of Lingayen Gulf that both MacArthur and Wainwright believed the decisive battle for the Philippines would be fought.

MacArthur and Wainwright were correct in their suspicions: Japan's General Homma was planning a massive airstrike on Luzon's airfields. Even if the five-hour time difference between Hawaii and the Philippines meant that the attack on Luzon could not coincide with the strike against Pearl Harbour, Homma still planned to maximize surprise by hitting Luzon shortly after dawn on 8th December. In the event dense fog over Formosa prevented the Japanese takeoff and gave the Americans several hours to mobilize and prepare their defences. But the delay worked to Japan's advantage. When at midday American aircraft – including the precious B-17s – put down to refuel after a morning spent fruitlessly patrolling over Luzon, Japanese bombers suddenly arrived. Within minutes MacArthur had lost most of his air force – another Pearl Harbor, but this time with less excuse.

During the next two days Japanese aircraft launched a relentless assault on northern and central Luzon. They destroyed torpedo stocks at Cavite, Manila Bay's naval base, making reloading impossible for Admiral Hart's submarines, and drove what was left of the American air force to bases at Mindanao, the southernmost island of the Philippines. By 10th December, the Japanese had achieved control of the air. That day they landed small forces at Aparri and Vigan in the north of Luzon and two days later further forces at Lagaspi in the extreme south. Homma was trying to divert MacArthur's troops from the shores of Lingayen

Gulf – he too had realised that it was the only practical coastal landing spot – but MacArthur refused to be sidetracked. His troops were so geared up for a major Japanese landing at Lingayen that they spent the night of 12th December blazing away at a small Japanese motor boat which had entered the Gulf. By dawn MacArthur's staff were claiming a major American victory and the Battle of Lingayen Gulf received widespread U.S. news coverage.

When the real Japanese invasion of the Gulf occurred on 22nd December, American glory was not much in evidence. Hart's submarines lay in wait, but when they sighted the Japanese warships, some inexperienced captains dived deep, while others who fired watched aghast as their torpedoes hit the Japanese hulls without exploding. That night the American Navy learned that most of its torpedo stocks were defective, but, in what became one of the great scandals of the Second World War, nearly eighteen months elapsed before the defect was remedied. By dawn the Japanese convoy, barely aware of the American submarine attack, had penetrated deeply into Lingayen Gulf. The mountainous surf which met 48th Division's landing forces almost put paid to Homma's plans, capsizing scores of invasion barges, drowning hundreds of overladen soldiers and washing up others without arms or equipment. Wainright seized the opportunity and ordered a Filipino reservist division under Brigadier General Clyde A. Selleck to attack. Thanks to MacArthur's decision to keep American soldiers in the north, Filipino divisions were all that were at Wainwright's disposal at this time. It should have been a great American victory, but

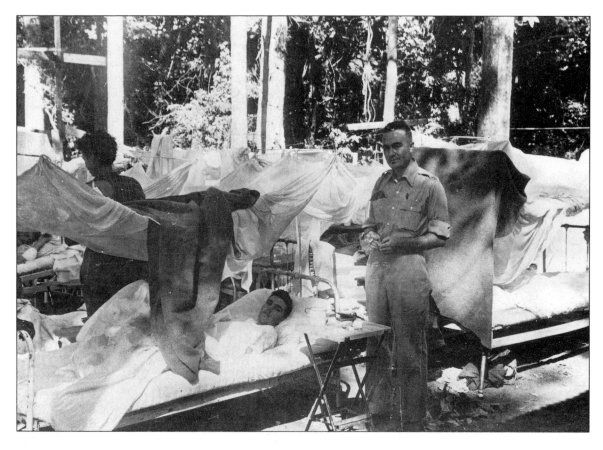

A primitive field hospital hacked out of Bataan's jungle. With few drugs, no running water and no covering for the beds - except a mosquito net -, the death rate from wounds and sickness was very high. MacArthur neglected medical arrangements in this notoriously unhealthy area - an oversight Bataan survivors found hard to forgive.

instead battalion after battalion of Filipinos refused to advance and, as the Japanese moved towards them, melted into the countryside, abandoning their equipment, including entire artillery batteries. By nightfall Homma had finally managed to land tanks and artillery and 48th Division began moving inland.

MacArthur, bitterly disappointed by the rapid disintegration of his native Filipino units, blamed Selleck and demoted him to colonel. But the fault was MacArthur's: Wainwright had never entertained any illusions about reservist Filipino fighting effectiveness and indeed had also tried to stem the Japanese advance by more reliable means – the regular Philippine Scouts whom he had ordered north from Manila Bay. For two days the Scouts, supported by a tank battalion, fought a running battle against the Japanese. By 24th December they seemed to be holding the Japanese at Rosario, a town twenty miles south of the Japanese beachhead. Wainwright intended to fall back from this position some ten miles to the Agno River, a natural defence line running across

the central plain of Luzon, but that very morning came a fresh blow – Homma's 16th Division landed at Lamon Bay, a hundred miles southeast of Manila on Luzon's eastern coast, and advanced on the capital. The news of this landing, followed by Wainwright's request that he be allowed to pull his forces further south to behind the Agno River, at last galvanised MacArthur to action: within hours he had notified all American units that WPO-3, the old plan for the defence of the Bataan Peninsula, was now in effect.

Over the next eight days and nights the road around the northern end of Manila Bay to the Bataan Peninsula was packed with convoys as Americans and Filipinos belatedly moved in supplies and prepared defensive positions. All the while Japan's 48th Division continued to push south from Lingayen through the central plain, while their 16th Division advanced northwest towards Manila from Lamon Bay. In contrast to the lacklustre performance of Filipino reserve divisions on 22nd December, American and Filipino regular units now conducted determined rearguard actions which

The beginning of the Bataan 'Death March' on 10th April, 1942. Thousands of American and Filipino soldiers sit in the burning sun without food or water. As the columns staggered north such rests became infrequent. Thousands dropped from exhaustion and were bayonetted by Japanese guards.

successfully slowed the rate of the Japanese advance. It was not until 2nd January, 1942, that the jaws of the pincers slammed shut with the advance guard of the Japanese 48th Division meeting the leading elements of 16th Division in the streets of Manila. The Americans had long gone, MacArthur having declared Manila an open city on 26th December. As far as Homma and the Japanese Imperial Headquarters were concerned the campaign was now over. All that remained was the mopping up of scattered American forces on Mindanao and other southern islands, and the rounding up on the Bataan Peninsula of forces which Homma believed were little more than a disorganised mob. Indeed, so confident were the Japanese that the veteran 48th Division was ordered south to help in the conquest of

the Dutch East Indies, and its place taken by 10,000 poorly trained, middle-aged reservists commanded by Lieutenant General Akiri Nara.

In fact some 80,000 American and Filipino troops were now in the Bataan Peninsula. Since 26th December MacArthur's forces had constructed a system of field fortifications which ran east and west of the forbidding, jungle-clad slopes of Mount Natib, a jagged volcanic cone which dominated the neck of the peninsula. Three divisions, backed by 200 guns, manned what the Americans called the Abaucay Line, which ran across the neck of the peninsula, except for a seven-mile gap at Mount Natib, which MacArthur believed impassable. In the eight days which had elapsed between MacArthur's decision to implement WPO-3 and the Japanese

**With their few possessions slung between bamboo poles, survivors of the Bataan 'Death March' stagger into Bilibid prison. During the preceding two weeks more than 10,000 (including some 2,300 Americans) had died on the sixty-five-mile long march. Ahead lay nearly three years of brutal captivity.**

Lieutenant General Jonathan Wainwright broadcasting his order for American forces throughout the Philippines to lay down their arms on 6th May, 1942. Throughout the day Wainwright had tried to confine his surrender to Corregidor but, exhausted and emotionally drained, he had finally capitulated in the face of a Japanese threat to massacre the island's garrison.

occupation of Manila the Americans had been able to move vast supplies of ammunition into Bataan, but because top priority had been given to military supplies they had stored only about thirty days' supply of food. More worrying still to MacArthur's staff was the shortage of medical supplies, particularly quinine, because Bataan was a notoriously malarial region. An additional problem was the hordes of civilian refugees who had crowded into Bataan – the Americans believed there were at least 26,000 – who made demands on supplies barely adequate for the soldiers. MacArthur's situation was anomalous: Bataan offered an excellent defensive position, but the logistic situation in everything except ammunition was precarious. MacArthur and key members of his staff, accompanied by the President of the Philippines, Manuel Quezon, soon moved from Bataan to Corregidor, the fortress island which lay two miles off the tip of the peninsula, and established a headquarters in the Malinta tunnel complex. From here MacArthur sent increasingly peremptory messages to Washington demanding the immediate dispatch of relief convoys. Unwilling to believe that America's situation was truly desperate, MacArthur urged his troops to fight on because 'help is on the way from the United States – thousands of troops and hundreds of planes are being dispatched'. It wasn't true but MacArthur didn't know this – besides, the message did serve to improve American and Filipino morale.

Confident of victory, on 10th January Nara's reservists advanced down the peninsula in two columns, one to the east and one to the west side of Mount Natib. At 3.30 p.m. a devastating artillery barrage hit the eastern column as it marched through sugar cane fields only twenty miles north of Marivales, a town at the very tip of the peninsula. By evening the western column was also involved in heavy fighting. Greatly outnumbered and without adequate air and artillery support, Nara's troops battered ineffectually at the Abaucay line for the next twelve days, while a regimental-sized task force probed and eventually found a route through the supposedly impenetrable jungles of Mount Natib. On 22nd January the Japanese burst out of the jungle to the rear of the Abaucay line. American and Filipino counterattacks on 23rd and 24th January failed to dislodge them,

and a day later MacArthur's forces were falling south. It might have developed into a rout but Nara's men were too exhausted to follow – they had suffered at least 1,500 dead and wounded in the battle, the first real test of their fighting prowess since the beginning of the campaign.

The retreating Americans and Filipinos managed to form a new line along an old cobbled road running across the peninsula twelve miles north of Marivales. The slopes of Mount Samat, an extinct volcano in the centre of the line, offered U.S. gunners a superb vantage point. Homma, dismayed by the unexpectedly effective American resistance, devised a much more complex plan for the rest of the campaign. On 23rd January small Japanese forces landed well behind American lines on the western side of the peninsula, and these probes were reinforced on 26th January by the landing of a battalion-sized force. Nara's men, supported by as much artillery as could be brought forward, simultaneously hurled themselves at the Samat line. American gunfire cut them down in swathes. The landings to the south fared no better – American and Filipino rear-echelon troops managed to contain the beachheads and after three weeks of bitter fighting, on 17th February, the last Japanese positions were overrun. Homma had already called a halt to the attacks against Mount

Samat on 8th February. Now reduced to 3,000 effectives (the Bataan campaign cost him 7,000 dead and wounded and 10,000 through disease), Homma feared an American counterattack. His admission to Imperial Headquarters that the campaign had foundered in disaster and his appeal for reinforcements signalled the end of his career.

Unlike the spurious 'battle' for Lingayen Gulf on 12th December, Americans and Filipinos had now won a genuine victory. Though elsewhere the tide of Japanese conquest rolled remorselessly forward, 'Old Glory' still flew over Bataan. The American press now referred to the Philippine's defenders as heroes and elevated their general to the status of demi-god. The defence of Bataan certainly improved morale within the United States, but paradoxically the morale of the defenders was now beginning to falter. MacArthur had long realised that hopes of relief were chimerical – his continued demands for reinforcements eventually produced an order from Roosevelt that the general, his family and key members

of his staff should escape to Australia when MacArthur considered the time was right. The main problem his men faced was hunger. By mid-February the garrison was subsisting on less than half normal combat rations and parties sometimes foraged deep behind Japanese lines. Malnutrition became widespread, and with it came diseases such as dysentery, beriberi and malaria. In mid-March medical officers reported that 60,000 were unfit for combat. Hunger and disease were succeeding where the Japanese had failed. MacArthur left for Australia on 11th March, appointing Wainwright to command with orders to fight to the end.

By early April Wainwright commanded only some 20,000 effectives and these now faced a Japanese army swollen to 50,000 by reinforcements. On 3rd April a massive barrage hit the lower slopes of Mount Samat, setting fire to the cane fields and incinerating American positions. A gap was torn in the American line and the Japanese surged through. Within three days they had crossed the mountains and were herding a now disorganised mob of Americans and Filipinos into Marivales. Wainwright, at his headquarters on Corregidor, forbad surrender but on 9th April his subordinates on Bataan disobeyed and ordered U.S. forces on the peninsula to lay down their arms. In all, 76,000 surrendered, and the Japanese were soon marching them the sixty-five miles north to the railway which would take them to Camp O'Donnel and imprisonment. Only 54,000 reached the camp alive after what became known as the Bataan Death March.

Wainwright still commanded 15,000 men on Corregidor, but most were administration troops untrained for combat. The Malinta tunnel complex sheltered some 6,000 of them plus more than 1,000 sick and wounded. Morale was generally low, except amongst the Marines and the soldiers who manned the beach defences. Corregidor had already become used to heavy bombing but now the Japanese moved some 200 guns to the heights above Marivales, including gigantic 240mm mortars, the largest they possessed. The bombardment began on 10th April and, growing heavier

each day, lasted without intermission for more than three weeks. The once lush island was reduced to a smoking moonscape. Even within the Malinta tunnel the force of the concussion caused nose and ear haemorrhages – above, the defender's heavy batteries were silenced one by one, the last, a thirteen-ton mortar, being blown 150 yards through the air by the force of an explosion. Just before midnight on 5th May the Japanese stormed ashore. The battle on the beach was short and violent, the invaders suffering heavy casualties, but shortly after dawn the Japanese were at the eastern end of the Malinta tunnel. Thousands of Americans sheltered behind the tunnel's steel gates but, unlike the men on the shore, they were little more than a frightened mob. In mid-afternoon an exhausted Wainwright met with Homma and surrendered not only Corregidor but all American forces in the Philippines. Three thousand miles to the south a furious MacArthur vetoed Roosevelt's suggestion that Wainwright be awarded the Medal of Honor.

It was widely believed during the war and for many years thereafter that the Philippine campaign seriously disrupted Japan's timetable by tying up her forces in an exhausting siege and giving other Allied forces a breathing space. It is now known that except for the fillip it gave Allied moral it had virtually no effect on Japanese operations elsewhere. The Philippine campaign, however, did have a considerable effect on the way America was to conduct the Pacific War. After MacArthur's arrival in Australia on 17th March and his pledge to return to the Philippines, Roosevelt had little option other than to appoint him Supreme Commander of the newly formed Southwest Pacific Area. Over the next two years the general was to use this position and his immense popularity in the United States to force upon the joint chiefs of staff the reconquest of the Philippines, in contrast to the Navy's strategy of bypassing the islands and driving directly across the Central Pacific towards Japan. MacArthur's dispute with the Navy was long and bitter and still influences the way historians view the Pacific War. Certainly after the heroic stand made there, it would have been hard for the United States to avoid further involvement in the Philippines. Even today many Americans still feel an odd tingle in the spine when they hear the names Bataan and Corregidor.

# THE BATTLE OF THE CORAL SEA

The Battle of the Coral Sea in May 1942 was the first battle ever fought at sea between two fleets that never even saw each other.

The closest they ever came to meeting was about fifty miles. The deciding weapons were no longer shells from big guns, but bombs and torpedoes from planes operating from aircraft carriers.

The Coral Sea lies off the northeast coast of Australia. It is encircled by a string of islands that separate it from the rest of the Pacific: Papua New Guinea; the Bismarck Archipelago and New Britain; and the Solomons and the New Hebrides.

By April 1942, the Japanese controlled the islands of the Bismarck Archipelago and were moving into the Solomons – Bougainville, Tulagi, and Guadalcanal. Their main base was Rabaul in New Britain, and they held the north of Papua New Guinea. Their next target on that

huge island territory was Port Moresby in the south, to be followed by Australia. Several Japanese naval forces were in the area, covering the landings at Tulagi and escorting the troopships heading for Port Moresby. Others were getting into position to head off any Allied forces that might interfere with their sea-borne invasions.

Together they amounted to two large aircraft carriers, the 30,000-ton sister ships *Shokaku* and *Zuikaku* of some, one smaller 15,000-ton carrier, the *Shoho*, nine cruisers and fifteen destroyers.

The overall Japanese commander, Vice Admiral Inouye, thought the most he would face would be one aircraft carrier, plus cruisers.

However, the American commander in chief in the Pacific, Admiral Nimitz, knew of the Japanese plans through the breaking of their naval code. Nimitz therefore despatched

The Battle of the Coral Sea was the first naval battle in which the opposing forces never came within fifty miles of each other. It was a carrier battle fought between forces of almost equal size, and if tactically it was a 'tie', strategically it was an American victory. Left: SBD Dauntless aircraft safely back on the USS *Lexington* after a strike against the Japanese carriers.

Top right: although the carrier was damaged by Japanese attackers, most of USS *Lexington*'s aircraft were already back on board. After the Japanese attack, destroyers (bottom right) removed those crewmen not needed for fire fighting from the USS *Lexington*. Destroyers also pumped water onto the starboard side of the carrier to try and stem the fires.

The big explosion (bottom left) which decided the fate of the USS *Lexington* was thought to have been caused by leaking gasolene. It made further fire fighting impossible, although Captain Sherman and other key fire-fighting personnel were still aboard.

Bottom far left: the USS *Lexington*, still burning, after being hit by two torpedoes and three bombs during the Battle of the Coral Sea on 8 May, 1942. At this stage, her crew abandoned the burning ship (top left).

another carrier, the USS *Lexington*, plus two more 8-inch gun cruisers and five destroyers from Pearl Harbor as reinforcements. The aircraft carrier USS *Yorktown* was already in the Coral Sea, escorting cruisers and destroyers.

In the following four days of manoeuvering and fighting, the opposing forces were very roughly equal. The Japanese had one small carrier extra, and a slight edge in the number of cruisers and destroyers. However, they also had Japanese transports to protect.

The Japanese began by occupying Tulagi, without meeting any opposition. In fact, the senior American commander there, Rear Admiral Fletcher, on the *Yorktown*, did not learn of this until the evening after the landing. Even then he learned it only from a land-based reconnaisance aircraft.

At this stage of the War, U.S. carrier-borne aircraft could not operate at night; their pilots were not trained for night flying. Next day, however, nearly a hundred U.S. carrier-borne aircraft raided Tulagi, sinking a Japanese destroyer and three other smaller vessels in the harbour. First blood to the Americans.

This success was partly due to the Japanese admiral's decision to use his aircraft carriers to ferry a small number of fighter aircraft to Rabaul instead of moving at speed into the Coral Sea.

The next two days saw the two aircraft-carrier fleets searching the Coral Sea for each other. At one stage they were as close as fifty miles, but never within gun range. Identifying ships from the air is seldom easy, and visibility over these two days was not good. Both sides would make a number of mistakes of identification or communication. Had these errors not been evenly balanced, the battle might have been settled at an early stage.

Japanese search planes were the first to find an enemy ship at sea, a tanker from which the USS *Yorktown* had just refuelled, together with its escorting destroyer. However, these were described to Admiral Inouye as an aircraft carrier and a cruiser. Thus they became the target for a full-scale Japanese attack, which sank them both.

Not to be outdone, an American reconnaisance plane from the *Yorktown* found what it thought to be two cruisers and two destroyers. They were reported, this time as a result of a coding error, as two aircraft carriers and four cruisers. The Americans therefore launched a full attack, using just under one

hundred bombers and torpedo-carrying planes.

In fact, the force that they had found was one commanded by Rear Admiral Goto, coming down to support the Japanese transports heading for Port Moresby. It included just one small aircraft carrier, the *Shoho*, under Captain Izawa, which was hit within minutes by a dozen bombs and seven torpedoes, and sank. About a hundred of her crew were rescued by an accompanying Japanese destroyer.

The sinking of the *Shoho*, which left each side with two large carriers, would be more important than was at first thought. It led to the recall of the Japanese force bound for Port Moresby.

Meanwhile, a force of cruisers, two Australian and one American, had been sent to intercept these transports and their escorting force. As these had turned back, they could not of course be found. Instead the cruisers came under heavy attack from both land-based Japanese aircraft and, by mistake, from U.S. Army Air Force planes flying out of Australia. Excellent ship handling enabled them to escape the attentions of both enemies and 'friends', though the Japanese claimed one battleship sunk and another torpedoed.

One must be careful not to overemphasise the muddle in battles of this kind, but to remind oneself that brave men were hazarding, and often losing, their lives in order to try and find and defeat the enemy. The next attack had to contend with that ever-present and impartial enemy – bad weather.

The Japanese aircraft carriers sent out a strike force to find the Americans. When they had not done so by dusk, they were forced to jettison their bombs and torpedoes and return home. On their way back they were intercepted by American fighters which shot nine down. Another six that tried to land on the *Yorktown*, believing her to be Japanese, were also destroyed. A further eleven Japanese aircraft were lost attempting night landings once they had found their own carriers. Only seven aircraft survived. It was not until 8 May, 1942, that the final battle was fought. By then each side had about 120 planes left. Each side's carriers had a roughly similar force of cruisers around them in defence.

For once the weather was less than impartial. The Japanese carriers were hidden by low rain clouds; the American carriers were exposed in

The beginning of the end for the USS *Lexington* in the Battle of the Coral Sea in May 1942. All her crew have now abandoned ship, and fires rage both above and below decks and in her superstructure. Hours later, the U.S. destroyer *Phelps* was ordered to sink the stricken carrier, and did so with five torpedoes.

bright sunshine. Both sides launched attacks.

The Americans failed to find the aircraft carrier *Zuikaku* but scored three bomb hits on the *Shokaku*. They lost thirty-three planes. The Japanese were more successful. They scored one bomb hit on the *Yorktown*, and hit the *Lexington* with two bombs and two torpedoes. They too lost some thirty planes to American fighters and anti-aircraft fire.

The attempt to save the damaged USS *Lexington* is part of history, and has been well documented in photographs. A stricken aircraft carrier is a particularly sad sight. Her bulky, flat-topped, apparently top-heavy shape gives her an extra air of vulnerability.

The *Lexington*, under Captain Sherman, though her engines were still intact, was listing to port, and was on fire in several places. Sherman was convinced there was a chance of saving her, although leaking petrol later caused one explosion, and others followed. Finally she began to lose power and further fire fighting became impossible.

Some four and a half hours after the first major explosion, the order was given to abandon ship. Destroyers rescued most of her crew, though 216 had been killed either in the Japanese attack or during the earlier struggle to save her.

Who then won the Battle of the Coral Sea ?

The Japanese sank the 35,000-ton American aircraft carrier *Lexington*; the Americans the 15,000-ton *Shoho*. Both sides had a large carrier damaged: the *Yorktown* was repaired within a month; the Japanese *Shokaku* remained in dock for over two months.

More importantly the Japanese were to find themselves ill prepared for the next big aircraft-carrier battle which was to come a month later at Midway. The damage to the *Shokaku*, and the loss of planes and trained crews on both her and the *Zuikaku*, meant neither of these two Coral Sea aircraft carriers was battleworthy.

If these considerations made the Battle of the Coral Sea a tie in a tactical sense, strategically it was an American victory. The Japanese were forced to call off their plans to sail round Papua New Guinea and capture Port Moresby – their chosen base for an attack on Australia.

The battle also constituted the first real check to the great Japanese drive south through the Pacific. At every point until then, from that first surprise attack on Pearl Harbor onwards, it had been a ruthlessly successful campaign.

# THE BATTLE OF MIDWAY

**Low-flying Japanese torpedo aircraft attack a U.S. aircraft carrier during the Battle of Midway. Midway was indubitably an American victory, but at several stages the battle could have gone either way. After a long series of victories, Japanese arrogance led them to commit several tactical errors, whilst the American admirals hardly put a foot wrong.**

Midway has been described as the first and biggest full-scale aircraft-carrier battle of all time. It was not. The Battle of the Coral Sea exactly a month earlier was the first, and bigger battles would follow. In the Battle of the Philippine Sea in June 1944, nine Japanese carriers faced twelve of those from the U.S.

Midway was important, constituting a decisive turning point in checking Japan's advance across the Pacific. It was indubitably an American victory, but it could easily have gone either way.

The exact strategies and detailed studies of the aircraft strikes have been exhaustively covered in such books as *Miracle at Midway* by Gordon W. Prange (McGraw Hill, 1982) and the fourth volume of *History of United States Naval Operations in World War II* by Samuel Eliot Morison.

These accounts make interesting and sobering reading, as one realises just how many

brave and gallant pilots and crews went to their deaths in this battle. Many of the American planes that were thrown into the fight, especially the TBF (Avenger) aircraft, which were making their debut, suffered heavy losses. They stood little chance against the powerful, highly-manoeuverable Japanese Zero fighters. The TBD (Devastator) torpedo bombers suffered equally badly. Midway proved to be a battle in which the shortcomings of many American aircraft were revealed. Only the Dauntless dive bombers proved truly effective, and they are credited with settling the outcome of the carrier battle.

It was the Japanese who chose Midway to be the battleground. The Japanese plan, carefully worked out by Admiral Yamamoto, was to capture the island, and lure the American fleet out into the Pacific before destroying it. The Japanese had missed finding the American aircraft carriers at Pearl Harbor,

so this would be their chance to stage a confrontation on a chosen site and sink them.

The Japanese sent out a huge fleet of more than eighty surface warships, plus another force that would make a diversionary attack on the Aleutian Islands off Alaska. Admiral Yamamoto was flying his flag aboard the biggest battleship in the world, the 64,000-ton *Yamato*. His main force included two other battleships, a light carrier, two seaplane carriers – each with a dozen midget submarines aboard – a light cruiser and eight protecting destroyers.

A guard force of four more battleships, two cruisers and a dozen destroyers was sailing independently. This was for use either with the main force or to be detached to protect the Aleutian expedition if needed.

However, the centrepiece was the first carrier striking force, commanded by Vice Admiral Chiuchi Nagumo, the victor at Pearl Harbor. This comprised four aircraft carriers organised in two divisions: the *Akagi* and the *Kaga*, the *Hiryu* and the *Soryu*. Between them they were carrying some 260 aircraft, divided almost equally between dive bombers, torpedo bombers and Zero fighters. The carrier fleet had a supporting force of two more battleships, both heavy and light cruisers, and another dozen destroyers.

Finally, there was the Midway invasion force itself, comprising two more battleships, nine heavy and light cruisers, an escort carrier, numerous destroyers and a fleet of transports carrying troops. There were other supporting forces including oilers and supply ships, seaplane carriers, and minesweepers.

Last but not least there were a submarine tender and ten submarines. These would spread out in a great fan-shaped forward patrol east of Midway, ready to report any American ships coming on the scene.

To oppose this formidable array, the Americans had some twenty-eight ships. They were centred on two carrier task forces, TF16 with USS *Enterprise* and USS *Hornet*, and TF17 with USS *Yorktown*. The three U.S. carriers had 233 aircraft between them, plus support from a goodly number of land-based aircraft on Midway, including B-17s (Flying Fortresses) and B-26s. The rest of the American warships were a mixture of cruisers and destroyers, together with nineteen submarines.

The Americans were heavily outnumbered and would have to be very careful not to be lured into the trap the Japanese had set for them. They had, however, some unseen advantages. U.S. intelligence was way ahead of the Japanese in providing information about

**The USS *Yorktown* under attack during an early stage of the Battle of Midway on 4/6 June, 1942. One of the Japanese errors was to try and combine two objectives at the same time: the capture of the island of Midway and the destruction of the American aircraft carrier fleet in the Pacific.**

During the battle, the USS Yorktown, flagship of Rear-Admiral Frank J. Fletcher, was hit and set on fire by Japanese carrier-borne aircraft.

enemy dispositions. In addition, the American carriers were equipped with radar, which gave them that extra advance warning that could make the difference between success and failure in a carrier fight.

As it turned out, the Japanese made a great number of mistakes, mainly attributable to the arrogance arising from their long series of triumphs in the Pacific and Indian Oceans.

The Americans would prove to have two further advantages: luck, and an admiral who outthought and outfought his Japanese opposite number. In fact, there were two American admirals who hardly put a foot wrong in this engagement: Rear Admiral Frank J. Fletcher aboard the *Yorktown* and Rear Admiral Raymond A. Spruance aboard the *Enterprise*. Spruance is generally given most of the credit, but Rear Admiral Fletcher, who was the senior of the two, gave Spruance just the right amount of support and freedom in his decision making. This of course is not always the case when two commanders of equal rank operate in tandem.

For the naval historian, the interest in Midway inevitably lies in what might have happened if things had worked out differently. Hindsight also provides us with an opportunity to judge what should have been done, and also to wonder why things that seem so obvious to us

now were not taken into consideration on 4 June, 1942, and on the two days which followed.

It seems clear to us now that Admiral Yamamoto's decision to bring up the rear with his main force was a mistake. At the time when it might have played a part in searching out the American carriers, it was miles away and, after the carrier battle had gone against the Japanese, the force was handled very indecisively.

For all the part the main force and the smaller carriers dispersed throughout the various Japanese groups played in the Battle of Midway, they might just as well have stayed at home and saved the fuel. Everything was left to Nagumo's First Air Fleet.

The first bit of American luck, or bad Japanese management, was the two American carrier task forces getting into position undetected, well to the northwest of Midway. The Japanese submarines were almost two days late in taking up their patrol arc east of Midway. The second Japanese failing was in not using reconnaissance aircraft to their full capacity.

Lacking radar, the Japanese were completely reliant on reconnaissance work, yet it came low in their priorities. Little training was given to pilots in this role, which was

**Left:** the USS *Yorktown* listing badly after being hit by a total of three bombs and two torpedoes.

**Right:** the scene on the listing deck of the USS *Yorktown*. Her crew struggled long and hard to save the carrier, but eventually she had to be abandoned.

looked down on as a defensive measure not in keeping with the offensive attitude of the Imperial Japanese Navy. A ten percent limit had been placed on the number of aircraft used for reconnaissance.

Thereafter, whilst Vice Admiral Nagumo made several tactical errors, Rear Admiral Spruance seemed to make the right decision every time. When American aircraft spotted Japanese forces heading for Midway, Spruance correctly judged that they were transports or escort forces, not the key aircraft-carrier group that he was to stop reaching Midway.

The Japanese, still not suspecting that American carriers were anywhere near at hand, then launched their first attack on Midway. 108 carrier-borne aircraft comprimising a mixture of level bombers, dive bombers and a strong fighter escort, took off.

Midway was ready for them. Its own bombers took off and its fighters and anti-aircraft guns put up a good defence, despite the superiority of the Zero fighters. Not as much damage was

done to the three airfields there as had been feared, and at least nine Japanese planes were shot down and another two dozen damaged.

The returning force signalled: 'There is need for a second attack wave'. Nagumo had kept half his strike aircraft loaded with torpedoes to deal with the American aircraft carrier, or carriers, should these appear. He then decided to unload the torpedoes and load his aircraft up with bombs instead.

This illustrates the problems arising from giving a naval force two separate tasks to carry out. Nagumo was told that his priority was to smash Midway so that it could be captured, but also that he should lure the American carrier force into the open and destroy it.

While he pondered his priorities, his ships were being attacked by land-based aircraft from Midway, albeit a very motley force of six TBF (Avengers), four B-26 bombers, and Vindicators and B-17s. Although several near misses occurred and some optimistic claims for hits made, the attackers succeeded only in

Japanese problems did not end with the carrier battle, in which all four carriers of Vice Admiral Nagumo's First Carrier Striking Force were eliminated. The following day, two of the heavy Mogami-class cruisers that had been part of the Midway bombardment force collided and were badly damaged. On 6 June, the two cruisers were found by U.S. aircraft and bombed (top and bottom left). The *Mikuma* sank, and the 69 *Mogami*, though seriously hit, was recovered and would be converted to an aircraft-carrying cruiser. She was finally sunk by U.S. aircraft, off the Philippines in October 1944.

irritating the Japanese. The Americans suffered heavy losses. The failure of these bombing attacks and of the fighters defending Midway added to Japanese overconfidence. Perhaps in this, and in the distraction they provided, lay the attacks' major contribution to victory.

Space allows only a brief summing-up of the actual battle here. Suffice to say, Spruance got it right again. He took his chief of staff's advice to strike at Nagumo just as the latter's planes returned from Midway, and to go for them with his full strength. 116 planes took off from the *Hornet* and the *Enterprise*. The *Yorktown*'s would follow an hour later.

It worked. Nagumo now knew that there were American aircraft carriers in the offing, and that he would have to attack them next, and not Midway. Before Nagumo had decided whether to send off his strike force, only half of whom were armed with torpedoes, or to delay, take on his returning aircraft and rearm the rest, the Americans were on their way.

American bravery, and luck, settled the carrier battle, and thus the Battle of Midway. The bravery came in the attacks pressed home by the torpedo-carrying planes once they found the carriers, which not all did. The luck came in an unorthodox search manoeuvre executed by the dive-bombers, which found the Japanese where they were not expected to be. Luck played its part again when the *Yorktown*'s dive bombers arrived to attack at the same moment, a piece of unplanned 'co-ordination'.

Victory was mainly due to the dive bombers' attacks. The *Kaga* was hit first just as planes were taking off, then two more bombs crashed through into the hangars below, fires were started and power lost. All those on her bridge were killed. A fourth bomb sealed her fate. Nagumo's flagship, the *Akagi* was also hit several times, and great damage inflicted when stacks of bombs not cleared away from the rearming exploded. The *Akagi*, by then a hulk, was sunk next morning by Japanese destroyers.

The *Yorktown*'s dive bombers also accounted for the *Soryu*. She was reduced to a wreck, abandoned by her crew, and despatched that evening by the U.S. submarine *Nautilus*. Having had three of his four aircraft carriers put out of action within six minutes, Admiral Nagumo might understandably have withdrawn at this stage, but he did not. Instead

he ordered two strikes against the American carriers from the surviving *Hiryu*.

Most of the forty attacking aircraft were shot down either by American fighters or by anti-aircraft fire, but a few got through. The *Yorktown* was hit by three bombs and two torpedoes and had to be abandoned. However, aircraft from the *Enterprise* found the *Hiryu* and inflicted so much damage that she barely survived the night, and actually sank the following day.

Admiral Yamamoto seemed determined to continue to make a fight of it. He called down his small carriers from the Aleutians, and brought up his heavy cruisers to join the main fleet. However he then appears to have lost heart. His aircraft-carrier force had after all suffered disastrous losses: four ships, 250 planes and over 2,000 officers and men. He cancelled a planned bombardment of Midway, and signalled his fleet to withdraw to Japan.

The Japanese troubles were not over. Two cruisers from the Midway bombardment force of Vice Admiral Takeo Kurita's close support group, the *Mikuma* and the *Mogami*, collided when turning to avoid an attack from the U.S. submarine *Tambor*. Both were badly damaged. They were found at 0800 next morning, 6 June, 1942, by Spruance's dive-bombers. The *Mikuma* was sunk, but the *Mogami* managed to get back to Truk.

Admiral Yamamoto now changed his mind again, and ordered cruisers to go after the U.S. carriers, turning his battle fleet back to provide support. Spruance again showed exemplary judgement. He withdrew to the east, to refuel from his fleet train and to avoid being trapped into a fight with surface ships. He had done his job.

The USS *Yorktown*, which some commentators claimed had been prematurely abandoned, was being towed by a minesweeper, and a salvage crew were working to save her. The U.S. destroyer *Hammann* was alongside, attempting to provide power for the salvage team. At this point the Japanese submarine I.168 fired two torpedoes into the *Yorktown* and another into the *Hammann* which sank with heavy loss of life. The *Yorktown* had to be abandoned again. She remained afloat throughout the night only to sink at dawn the following day.

As in the case of HMS *Ark Royal*, torpedoed in the Mediterranean a year earlier, it is now felt that, had the salvage teams made more

Fleet Admiral Isoruku Yamamoto, commander in chief of the Japanese Imperial Navy, and the man who planned the attack on Pearl Harbor. He was overall commander of the Japanese operation against Midway and led one of the greatest naval forces ever assembled at that time, comprising eighty surface warships. However, he seems to have left too much to the Japanese carrier force and, when decisions had to be made, was uncharacteristically indecisive. Less than a year later he was killed when U.S. fighters from Guadalcanal shot up his transport aircraft at Bougainville.

effective use of counterflooding, the USS *Yorktown* might have been saved. However, this is precisely the kind of knowledge gained with hindsight and greater experience.

As a footnote to Midway: on 18 April, 1943, Admiral Isoruku Yamamoto, Commander in Chief of the Combined Japanese Fleet, was killed as his aircraft landed at Bougainville airfield. Intelligence decrypts had alerted the Americans to his visit, and his aircraft was shot down by U.S. P.38s from Guadalcanal.

# CHAPTER SIXTEEN

# THE BATTLE OF EL ALAMEIN

Rommel briefs senior commanders from a half-track vehicle. Note the *Panzerarmee Afrika* symbol on the door. The Field Marshal was famous for leading from the front - he would often abandon his headquarters for the front line and, on occasion, take over personal command of encounters with 8th Army.

The triumph of Gazala and Tobruk behind him, Field Marshal Erwin Rommel lost no time in driving deep into Egypt – his goal of the Suez Canal at last in sight. An attempt by rallying elements of the British 8th Army to hold him at Mersa Matruh was shattered on 27th and 28th June when another forty tanks were destroyed and a further 6,000 disconsolate POWs began the long, thirsty trudge back towards Tripolitania.

However, four factors began to affect his brilliantly extemporized exploitation of the British defeat. First, the inexorable laws of 'the diminishing power of the offensive' began to exert their hampering influence. Second, the Desert Air Force, now operating from its nearby bases, slowed his speed of advance. Third, his pleas to the Fuehrer for just a pair of fresh German divisions to enable him to clinch his success in the Middle East, fell on uncomprehending ears, for the impending summer drive towards the Caucasus in the U.S.S.R. was taking all Hitler's attention. And fourth, in July, three out of the four Axis tankers conveying vehicle fuel to North Africa would fall victim to Allied operations mounted from

unsubdued Malta.

As a result, General Claude Auchinleck was afforded just sufficient time to prepare another line – and a real one this time – seventy miles west of Alexandria. It was to go down in history as 'the El Alamein position' and, before 1942 was out, would be not only the decisive turning point in the Desert War, but also in Britain's fortunes overall in the Second World War. But none could guess this in late June 1942, when 8th Army was, although brave, both baffled and defeated.

Reconnoitered by General Sir James Marshall-Cornwall earlier in the summer, the Alamein line ran for about thirty miles from the Mediterranean coast near the small railway station of El Alamein to the cliffs edging the Qattara Depression, which was a vast area of impassable, low-lying salt marshes that effectively closed the desert flank. Flat and sandy on the coastal sector, the centre comprised a number of rocky ridges and escarpments. Both areas presented bad going for armour. Auchinleck estimated that two reinforced armoured divisions and two well-sited infantry divisions could hold this position

Winston Churchill lost confidence in General Auchinleck and sent him to India. In his place he appointed two new commanders: General Sir Harold Alexander (left) as Commander-in-Chief Middle East Land Forces, and Lieutenant General Sir Bernard Montgomery as Commander 8th Army. 'Monty' was soon to have Rommel's measure.

against superior numbers. The coast road and the railway provided good lines of communication to the rear, so long as the RAF could maintain air supremacy. Naval vessels could overhang the coast in front of the position. Lieutenant General Norrie at once put his weary and disheartened men to work, aided by troops of the new X Corps of Lieutenant General Holmes, whilst Gott's XIII Corps held the ring. Four defended localities were prepared: the largest around El Alamein; the next along Ruweisat Ridge; the third about Abu Dweiss and the fourth at Deir el Shein. The headquarters of 8th Army were close behind the Ruweisat position, where the supply dumps and airfields of Alexandria and the Delta were within easy range to the east.

To hold the area, Auchinleck could call upon 35,000 men and just 160 tanks. Reinforcements were promised – including a convoy of new American Sherman tanks provided by Roosevelt – but these would not arrive before September. Rommel could not be expected to be so helpful as to delay his next offensive until then, so could the line be held? The available troops were split into battle groups, and Auchinleck massed his artillery under Army HQ, and did what he could to create 4th Light Armoured Brigade. But to guard against disaster, he also began to prepare defences in the Delta.

Fortunately for the British, Rommel also had his problems. At the extremity of his advance he had only sixty German and thirty Italian tanks, some 1,500 German soldiers and 5,000 Italians, so small had *Panzerarmee Afrika*

**The Battle of Gazala. Rommel's main swoop to the south with his *Afrika Korps* - an attempt to avoid the heavy defences of Ritchie's Gazala Line - was spotted by the British the evening that the 'Fox' set out. Ritchie, convinced the move was a feint, steadfastly believed that Rommel would strike the British defences in the centre of the Line and so initially failed to divert his armour to the south to counter Rommel.**

become.

Small wonder he pleaded, albeit unsuccessfully, for reinforcements. Typically, however, he paid scant heed to the 'quartermaster's nightmare' of his position, and at once set about planning a repeat of Mersa Matruh and Gazala, which meant diversions in the north by the Italians, strengthened by 90th Light Division, combined with a drive by what remained of the *Afrika Korps* in the distant south to penetrate the desert flank. He believed this bluff would break what little he believed was left of Ritchie's nerve. Here he made a major miscalculation, for Auchinleck had replaced his army commander, and had himself devised an effective plan of defence. This was first to block Rommel's attack and then to launch counter-thrusts against the weaker Italian formations, compelling the German armour to divert from its own purposes to the task of bolstering their allies.

Rommel struck on 1st July. By last light all his attacks had petered out. The long defence by Indian troops of the Deir el Shein box and the damage inflicted by heavy artillery fire on 90th Light Division halted the diversionary attack, whilst the *Afrika Korps*, severely hampered by bad going and incessant air attacks, had to abandon its envelopment plan. But when Auchinleck launched XIII Corps in a counter-strike towards the coast on 2nd July, it made little ground, apart from reducing Rommel's tanks to twenty-six 'runners'. Risking all to gain – or lose – all, the next day Rommel threw everything against the coastal sector and broke in as far as Alam Baoshala, before again being halted. 'Our strength has faded away' remarked the German commander. Time was now on Auchinleck's side. The efforts of the New Zealand infantry and 1st Armoured Brigade had reduced the Italian *Ariete* Division to a mere five tanks. Rommel unwillingly accepted the inevitable: he ordered his formations to dig in.

There followed three weeks of attritional warfare. Applying his operational plan, Auchinleck struck time and again at Italian positions, forcing the *Afrika Korps* to dance to his tune. Rommel bided his time, waiting for the arrival of 260 reinforcement tanks from Tripoli, together with 164th Infantry Division that had very belatedly been made available to him from Crete. But 8th Army lacked real drive:

the 'battle groups' were disliked, and the South African troops were critical of the fate of their compatriots at Tobruk. On 9th July, Rommel occupied 'Bel Q', jubilant to find it undefended, but the next day the new 9th Australian Division routed the Italian *Sabratha* Division at Tell el Eisa, forcing Rommel to divert 15th *Panzer* north. Two days later, Auchinleck routed the Italian *Trieste* Division and again Rommel was forced to respond. On 14th July the New Zealanders and 5th Indian Brigade routed the Italian *Brescia* Division in its turn, and all Ruweisat Ridge was cleared of the enemy. The Italian *Pavia* Division was captive or in full flight behind *Brescia* Division and Rommel, desperate, had to use his dwindling number of tanks to patch the line. On 17th July, he was about to launch an all-out armoured blow against 8th Army's centre in a new breakthrough attempt when he learned that *Trieste* and *Trento* had been routed in their turn by the Australians on the coastal sector, and

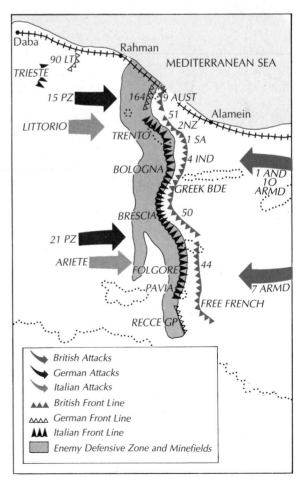

Facing page top: a feared German 88mm artillery piece in action in the Western Desert. This gun, originally designed as an anti-aircraft weapon, proved equally effective in an anti-tank role and achieved many 'kills' against British armour. The '88' was probably the most successful dual-purpose gun of the entire war.

The arrival of the first American Sherman tanks (facing page bottom) swung the advantage in armour to the British. Weighing thirty tons and boasting a top speed of thirty miles per hour, the Sherman was equipped with a 75mm main armament in a turret capable of 360° traverse. At the battles of Alam Halfa and Second Alamein it proved to be 'Queen of the Battlefield'.

Right: the battle begins as a twenty-minute bombardment by 600 British guns heralded the beginning of Montgomery's Second Battle of Alamein. Under its cover, sappers went forward to detect and lift enemy mines to create corridors for the armour of X Corps. Unfortunately, they failed to detect a second minefield area, and serious problems resulted.

90th Light Division had come off the worse in a contest with 4th Light Armoured Brigade west of Alem el Onsol, after making a limited penetration southeast of the El Alamein defended zone.

Rommel had failed. His health was breaking down – he was suffering from a liver complaint, a duodenal ulcer and severe nasal catarrh. Even worse, he found himself militarily 'off-balance'. But to convert defeat into disaster for the Axis proved beyond Auchinleck's skill. Between 21st and 26th July he used XIII Corps in a northward drive, seeking Rommel's communications; but, as General Bayerlein recorded: 'our counter-measures succeeded in preventing a catastrophe', and Auchinleck emerged with only complete possession of Meteirya Ridge to show for his efforts. Although 8th Army still possessed 119 tanks, whereas Rommel was reduced to a mere twenty-six, both armies were now totally exhausted, and five days later the First Battle of Alamein simply petered out.

Auchinleck had lost 13,000 casualties since 1st July. But he was expecting two new armoured divisions from the canal base – namely 8th and 10th – two new infantry divisions (44th and 51st Highlanders reconstituted after the disaster following Dunkirk) and a hundred self-propelled guns. Furthermore, he had inflicted 22,800 losses on the enemy, including 7,000 prisoners, and yet had managed to leave Rommel with just a sufficient illusion of success to persuade him to hold his position face-to-face with 8th Army, rather than to retire westwards to his bases.

Auchinleck was not destined, however, to reap the benefits of his achievement. On 3rd August, Winston Churchill arrived in Cairo, and five days later informed Auchinleck that he was to hand over to General Alexander, Commander in Chief of the Middle East. The Prime Minister's intention that Gott should command 8th Army was shattered when that officer died in an air crash. Instead, Churchill summoned Lieutenant General Bernard Montgomery to assume the role. On 15th August, the handovers were complete, and a disappointed Auchinleck departed to command in India.

Montgomery immediately set about creating better morale and a new army based around a *corps de chasse* of powerful armour. He courted the rank and file of Britain's citizen army like no commander before him. He brought in new generals – Brian Horrocks for XIII Corps, Sir Oliver Leese for XXX Corps, and Frederick de Guingand as Chief of Staff. He even insisted upon a new Chaplain General, hopeful of more effective prayer. The X Corps received two armoured divisions and the New Zealanders. He declared, erroneously, that he had destroyed '.. all plans for further retreat', and that he was going '.. to hit Rommel for six out of Africa'. These strident, even bombastic, claims had an amazing effect. General Sir Harold Alexander was happy to allow his subordinate his head – and large convoys of munitions were due to arrive any day. Better still, Ultra intercepts revealed that Axis shipments into Africa had dropped from 30,000 tons a month to only 6,000 tons in July.

Rommel was aware of the 1,200 miles separating him from his base at Tripoli, and knew that 8th Army was expecting important reinforcements. Already it had 767 tanks, good air support and plenty of fuel. Typically, he decided to try the mettle of the new British command without delay, in a last great fling to forestall the arrival of yet more Allied reinforcements. By late August he had amassed 226 German and 243 Italian tanks. Accordingly, on 30th August, he suddenly attacked, in what the Germans dubbed 'the Six-Day Bicycle Race', and drove for the Alam Halfa Ridge southeast of El Alamein. As Italian XX Corps attacked on the left, the *Afrika Korps* drove for the centre. From the outset, air attacks and minefields imposed delays. And Montgomery was ready for him. With XXX Corps on his right, XIII Corps on his left and with 7th Armoured Division (the 'Desert Rats') to the fore as a lure, he held Ruweisat Ridge and allowed his left wing to be pressed back towards a series of strong, new positions facing south, of which the key was Alam Halfa Ridge. Against the dug-in tanks and new 6-pounder, anti-tank guns, Rommel struck in vain. With his fuel low, on 2nd September he called off the battle and fell back to his starting positions. Montgomery made no serious attempt to follow, merely re-occupying his original line in the south. He was determined to bide his time. Rommel had lost forty-nine tanks, 2,900 men, fifty-five guns and 395 vehicles to 8th Army's sixty-eight tanks, eighteen anti-tank guns and 1,640 casualties. Montgomery also knew that a major Allied landing in northwest Africa – Operation 'Torch' – would occur west of Tripoli in November. So he played Rommel along, keeping his attention fully eastwards, whilst 8th Army grew steadily stronger.

Rommel fell for the bait, and stayed facing El Alamein, putting down new minefields and absorbing 164th Infantry Division, before departing on Hitler's order for hospital in south Germany, leaving General von Stumme in command. By mid-October the Germans had built a forty-five-mile line, faced with a double row of minefields, five-miles deep in all. On the coast stood 90th Light and 164th Infantry divisions. To its south was placed the Italian XXI Corps, strengthened by German paratroop

battalions. On the right was the Italian X Corps. Close in the rear stood the armoured reserve, the veteran 15th and 21st *Panzers* and the two armoured and one motorized divisions of the Italian XX Corps in two groups – fielding in all 200 German and 300 Italian tanks, 53,000 German troops and 55,000 Italians.

Montgomery was now almost ready. On his right was XXX Corps, five infantry divisions strong. On his left was XIII Corps, two infantry divisions plus the 'Desert Rats' of 7th Armoured Division. In the rear waited X Corps – two armoured divisions (1st and 10th) with parts of a third (8th) divided between them, and the New Zealand Division. In all 220,000 Allied troops and 1,351 tanks, including new Shermans and trusty Grants, and a reinforced Desert Air Force (500 aircraft) stood waiting the order to advance and attack in Operation 'Lightfoot'. This was deliberately timed for 'Torch minus 13'. Montgomery refused all Churchill's orders for an earlier offensive. He had a master plan.

The nine infantry divisions and three armoured divisions, equipped with 285 Sherman tanks with their 75mm guns, 246 Grants and 421 Crusaders, 850 6-pounder and 550 2-pounder anti-tank guns and fifty-two medium and 832 field guns – amounted to a formidable 8th Army; in its ranks were Australians, New Zealanders, Indians, Greeks and Frenchmen, as well as British soldiers. Facing it stood four reinforced Axis armoured divisions (two German and two Italian), a pair of motorized divisions (one of each nationality) and eight infantry divisions, seven of them Italian. In overall terms Montgomery enjoyed a 2:1 advantage in manpower and a 3:1 advantage in tanks. Overhead, the Desert Air Force of Air Vice Marshal Tedder (which had been reinforced by two fighter and two light bomber groups) held undisputed sway over the *Luftwaffe* and *Regia Aeronautica*. The numerical advantage that Montgomery had demanded had been achieved. He entered the battle in an enviable position: Rommel was away sick, and come what might Montgomery could hardly lose, for once Operation 'Torch' opened in Tunisia and Algeria on 8th November, the Axis would be compelled to retreat to save Tripoli. However, there was some anxiety over the size and extent of the Axis minefields which had been partly probed in two brigade attacks on 30th September;

A powerful self-propelled German gun captured intact during the desert battles of autumn 1942. The chassis proved to be of French manufacture and was probably made in the Renault works in Paris which the Germans had taken over.

accordingly, in tune with the latest intelligence reports, Montgomery adjusted his plan.

Originally, this had conceived of a simultaneous attack by XXX Corps in the north and XIII Corps in the south, which were to break into the Axis positions and clear corridors for the armour of X Corps to exploit; the tanks would then sever the enemy's hostile lines of communication. Now, on 5th October, he decided to attack in the north with both XXX and X corps and employ both simultaneously. Two busy weeks of final preparations and exercises ensued.

On the night of 23rd to 24th October, 1942, some 900 guns suddenly delivered a hurricane bombardment, and the mine-clearing parties moved forward. The Second Battle of El Alamein had begun. The Axis were taken by surprise, but soon rallied to their pre-arranged defensive tasks. The southern of the two thrust lines made good progress, and the New Zealanders rapidly captured Miteirya Ridge. Behind them, however, 10th Armoured Division hesitated to

pass through, having run into more mines. Further north, the Australians made less progress against heavy resistance, and 1st Armoured Division became bogged down between the two minefields. The static tanks made excellent targets for the pre-registered Axis artillery. On the other hand, German General Georg Stumme died of a heart attack caused by an exploding mine. On 25th October, Rommel hurried from Germany to find the Allied operation still stalled in the north and making scant progress in the south, where 44th Division and 7th Armoured had also come to a halt.

On 26th October, Montgomery ordered a pause to adjust the plan. He now enjoined XIII Corps, led by the Australian 9th Division, to strike northwestwards towards the coast. On 27th October, some progress was made, but then Rommel's armoured counter-attacks against Miteirya and Kidney ridges, although ultimately forestalled, restricted forward progress. Churchill cabled anxiously for news, aware that 'Torch' was now imminent. So Montgomery for the second time changed his

**Crusader tanks armed with 6-pounder main armaments are seen in full 'hue and cry'. The breakthrough achieved, the German *Panzers* beaten and Rommel in full retreat, it was time for the British medium tanks to sweep forward in pursuit.**

plan. By Operation 'Supercharge', the Australian attack on the coast was to continue, but the main thrust would be further south. While XIII Corps pressed forward, X Corps was to strike northwestwards to distract and defeat Rommel's *Panzers*. The new assault began early in the morning on 2nd November. Rommel, his petrol almost gone, was told to 'stand and die' by Hitler. More realistically, he decided to break off and retreat, taking all Italian transport for his German troops. Victorious 8th Army had lost 13,500 more casualties and 500 tanks (150 of them destroyed), but in turn had inflicted 59,000 on the Axis and accounted for 454 tanks and 1,000 guns. It had been a battle of direst attrition, but numerical advantages had told in the end

By 4th November, X Corps was in full pursuit, but then heavy rain bogged the armour down and Rommel was free and away. Fighting bitter rearguard actions, he was pressed back through Tobruk by 13th November and Msus by 17th November, and the British re-entered Benghazi on 20th November. Montgomery paused before El Agheila where Rommel turned to face him once more, but on 13th December the Axis moved to the west again. Boxing Day found Rommel in a new position at Buerat, but on 13th January, 1943, he again pulled out just before Montgomery launched an assault. So, on 23rd January, the British at last entered Tripoli as Rommel entered Tunisia. The battle for the Western Desert was over, although much bitter fighting remained against field marshals von Arnim and Rommel who now, far too late, received strong reinforcements from Germany. But there was no denying the importance of Montgomery's victory at El Alamein. It was the only great land battle won by British and Commonwealth forces without direct American participation and, together with the German surrender at Stalingrad in February, 1943, it marked the turning point of the war. 'It is not the end', Churchill warned the jubilant British public at a review of the victorious 8th Army in Tripoli; 'it may not even be the beginning of the end. But it is undoubtedly the end of the beginning'.

# GUADALCANAL

By the summer of 1942 Japan controlled an area which extended from the eastern borders of India to the islands of the Central Pacific, and from the Aleutians to the Solomon Islands. In early June, at Yamamoto's urging, the Combined Fleet had sought to annihilate the remnants of the American Navy off the island of Midway, 1,000 miles west of Hawaii, and had suffered its first serious reverse. But even after the loss of four carriers, the Imperial Navy still dominated the Pacific. Nevertheless, this failure caused Japanese attention to turn to the South Pacific. Japan's new plan was to consolidate her hold on the Solomons, a group composed of seven large, mountainous, jungle-clad islands and many smaller ones that extended 800 miles southeast from her main South Pacific base at Rabaul. A 1,500-man garrison had already occupied Tulagi, a small island which had served the British as an administrative headquarters. Fifteen miles south of Tulagi lay Guadalcanal, one of the southernmost islands of the group. Ninety miles long by fifteen wide, the northern shore of this rugged, heavily forested island was fringed by a narrow coastal plain. On 1st July 2,000 Japanese construction troops landed on this shore at Lunga Point and began clearing an airfield. It was intended that aircraft flying from Guadalcanal would provide air cover for the next stage of Japan's expansion – the occupation of New Caledonia and Fiji that would cut the flow of American supplies to Australia.

Unknown to the Japanese, their activities were being closely observed by a team of 'Coastwatchers' – Australian and British planters and officials who had volunteered to stay behind in Japanese occupied territory. Those on Guadalcanal were commanded by Captain Martin Clemens, a Cambridge graduate and former athlete. Within hours of the landing, he had given America's South Pacific Headquarters in Noumea a clear picture of Japanese intentions. The American Commander in Chief Pacific (CINCPAC), Admiral Nimitz, responded with characteristic energy. On 7th July he ordered the only American unit in the South Pacific considered combat worthy, New Zealand-based 1st Marine Division, north to seize the airfield. The Division's commander, Major General James A. Vandegrift, protested vigorously. Apart from a handful of long-serving NCOs and officers, his division was composed of raw recruits, inexperience which showed when a rehearsal for the landing collapsed into chaos. But Nimitz remained adamant. If the Japanese were allowed to complete their air base, the strategic outlook in the South Pacific would be bleak.

On 26th July, 1942, the largest task force the United States had yet assembled in the South Pacific rendezvoused off the island of Kora, some 350 miles south of Fiji – an amphibious strike force – TF 62 – commanded by Rear Admiral Richmond Kelly Turner and composed of twenty-three transports carrying 18,000 Marines escorted by eight cruisers and fifteen destroyers, and a covering force – TF 61 – commanded by Rear Admiral Fletcher and composed of three aircraft carriers, a battleship, six cruisers and sixteen destroyers. Eleven days later, when the fleet was sixty miles south of Guadalcanal, TF 61 detached itself and remained in open waters. Meanwhile, TF 62 sped north, rounded Cape Esperance, the northwestern point of Guadalcanal, on the evening of 6th August and entered Sealark Channel, which separated the northern shore of Guadalcanal from Tulagi. About five miles west of Savo Island – a volcanic cone which rose precipitously from the channel – TF 62 divided into two groups; one heading for Tulagi, the other for Lunga Point.

At dawn the Marines of Colonel Mike Edson's 1st Raider Battalion stormed ashore on Tulagi. It was America's first assault landing since 1898. The Japanese commander, seeing the size of the American task force, radioed to Rabaul:

Assault groups of U.S. 1st Marine Division practise landing operations on Koro Island in the Fiji group on 28th July, 1942. Shortly after this picture was taken, the landing-craft ground onto Koro's reefs, and the exercise degenerated into a shambles. Ten days later the Marines' commander, Major General A.A. Vandegrift, approached Guadalcanal with deep misgivings.

Right: photographed
from a dive-bomber of
the U.S. Carrier
*Dauntless*, landing
craft carry Marines of
Colonel Edson's
Raider Battalion to the
shore of Tulagi on 7th
August, 1942. This was
the Marines' first
assault landing since
1898.

Inland from the
beachhead Marine
patrols (below) found
the going difficult.
Dense jungle
interlaced with vines
and creepers slowed
progress to a few
hundred yards per
hour. Fortunately for
the Marines, the
Japanese found
movement just a
difficult.

'enemy troop strength is overwhelming. We will fight to the last man.' He was as good as his world; the heavily reinforced Raiders took three days to exterminate the garrison.

On Guadalcanal, things had gone differently. The bulk of 1st Marine Division landed on a beach two miles east of Lunga Point shortly after 9.00am, advanced southwest to the airfield and discovered that the Japanese had fled inland. This was fortunate because the landing had been even more confused than the practise run. Supplies were dumped in hopelessly mixed-up piles and men wandered around waiting for orders.

Japanese headquarters in Rabaul was at that time much more interested in their invasion of Papua, 1,000 miles to the west of Guadalcanal, than in anything that was happening on the island. They simply did not have the men to reinforce their Guadalcanal garrison substantially, nor did they take the threat seriously. Confident in the ability of their air and naval forces to cut the Marines' supply line, they decided they could deal with the Americans by only sending a 5,000 strong detachment of General Hyakutake's 17th Army, which was then based on Guam. Although they knew it would take at least ten days for the detachment to reach Guadalcanal, they were

certain that by then their navy and air force would have won the battle.

Rabaul's strategy nearly worked. Heavy Japanese air attacks during 7th and 8th August cost Admiral Fletcher twenty-one of his ninety-nine fighters, and on the night of 8th August he radioed Turner to say that he was withdrawing his carriers out of range. The loss of air support this entailed meant that Turner had no option other than to withdraw TF 62. During the evening of 8th August supplies were dumped on the beach and the task force prepared to leave. At 1.00am disaster struck. When the first news of the landing reached Rabaul a Japanese

cruiser and destroyer force had sped south. It now surprised Turner's cruisers and in a violent, thirty-minute action off Savo Island sank four.

As dawn broke on 9th August the men of 1st Marine Division knew they were completely alone on an isolated beachhead 1,000 miles from the nearest Allied base. Their supposedly imposing navy had fled, leaving only debris and the still-burning hulls of the cruisers. For many, the situation seemed very close to that which had faced MacArthur's beleaguered forces on Bataan four months earlier. A determined Japanese ground attack at this time would almost certainly have destroyed the beachhead. Instead, the Japanese confined their activities to air raids and naval shelling – unpleasant enough, but it gave Vandegrift time to construct a perimeter centred on Lunga Point, about three miles wide by three deep, which encompassed the airfield. Engineers worked feverishly to complete the runway, now named Henderson Field after a hero of Midway. On 20th August thirty-one Marine Corps aircraft flew onto the just-completed airfield – twelve Dauntless dive-bombers and nineteen Wildcat fighters – which lessened the Marines' sense of isolation and allowed them to hit back.

The Marines had also discovered that they had friends on the island. Captain Clemens and a party of Solomon Islands constabulary had emerged from the jungle with accurate intelligence on the island's topography and on Japanese positions – the first real intelligence Vandegrift had received. On 19th August one of the constables, Jacob Vouza, while patrolling to the east of the perimeter, ran into a large force of Japanese. He was tortured, bayoneted,

and left for dead, yet was able to crawl back to the beachhead with the news that an attack was imminent.

Vouza had stumbled across an 800-strong advance guard of the detachment from Guam which had landed by destroyer on 18th November. Its commander, Colonel Kiyono Ichiki, was an arrogant and headstrong officer who believed that even a small number of boldly led Japanese could defeat many times their own number of white soldiers. Rather than wait for the rest of the detachment, he decided to attack. During the evening of 20th August his troops infiltrated through a coconut plantation just to the east of the Marines' perimeter and at 1.20am on 21st August they burst from the trees and charged towards the Marines' foxholes across a sandbank at the mouth of the Tenaru River. The forewarned Americans cut them down with 37mm canister shot and machine-gun fire. By dawn, counter-attacking Marines had trapped Ichiki and his men in the coconut plantation. Dauntless dive-bombers from Henderson strafed the area again and again and the Marine's Stuart tanks then rolled in, crushing the Japanese beneath their tracks. 'The rear of the tanks', Vandegrift recorded, 'looked like meat grinders'. At the end of the day, 800 Japanese and thirty-five Americans were dead.

This action, which the Americans named the Battle of Tenaru, finally convinced Japanese headquarters that substantial reinforcements would have to be diverted to Guadalcanal. The American High Command, too, realized that 1st Marine Division was going to need large reinforcements if it was to retain to its precarious beachhead. Guadalcanal now became a vortex, sucking in all available Japanese and American manpower and material in the South Pacific – a gruelling battle of attrition was in prospect. As the Americans held Henderson Field (by 30th August more than sixty aircraft were operating from it), they could control the waters around Guadalcanal by day and provide cover for their own supply convoys. The Japanese were obliged to reinforce at night. From 22nd August onwards the fast transports and destroyers of Admiral Raizo Tanaka's 'Tokyo Express' made the nightly dash down through the straits of the Solomons to deposit men and supplies on open beaches. In order to cut each other's

Below: a Marine Stuart tank rolls towards the coconut plantation on the Ilu River late on 21st August, 1942. Nearly 800 Japanese had already been killed in the plantation, many being crushed by the tanks.

Only some 1,000 yards south of Henderson Field a Japanese Juki machine gun and its dead crew mark the point where the last attempt to take the airstrip was finally brought to a halt on 26th October.

supply lines, the Americans and Japanese fought a series of complex and bloody naval and air battles between 22nd August and 30th November. Some, like the Battle of the Eastern Solomons (22nd to 25th August) and the Battle of the Santa Cruz Islands (26th to 27th October), were long-range duels between carrier aircraft as Yamamoto attempted to lure the Americans into a climatic battle of annihilation. Others, like the Battle of Cape Esperance (11th to 13th October), the Naval Battle of Guadalcanal (12th to 15th November) and the Battle of Tassafaronga (30th November), were close-range clashes between surface fleets fought at night. American and Japanese naval losses were about equal, but American shipyards could replace the losses, while those of the Japanese could not.

The key to the campaign was the control of Henderson Field. All the land fighting was designed to achieve this – the Japanese either had to capture the field or put it out of action, while the Americans had to hold it at all costs. Between 22nd August and 12th September, Tanaka's nightly convoys increased Japanese strength on Guadalcanal to 5,200 men. Vandegrift, in the meantime, engaged in

aggressive probing. In early September, reports from Clemens' scouts of a powerful Japanese concentration to the south of the beachhead caused Vandegrift to suspend the probes and concentrate on strengthening the perimeter. On 10th September he brought Edson's Raiders across from Tulagi and positioned them on a low ridge to the southeast of the airfield, opposite the reported Japanese positions.

The Raiders did not have long to wait. At 9.00pm on 12th September a Japanese cruiser and three destroyers began shelling the southeastern side of the perimeter, and twenty minutes later 2,000 Japanese charged out of the jungle. The Raiders, dug in at the base of the ridge, met them with concentrated fire, and then fell back northwards up the ridge to higher ground. During the following day they dug in furiously and laid barbed wire. At 6.30pm the Japanese came on again. Their sheer weight of numbers overwhelmed Edson's right flank. Some surged along the American line, others made for the airfield. Three who burst into Vandegrift's command bunker were shot dead by the general's clerks. Some of the Americans came close to panic, but were rallied by Edson with the Marines' cry of 'Do you want to live forever?' He called in artillery fire closer and closer to his own positions until it rained like a wall between his men and the Japanese. Dawn revealed a field of carnage. More than 600 Japanese lay where they had fallen along what the Marines were already calling 'Bloody Ridge' and 500 more had been wounded or were missing. The Americans, too, had suffered heavy losses – 260 killed or wounded – but they had held on.

Despite this victory Vandegrift's position was far from enviable. Japanese naval shelling at night was relentless and during the day Japanese bombers still made it through the protective screen of Wildcat fighters. Heavy rain, which began on 1st October, filled foxholes and added to the Marines' discomfort. Meanwhile, the Japanese prepared to make yet another assault. On 9th October Lieutenant General Harukichi Hyakutake, commander of Japan's 17th Army, landed on Guadalcanal, along with the bulk of his 2nd Division, a squadron of medium tanks and a regiment of 150mm howitzers, which were soon shelling the beachhead. Four nights later, the battleships *Kongo* and *Haruna*, cruising off

Lunga Point, bombarded Henderson Field with 918 14" shells in just two hours. At dawn the airstrip resembled a moonscape – half the Marines' aircraft had been destroyed, and, although only forty-one men had been killed, hundreds were wandering about dazed, the victims of extreme 'battleshock'. On the following two nights Japanese cruisers poured in another 2,000 shells. Yamamoto's fleets now moved into the waters of the southern Solomons to force the American Navy to battle, while Hyakutake's forces, 20,000 strong, closed on the Americans.

Unlike the crude frontal attacks which had produced disaster at the battles of Tenerau and Bloody Ridge, Hyakutake planned to employ finesse. A tank and infantry force commanded by Major General Tadishi Sumiyoshi was to strike at the western side of the perimeter across the Matinikau River and divert the Americans' attention, while the main attack force under Lieutenant General Masai Maruyama moved along a jungle trail around the beachhead and struck from the south. Fortunately for the Americans, Maruyama's movement was delayed by thick jungle and

A Japanese battle flag captured during the fighting on 26th October, 1942 – a photograph which was of immense symbolic importance for the American public. The Marines stretch the flag, displaying the rent their bullets have torn across the centre.

**The guns of the destroyer U.S.S. *Laffey* blaze at the Japanese battleship *Hiei* at 2.00am on 13th November. This encounter was one of the most dramatic in the four-day naval battle of Guadalcanal, the titanic slugging match which gave the Americans control over the waters around the island and sealed the fate of the Japanese.**

he urged postponement. Hyakutake agreed, but his order to delay the attack did not reach Sumiyoshi. At sunset on 23rd October Sumiyoshi's tanks rolled across a sandbar at the mouth of the Matinikau River and were smashed by the concentrated fire of the Marines' 37mm anti-tank guns. Five hours later, Maruyama's troops were at last in position, slightly to the east of Bloody Ridge. At 11.00pm they attacked in blinding rain.

Colonel Toshari Shoji's 29th Regiment led the assault and actually broke through the American perimeter. Charging north they crossed a flat, grassy space. An ecstatic Shoji radioed that he had captured Henderson Field and, on his flagship far to the north, Yamamoto rejoiced and ordered his fleet to close on Guadalcanal. But Shoji hadn't reached the field. One ridge still remained between Shoji and the airstrip – a ridge which 7th Marines

defended to the death. Bitter hand-to-hand fighting raged throughout the night and at dawn Maruyama called his force back to consolidate, leaving behind 900 dead. All day long, Japanese aircraft strafed and bombed the ridge and in the intervals between the raids 150mm howitzer shells screamed down. It was a Sunday – later to become known throughout the Marine Corps as 'Dugout Sunday'. At dusk, Maruyama's men charged again, and again were cut down. By dawn on 26th October he had had enough and withdrew into the jungle, having sacrificed 3,500 men.

Hyakutake was disappointed by this reverse, but had not yet given up hope. He determined to bring in 11,000 men of his veteran 38th Division to reinforce the 30,000 Japanese then on the island and crush the beachhead by sheer weight of numbers. The attempt to convoy

these troops to the island, however, ended in the disastrous naval battle of Guadalcanal, described by Admiral Richmond Kelly Turner as 'the fiercest naval battle ever fought'. Battleships blazed away at point-blank range, but the issue was decided by Henderson's aircraft, which tipped the balance in America's favour. The convoy carrying 38th Division was all but destroyed, only some 2,000 troops making it to the island. Worse still for the Japanese, the battle had given the Americans control over the waters of the southern Solomons by both day and night. The Japanese now realised that they had 30,000 men on a tropical island whom they could not keep adequately supplied. Tanaka's destroyers still raced along the coast at night, but they could no longer risk stopping to unload supplies – instead they threw supplies, sealed in drums, overboard in the hope that some would drift ashore. Almost incessant rain heralded the onset of malaria, a disease soon supplemented by dengue fever and amoebic dysentery. By early December malnutrition, too, was widespread and by mid-December the Japanese were beginning to die in large numbers.

The Marines had also been suffering, but they did so on relatively full stomachs, and their malaria had been held in check, to some extent, by the new drug atabrine. A major difference was that sick Marines could be evacuated by air – of the 8,580 Americans who had been hospitalized since the beginning of the campaign, 3,919 had been flown to New Caledonia by the end of November. In early December entire 1st Marine Division was evacuated by sea – about one third were considered medically unfit for duty – and were

replaced by 2nd Marine Division and the American Division, formed from U.S. Army units which had been garrisoning New Caledonia. An exhausted Vandegrift also left, handing over command to an Army officer, Lieutenant General Patch. Japanese intelligence had informed the High Command of these changes, and Tokyo knew that their own emaciated forces were no match for the fresh Americans. On 31st December an Imperial conference took the only decision possible: even though it was extremely hazardous, the entire force was to be evacuated at night.

By the beginning of January, 1943, Patch's fresh divisions were driving the Japanese steadily westwards towards Cape Esperance. Even on their last legs, the Japanese put up tenacious resistance, but as they intended to evacuate from this cape, they fell back before the Americans. On seven consecutive nights, from 1st to 7th February, fast destroyer convoys rescued 13,000 survivors from open beaches – the most skilful evacuation since the British left Gallipoli twenty-six years earlier. But the Japanese had left 25,000 dead behind. The Americans had lost 1,592 killed and 4,300 wounded. No amount of rationalization by the Japanese could disguise the fact that they had suffered a major defeat.

Unlike the freakish American victory at Midway, the gruelling attritional struggle for Guadalcanal tested not just the American and Japanese armed forces, but the economies and societies which sustained them. It was precisely this sort of battle which Yamamoto had hoped the Pearl Harbor attack would obviate, for he knew that in any contest of brute force, America was bound to win. And so it proved. In the immediate aftermath of Savo Island, the Japanese could have destroyed the beachhead had they thrown substantial forces at it. The delay gave the Americans time to prepare defences – thereafter Japanese attacks battered themselves to pieces on an ever-stronger perimeter. The capture of Guadalcanal was the key to the reconquest of the Solomons, which, in turn, made possible the isolation of Rabaul and the eventual reconquest of the Philippines. From 7th February, 1943, the initiative in the Pacific War was clearly with the Americans.

Japanese stragglers who missed the last evacuation barges of 7th February, 1943 and were captured by the Americans two weeks later. Emaciated and sick, they received much better treatment at the hands of the Americans than did the few Marines who had the misfortune to fall into Japanese hands.

# CHAPTER EIGHTEEN

# THE BATTLES OFF GUADALCANAL

**Sunset over the Pacific makes a photogenic study, but the fighting to wrest the islands there from the Japanese would include some of the most bitter warfare of the Second World War. Getting the troops to the beaches and supporting and supplying them whilst there would inspire the development of a whole new science of amphibious warfare.**

Midway marked the first major check to Japanese aggression and expansion since their attack on Pearl Harbor. It was a significant American victory. However, wars are only won on the ground. Lost territory must be recovered and, ultimately, the enemy's capital must be occupied.

More than three years' hard fighting, on land and against a determined enemy, lay ahead of the United States. Although her Australian and New Zealand allies were also sometimes fully involved, the Pacific island battlegrounds were mainly American. Land battles would not concern us here, were it not for the fact that 'island hopping', as it came to be called, inevitably meant the use of amphibious forces.

The U.S. Marines, and the U.S. Army divisions that followed them, had to be escorted to their landing places offshore. They required as much support and protection as possible, and they

had to be continually supplied and reinforced as they fought their way towards Tokyo. The warships also had to stop enemy supplies and reinforcements getting through.

The first U.S. objective was Guadalcanal, one of the British Solomon Islands on the northern edge of the Coral Sea. The assault, originally planned for later in 1942, was brought forward to August. This was because the Japanese, who already had a seaplane base on nearby Tulagi, were discovered to be building an airfield in the jungle in the north of Guadalcanal. This would become Henderson Field, a key to the six-month battle for the island which followed.

The amphibious forces for the landing were under the command of Vice Admiral Robert Ghormley U.S.N. Task Force 62, under Rear Admiral Turner, had nineteen transports, carrying 19,000 U.S. Marines. It was escorted by three 8-inch gun cruisers, one 6-inch gun cruiser, and eight destroyers. This escort force included

Australian ships, and was commanded by British Rear Admiral Victor Crutchley R.N., who had won a Victoria Cross in World War I. There were also four more cruisers and six more destroyers making up two fire support groups.

Operating to the south was the powerful Task Force 61, under the command of Rear Admiral Fletcher. Along with the three aircraft carriers, the *Saratoga*, the *Enterprise* and the *Wasp*, this force also boasted a fast new battleship, the USS *North Carolina* and six 8-inch gun cruisers.

Opposing them was the much smaller Japanese Eighth Fleet, based to the north at Rabaul in New Britain. It was commanded by Vice Admiral Gunichi Mikawa, second in command of the attack on Pearl Harbor, and also at Midway. His force included five 8-inch gun cruisers, two smaller cruisers and destroyers. Added to this were naval aircraft operating from land: twenty-four bombers and thirty fighters.

At this stage the main Japanese fleet was far away, though heavy reinforcements would arrive for later battles off Guadalcanal. For Guadalcanal was a whole series of naval battles, not all of which the Americans won. At least two were disastrous in terms of losses. In his

excellent book, *Naval Battles of World War II*, Captain Geoffrey Bennett R.N points out that the U.S.A. fought as many sea battles around Guadalcanal as the Royal Navy had fought in the whole of World War I.

D-day at Guadalcanal and Tulagi was 7 August, 1942. The fact that the date had been advanced meant that the U.S. Marines were only able to stage one practice landing at Fiji. Nor had the supporting force, of mixed Australian and American cruisers, had the chance of working together before going into action.

In fact, the landings went surprisingly well. By the following afternoon, after fierce fighting, 6,000 marines had captured Tulagi. 11,000 marines landed on Guadalcanal with virtually only one Japanese labour battalion engaged on building the airfield to resist them. However, there were still more men to land and supplies to get ashore. The naval fire support groups and Rear Admiral Crutchley's cruiser force were then reorganised to cover any Japanese naval intrusions from either east or west.

The chapter of accidents that followed was blamed by some on the British admiral's dispositions. Either out of tact, or in the cause of Allied solidarity, he was not criticised by the

An apparently peaceful Pacific island (left), where the Guadalcanal waterway meets the Pacific, was actually the site of the battle of Matinakau. Wrecked Japanese tanks can be seen in the Matanikau River.

U.S. Marines are seen soon after landing with their jeeps (right) from what was, in 1942, a new type of landing barge. Jeeps came into their own as ideal vehicles for the kind of fighting that took place on Guadalcanal and other Pacific islands.

American commander in chief, Admiral King, in a later summing-up of the battle.

Instead of deploying his force well out to the west, with a destroyer screen even further out, Rear Admiral Crutchley chose to stay east of Savo Island, situated just to the north of Guadalcanal. He also managed to be away attending a conference with the Americans, when the Japanese arrived. He had travelled to the conference on his flagship, HMAS *Australia* instead of using one of the destroyers, thus splitting the defending forces even more.

The conference had been called after Rear Admiral Fletcher, commanding the aircraft carriers, gave notice that he was withdrawing his force that night and would not provide air cover for the third day's landings. Rear Admiral Turner, in charge of the landings, protested, but Fletcher was senior to him. Remembering his loss of the *Yorktown* at Midway, Fletcher stuck by his decision. A month or so later, Fletcher would be relieved of his command of aircraft carriers, and 'promoted' to take charge in the

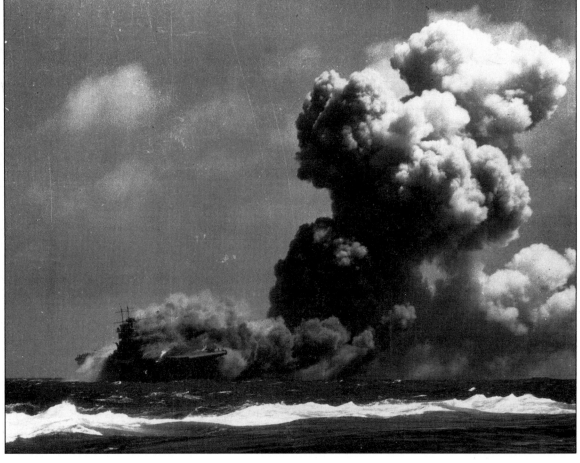

Top left: the liner *Kinugawa Maru*, a Japanese casualty at Guadalcanal. After failing to defeat the U.S. Navy in a series of battles off Guadalcanal, the Japanese were reduced to running fast night-time 'Tokyo Express' convoys in an attempt to land reinforcements on the islands the Americans were attacking.

Bottom left: the U.S. aircraft carrier *Wasp*, one of the two American carriers to be lost during the series of naval battles off Guadalcanal.

Right: three Americans lie dead on a beach at Buna in New Guinea. U.S. policy about showing the bodies of Americans killed in action in the official pictures of battle scenes changed in early 1943. It was felt that the public should be made to understand the real cost of war and the sacrifices involved.

Left: Australian troops about to land from American landing craft at Sadau, an island six miles north of Tarakan, Borneo. As island hopping continued through the latter part of the war in the Pacific, the Australians became involved in action in many places.

remote backwaters of the North Pacific Area.

The Japanese did exactly what they might have been expected to do – they headed straight for Guadalcanal and the vulnerable transports. Led by the large 8-inch gun cruiser *Chokai*, their force was now about the same size as that guarding the western approaches, given that HMAS *Australia* was absent and other cruisers had been detached to guard the east. The forces might have been equal in gun power, but the Japanese were three times as powerful in terms of torpedoes. A total of forty-eight Japanese torpedo tubes were able to use the Japanese Long Lance 24-inch torpedo.

The Japanese were sighted early on by a U.S. submarine, which had to dive under the passing ships, being too close to fire her torpedoes. In the darkness the submarine underestimated the enemy's strength in her subsequent radio report. The Japanese then steamed right past the two patrolling picket destroyers that Crutchley had placed. Nobody had thought of coordinating their sweeps. Thus when they were each at the end of their patrol there was a gap left in the middle. Vice Admiral Mikawa's force passed straight through this, undetected by either picket's radar or lookouts.

Most of the details of the one-sided battle that followed are best forgotten. Suffice to recall that half the crews on the Allied cruisers were asleep and that their guns were all trained fore-and-aft. The Japanese launched their attack unseen, and HMAS *Canberra* was hit immediately by two torpedoes as well as by broadsides from Japanese guns. The USS *Chicago* was hit by another torpedo.

The U.S. cruiser fired star shell but none of it ignited. Eventually the *Chicago* steamed off in pursuit, but Mikawa's ships had split and no contact was made. The *Chicago*'s next move, on what was admittedly an extremely dark night, was to return and fire shells at the destroyer USS *Patterson*, standing by the stricken *Canberra*. Luckily none of the shells scored a hit.

The Japanese continued to wreak havoc, smashing three U.S. cruisers, the *Astoria*, the *Quincy* and the *Vincennes*, with broadsides, scoring hits with torpedoes, and setting all three ablaze. Two sank, and the *Astoria* survived only as a burning hulk. There was a total loss of 900 lives.

Despite this catalogue of disasters, the Allied naval forces fulfilled their primary objective of protecting the transports. They did so only because Vice Admiral Mikawa lost control of his divided force, and had to sail north to regroup them. There, fearing that next day he would be attacked by planes from the American aircraft carriers that he thought were still in the area, he decided to head back to Rabaul, the main Japanese base.

On the way, the U.S. submarine S-44 managed to torpedo and sink the cruiser *Kato*, the only outright Japanese loss in this battle.

This unhappy first battle off Guadalcanal – the Battle of Savo Island – illustrates so many of the overall problems of battle at sea. There were the usual communication and reporting difficulties, there were problems of command and tactics, but above all there was a failure to appreciate the enemy's potential.

In fighting a truly determined and professional force, which is what the Japanese Navy proved, the Allied cruisers had failed to measure up and it had cost them dearly. However, it was a good introduction to what they would be up against, both on Guadalcanal and on other Pacific islands.

Several of the subsequent battles at sea off Guadalcanal concerned the so-called Tokyo Express convoys of destroyers and transports taking reinforcements to the island. These fast-moving convoys were protected by their own aircraft carriers and battleships, and challenged by those of the Americans.

A little over two weeks after the Battle of Savo Island, the Americans sank the small carrier *Ryujo*, but suffered serious damage to the USS *Enterprise*. A week later, a Japanese submarine torpedoed the USS *Yorktown*, putting her in dock for three months. On 15 September, 1942, another Japanese submarine attacked a force covering some American transports. It sank the U.S. aircraft carrier *Wasp* and a destroyer, and also damaged the battleship *North Dakota*.

The next battle, Cape Esperance, was a clear U.S. victory, except in its failure to stop the Tokyo Express reinforcements getting through. In this conflict the American force sank an 8-inch gun cruiser and a destroyer, badly damaged another Japanese cruiser, and killed Rear Admiral Goto of Coral Sea fame.

On 22 October, the Japanese Fleet was present in strength as their land forces made a fierce attempt to capture Henderson Field. Three powerful Japanese naval forces, including four carriers, steamed southwards to intercept Task Force 64, under Vice Admiral Lee. Taskforce 64 consisted of a battleship and three cruisers. Unbeknownst to the Japanese, two other American task forces, each including an aircraft carrier, were also preparing to engage.

When they did eventually locate all these forces, more than 130 Japanese aircraft flew off from the four carriers to attack. The USS *Hornet* was seriously damaged, and later sank, the USS *Enterprise* only slightly so. In return, U.S. aircraft caused extensive damage to two Japanese carriers, the *Zuiho* and the *Shokaku*, putting the latter out of action for six months. In addition the Japanese lost many more aircraft than the Americans.

This battle was seen as a tactical victory for the Japanese, but one which they failed to exploit fully. They missed a golden opportunity to pursue and sink the *Enterprise*. Furthermore, they did not capture Henderson Field, which the Marines tenaciously managed to maintain.

The next battle, the Battle of Guadalcanal, came in November. In the first stage, a force of American cruisers and destroyers bravely intercepted a stronger Japanese force that included two capital ships, the *Hiyei* and the *Kirishima*.

In the night action that followed the Americans would lose two cruisers, the *Atlanta* and the *Juneau*, and four destroyers. The Japanese lost just two destroyers, but the *Hiyei* was so badly damaged she had to retire. She would be torpedoed next day by aircraft from the USS *Enterprise*, bombed by shore-based aircraft, then eventually abandoned and scuttled.

These losses more or less balanced out to make battle honours even. However, the Japanese had again been stopped from getting at the American transports that were continuing to land men and supplies on Guadalcanal.

Next day, 14 November, 1942, other Japanese forces bombarded Henderson Field, destroying or damaging fifty aircraft. Nevertheless, the airfield could still be used and torpedo planes from it seriously damaged two Japanese cruisers, one of which, the *Kinugasa*, was later sunk by torpedo bombers from the *Enterprise*.

The final stage of this series of battles within a battle saw aircraft, from both Henderson

**Burning oil tanks ashore on Sadau, as the Australian force heads inwards. The following day there were landings on Tarakan itself.**

Top right: U.S. rockets being used very effectively prior to the landings on Tarakan by the Australians.

Top far right: a Japanese aircraft shot down while attacking U.S. forces off Saipan in the Marianas. Taken by a U.S. Navy photographer, the picture was one of those chosen to represent the best one hundred World War II pictures.

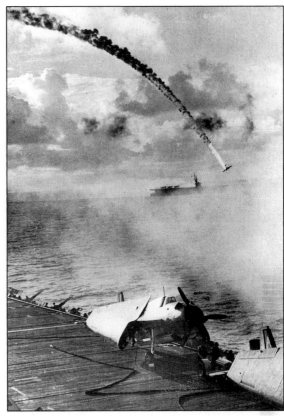

Field and the *Enterprise*, attacking Japanese troop transports heading towards the airfield. These ships were supported by a large bombardment force consisting of the remaining Japanese battleship, the *Kirishima*; four cruisers and eight destroyers.

Heading to intercept them was a force, under Vice Admiral Lee, of two battleships and four destroyers. These battleships, the *Washington* and the *South Dakota*, were brand-new sister ships, heavily armoured and equipped with radar. The Japanese did not yet have radar.

Another confused night action followed, in which the Americans were hindered by the malfunction of the *South Dakota's* radar. The *South Dakota* was lucky to escape more than thirty torpedoes fired at her. However, she was hit by 14-inch shells from the Japanese battleship and 8-inch ones from two cruisers. She pulled out of the battle with a hundred casualties, and had to go back to the U.S.A for repairs. The radar on the *Washington* worked well. She shattered the *Kirishima*, which was later scuttled.

The real American triumph came when

Admiral Kondo decided to withdraw and not to bombard Henderson Field after all. When the Japanese transports arrived at dawn and prepared to land their troops, they were fiercely attacked by planes from the still functioning Henderson Field. Only about 2,000 out of the intended 11,000 reinforcements finally reached Guadalcanal.

Fighting in the seas off Guadalcanal continued for another two months, although the Japanese were now restricted to making quick Tokyo Express supply trips and did not try any further major landings.

Cataloguing the losses on either side at Guadalcanal depends on where you start counting. In general the Americans would seem to have won a slight edge. Overall they lost two aircraft carriers, nine cruisers, eighteen destroyers, and several transports and auxiliaries. The Japanese lost two carriers, although one was fairly small, two battleships, eight cruisers and thirty-eight destroyers.

In January, the Japanese decided to abandon Guadalcanal. By February they had all slipped quietly away. The first link in the island chain had been forged.

# STALINGRAD – THE TURNING POINT

After their failure to win their Russian war outright in 1941, the Germans hoped that a fresh effort in the summer of 1942 would finally see them victorious. Their plan was admittedly a little less ambitious than that of the previous year, having only two main spearheads – from Kharkov to Stalingrad and from the Crimea to the Caucasus – rather than the three in 1941 that had been halted before Leningrad, Moscow and Sebastopol respectively. Nevertheless, the new eastwards push was still very grandiose and ambitious in its way, since it included some seventy-eight Axis divisions – a total of almost two million men. Its purpose was to shut down Stalin's vital supply lines through the Caucasus and along the Don and Volga rivers, thereby effectively cutting him off both from the Caucasian oilfields and from Western 'Lend Lease' aid coming in through Persia. If these targets had been achieved, the result would surely have been an utterly decisive victory, since the Russians would have had little option but to sue for an early peace.

When the Nazis failed to reach their objectives, they were no less decisively introduced to the hitherto unthinkable idea that they might not win the war. Their crack 6th Army of 300,000 men was entirely destroyed in Stalingrad itself, with enormous additional casualties being suffered by its many supporting formations. The Reich went into mourning, and for the first time came to accept that its economy had to be put on a full war footing. Dr Goebbels' propaganda adopted a newly sombre tone, while in the front line it became plain that the despised Red Army actually did know a thing or two about the art of modern warfare, after all.

All these truly momentous implications emerged from what history remembers as just 'one single battle' at Stalingrad. However, it would probably be nearer the truth to think of the event as rather 'a very protracted period of intense campaigning at the very height of the war, spread across most of the active sectors of the Russian front'. The operations covered a circular area of more than 500 miles in diameter; from Voronezh in the north to Sebastopol and Rostov in the south, and from Kharkov in the west to Grozny in the east – and they lasted nearly an entire year. In essence, German

plans had been complete on 28th March, 1942, and fighting was already approaching the Stalingrad area by 17th July: yet 6th Army's final surrender wasn't to come until the following 2nd February, and it would be 24th March before the spring thaw closed down the related flank and rear operations. The whole event added up to the biggest and most important clash of armies in the whole of the Second World War, so it would be quite misleading to dismiss it simply as 'just another battle'.

Initially, the main German objective had not been Stalingrad, but the maximum destruction of Soviet forces, followed by the seizure of Caucasian oilfields and communication routes. Stalingrad itself had originally been no more than a tertiary objective, although it became increasingly more important as events unfolded. Hitler gradually developed a personal obsession with the city, which was, of course, Stalin's city, whence Stalin had personally launched a brilliant offensive down to the mouth of the Don in 1920. Hitler was also under acute stress in this period, to the point where he would permit no avoidance or by-passing of the city, nor any retreat from it once it had been entered. As the strategic reports became successively worse, Hitler withdrew into his shell, refusing to take any decisions that might imply a change in the operational layout – indeed, he appeared to equate change with defeat. It is significant that between 7th and 23rd November, 1942, – at precisely the peak of the 'Torch'-Stalingrad crisis, when conceptual innovation was surely needed most of all – he deliberately removed himself from his main headquarters in order to 'rest' at his country retreat at Berchtesgaden.

Hitler was a brilliant, inspirational leader, capable of successfully cutting through the traditional formats of war, but he had never received technical training in the vital skill of managing multiple, simultaneous international crises – least of all when a superior enemy was persistently daring to fight back. Hitler's inflexibility about Stalingrad illustrates his awkwardness as an international operator, and vividly explains how a year of flexible, armoured manoeuvres could come to be focused upon such a tiny area of broken concrete and rubble

**Facing page top:**
Marshal S. K. Timoshenko near the front line in the summer of 1942. He was responsible for the failed offensive to Kharkov, then the phased retreat before Army Group B to Stalingrad. He did not, however, lose his standing in the Red Army, and was the only pre-war general to survive the war with his reputation unscathed.

**Facing page bottom:**
General Lindemann points out some topographical features to General von Bock, commander of German Army Group B in the initial drive to Voronezh. Von Bock was replaced on 15th July due to his disagreements with Hitler.

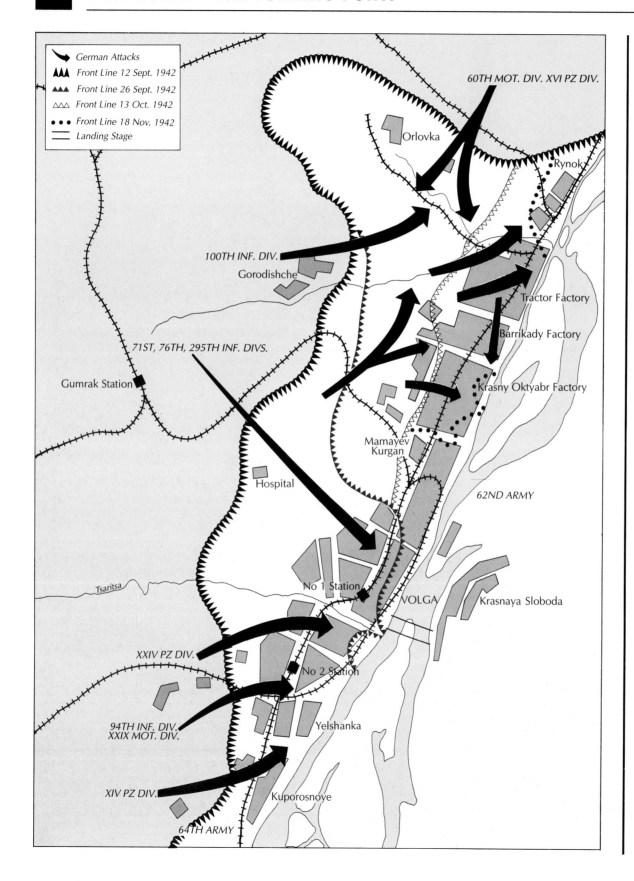

Von Paulus moves to take Stalingrad on 19th August, 1942, although he has yet to be joined by Hoth's 4th *Panzerarmee*. By 14th September, the Soviet garrison was hemmed into a narrow strip along the west bank of the River Volga. Increasingly mesmerised by Stalingrad, Hitler insisted that the city be taken, but, as the winter arrived, this task was clearly beyond von Paulus' strength.

**Legend:**
- German Attacks
- Front Line 12 Sept. 1942
- Front Line 26 Sept. 1942
- Front Line 13 Oct. 1942
- Front Line 18 Nov. 1942
- Landing Stage

**Map labels:**
60TH MOT. DIV. XVI PZ DIV.
Orlovka
Rynok
100TH INF. DIV.
Gorodishche
Tractor Factory
Barrikady Factory
71ST, 76TH, 295TH INF. DIVS.
Krasny Oktyabr Factory
Gumrak Station
Mamayev Kurgan
62ND ARMY
Hospital
Tsaritsa
No 1 Station
VOLGA
Krasnaya Sloboda
XXIV PZ DIV.
No 2 Station
94TH INF. DIV.
XXIX MOT. DIV.
Yelshanka
XIV PZ DIV.
Kuporosnoye
64TH ARMY

**Urban warfare in the late summer of 1942: a German platoon - bunched dangerously close together - moves up under the cover of a captured barricade.**

in the centre of that city. It also explains how a merely local military reverse could turn remorselessly into a disaster of such world-shaking proportions.

Ironically, the first phase of the German 1942 operations ran even better than expected, since Stalin was obsessed with the defence of Moscow and refused to believe plentiful evidence – not excluding a captured copy of the complete plan – that the primary target would lie elsewhere. When, finally, he launched a big attack south of Kharkov from 12th May, it was quickly met and destroyed by the agile manoeuvres of *Panzer* forces. After this, the *Wehrmacht* went on to clear the Crimea of resistance, until in June the way lay open for a rapid drive towards the east, with List's Army Group A providing the main spearhead, and Bock's (later Weichs') Army Group B covering its northern flank.

Only in July did hitches and delays start to appear in the German operations. These were small in number at first, but they gradually built up to the point where a distinct sense of unease came to pervade headquarters. There were disputes over whether Voronezh should be a prime target, and then whether the bulk of the armour should be aimed along the southerly route towards the oilfields. Hitler said he wanted to advance on the broadest possible front, but this left him overstretched at every point and vulnerable to hold-ups in front of enemy centres of defence, especially in the difficult mountain terrain of the Caucasus. Nevertheless, as late as his Directive No. 45 of 23rd July, he still envisaged Stalingrad as merely a secondary objective to cover his northern flank. However, by August he began to move his centre of attention towards the city, just when the Soviet forces appeared to be breaking up under the pressure, but also when the German spearheads were encountering difficulties caused by the depletion of their supplies.

On 7th August Colonel General H. Hoth's 4th *Panzerarmee* came within thirty kilometres of Stalingrad from the south, and then Paulus'

6th Army arrived from the west to commence its main assault on 23rd August. There was a massed aerial bombardment that destroyed much of the suburbs and helped to push the Soviets back to their second – or middle – line of defence. Thanks to the German bombing, towards the centre of the city the big factories and flats had been converted into easily defensible rubble. Resistance was successfully improvised and included the widespread impressment of the city's population, as well as the diversion of many regular formations from other tasks into the city. A system was set up whereby a trickle of men and supplies could be brought in at night from the far bank of the Volga River. Energetic leadership was also provided from 23rd August by Colonel General Andrei Ivanovich Yeremenko, with the collaboration of Party Commissar, Nikita Khruschchev. Three weeks later this team would be completed with the promotion of Lieutenant General Vasily Ivanovich Chuykov as commander of 62nd Army – the army that was to bear the brunt of the close fighting in the city.

At the time of the Stalingrad battle, Soviet forces were still notoriously inefficient in co-ordinated manoeuvres and ignorant of the finer points of battle-handling. Their furiously repeated counter-attacks to push the invader out of Stalingrad achieved only negligible successes, apart from the purely sacrificial one of maintaining the pressure of attrition. Nevertheless, they did manage to hold a defensive line, and compressed the battle into a style of brutal but basic house-to-house combat in which German technology and mobility was virtually redundant. The Russians' trump card was their courage and endurance as infantry; but it was a card they could play only when – as now – the fast-moving thrust and parry of mechanized warfare on the steppe had been replaced by a slow-moving slugging match in the town.

By the end of the first week of September Hitler suffered a crisis of confidence, as he realised that his offensive was failing to cut cleanly through the enemy. It was only on 10th September that 4th *Panzerarmee* reached the Volga; and it would be 18th October before 6th Army even managed to capture the Tractor Factory. The Barricades Factory followed on 23rd September, and half the Red October Factory soon afterwards. Yet despite major pushes by the attackers on 14th October and 11th November, the dogged defence line – by then split into three isolated sections, and with the river only too close behind – was never to be reduced. The Fuehrer raged mightily, and replaced a number of his generals: but he

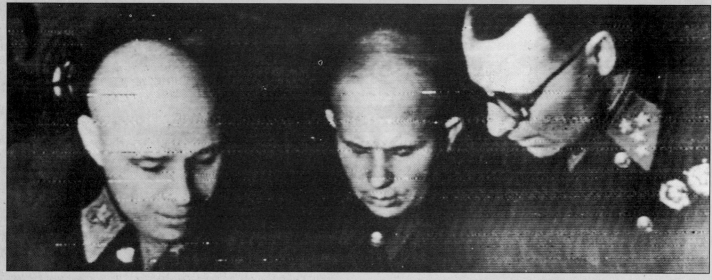

could do nothing to speed up the advance.

While all this was happening in the overt 'frontal' battle for Stalingrad, the Soviet staff was secretly proceeding with plans to launch a parallel flanking' battle – a grand double envelopment that would roll 6th Army into a vast pocket, and so bring about its complete destruction.

General Georgi Zhukov and Colonel General Alexander Vasilevsky had already visited the front on 2nd September, with instructions to examine the wider possibilities for a counter-offensive. As Stalin now knew he was free to release his large reserves from the Moscow area, he was in a position to contemplate operations a great deal more ambitious than the Germans at this stage believed possible. His two generals were especially interested to find that the Don River line on either side of Stalingrad was secured by Axis allies of dubious quality, who would probably not fight as stoutly as the Germans in the city itself. To the north of Stalingrad lay the Hungarian 2nd, the Italian 8th and the Roumanian 4th armies; and to the south the Roumanian 3rd Army. In the event none of these formations were strengthened with the stiffening of German elements that several commanders had wanted. Zhukov and Vasilevsky did not therefore take long to realise that well-prepared assaults against these weak links at the extremities of the enemy's chain

might mortally ensnare the stronger ones at its heart. A secret and complex build-up began to be conceived, codenamed 'Uranus'.

Nazi over-confidence in Russia received its final comeuppance through the total success of this silent Soviet concentration comprising a million men, 1,500 tanks, 6,000 guns and 10,000 mortars. Using the series of deception, disinformation and security techniques that are known collectively as *Maskirovka*, Stalin's generals managed to emplace five armies of the Southwest Front and Don Front to the north of the city, and two armies of the Stalingrad Front to the south, without raising any major alarm at Hitler's headquarters. The Roumanians themselves knew that something big was brewing locally for them; but their warnings were dismissed higher up as 'exaggerated'. When the storm finally broke on 19th November, however, even the Roumanians were found to have underestimated the full danger.

The two Roumanian armies that were initially attacked were both swept away almost instantaneously, leaving wide gaps in the Axis line on either side of Paulus' army. The German XLVIII *Panzer Korps* put up some resistance in the north, as did 24th Motor Division in the south, but on 23rd November – after five days that won the war' – the two attacking spearheads were able to join hands at the Kalach Bridge and complete 6th Army's encirclement. In the ensuing days they worked

*Luftwaffe* field troops, carrying the ageing Steyr-Solothurn S100 sub-machine gun and smoking casually, flush a Stalingrad inhabitant from her air-raid shelter. Although the scene looks outwardly relaxed, her chances of survival must have been slim indeed.

Facing page top left: Joseph Stalin, General Secretary of the Communist Party of the Soviet Union and Commander in Chief of her forces, in his marshal's uniform, March, 1943.

Facing page top right: Field Marshal Erich von Manstein poring over a map with his advisers - an activity that came to occupy him almost round the clock. Manstein, an aristocratic officer of the old school, rarely left his headquarters to visit the front, yet his operational decision-making was unsurpassed.

Facing page bottom: Red Army infantry counterattack in a photograph that was probably posed. Note the padded jackets, thick boots and fur hats for winter warfare, and the mass-produced PPSh SMG for close-quarter fighting. The man in the right foreground carries a captured Schmeisser.

Sub-zero conditions immobilized Paulus' Sixth Army in Stalingrad. The snow made air re-supply operations difficult while it increased the requirement for fuel and other materials. It also persuaded the Germans that it was better to stay in the relative shelter of the city than to attempt a break-out onto the still less hospitable open steppe.

hard to reinforce their inward front against any attempted break-out, simultaneously pushing additional forces further to the south and west to extend the breadth of the corridor against break-ins from outside.

In one sense, Soviet fears of a break-out turned out to be excessive, since Hitler's immediate reaction to the encirclement was to overrule Paulus' pleadings, and forbid any attempt at a retreat – a decision psychologically consistent with his almost simultaneous denial of Rommel's desire to evacuate his army from Africa following El Alamein and the 'Torch' landings. Relying on Goering's hopelessly over-optimistic (and uninformed) personal assurances that the *Luftwaffe* could keep 6th Army supplied, he thus wilfully ignored the need to re-open an overland line of communication. This did not, however, alter the fact that there simply were not enough transport aircraft available to do the job, or that those available would encounter intense difficulties with both the weather and Soviet air defences. The result was that whereas 6th Army's minimum requirement was for some

600 tons of supplies each day, only around 100 tons could actually be airlifted to it. Paulus' command started to run out of war material, making a break-out ever more difficult at precisely the same time as it became ever more urgent.

Nevertheless, Hitler did contemplate a break-in to relieve beleaguered 6th Army from the west, and appointed Field Marshal Erich von Manstein to arrange it, as commander of a new 'Army Group Don'. However, that professional soldier's task was enormously complicated by three central factors. In the first place, his freedom of action was seriously undermined by Hitler's intransigence and constant interference, even in the smallest details. Secondly, he had very few reserves with which to counter the vast new forces that Stalin had suddenly seemed to create from nowhere. He did manage to collect eleven divisions for the relief – Hoth's Operation 'Winter Tempest', which started on 12th December – but it was never enough. Finally, Manstein's attention always had to be diverted away from Stalingrad itself to the rescue of Army

The defeated face of recently-promoted Field Marshal Paulus during his interrogation at the Russian headquarters. He led his army effectively at first, but in the later days of the struggle he seemed to lose his grip.

Below: captive German generals on their way out of Stalingrad in bitter winter conditions.

Group A from a potentially still more awful encirclement in the Caucasus. As Soviet confidence grew, so their plans were extended from the locality of Stalingrad itself towards Rostov, the target of Operation 'Saturn' which was intended to cut off all German forces further to the east.

Manstein eventually succeeded, not a moment too soon, in persuading Hitler to authorise the withdrawal of Army Group A from the Caucasus from the end of December. Protected by some impressive mobile defensive actions along the Chir River line, the endangered forces eventually managed to slip back before the trap closed. However, this did not remove the Soviet stranglehold around Stalingrad, and the Chir battles served rather to draw German resources away from the attempted relief efforts. As 6th Army's reserves of fuel and ammunition dwindled away, its freedom of action also declined to the point where it could no longer move to break out. The men found some shelter in the ruins of the city at least, whereas, in the depths of winter, it was scarcely alluring to venture out onto the

open steppe. In a series of fierce arguments between 18th and 20th December, therefore, Paulus insisted that he could not move, but would hold out in position until Easter.

By January, however, not even Paulus' defensive plan could be seen as realistic. On 22nd December the Russians captured Tatinskaya airfield, then on 10th January their major offensive – Operation 'Ring' – sliced 6th Army into two. The northern pocket was finally crushed on 30th January, and fighting ceased in the southern pocket on 2nd February. Near the end, Hitler promoted Paulus to field marshal – hoping he would commit suicide, since no German field marshal had ever been captured alive – but Paulus accepted the honour while ignoring the hint, and passed into captivity with the ragged remains of his command.

The battle of Stalingrad was over, and Soviet military power had been dramatically re-born. Stalin's supply routes and oilfields had been saved from the *Panzer* spearheads and – perhaps most importantly of all – the totality of the war had been brutally brought home to the German people. The Third Reich had entered its fatal final phase.

**A column of German prisoners starting their march away from the snow-bound, devastated city in which they had been trapped. They might perhaps be counted lucky not to have been killed in the fighting that cost 100,000 German lives, but less than ten per cent of them would get back to the Fatherland alive.**

# OPERATION TORCH

Propaganda headlines announcing the North African landings claim them as the long-awaited 'Second Front' to help USSR. The newspaper emphasizes the American contribution since this was the first action in the West in which U.S. troops were seriously engaged.

'Torch' was the final codename for the Allied landings in French Morocco and Algeria on 8th November, 1942. It had originated a year earlier as an all-British operation known as 'Gymnast' and then, when American participation was added, as 'Super Gymnast'. In the event it constituted a grandiose – almost global – undertaking, with over 670 ships and 1,000 landing craft sailing from two different continents to land in a third. Participating units came from bases as far distant as Malta and Alexandria in the Mediterranean; the Gambia and Sierra Leone in West Africa; Glasgow in Scotland; and Norfolk in Virginia. At the time it was the largest amphibious operation that had ever been mounted, with an attack frontage no less than 900 miles long; a landing strength of 65,000 troops, and a planned build up to some 1,700 aircraft. In many ways it was the major dress rehearsal for D-Day eighteen months later, and certainly much larger and more important than the costly Dieppe raid of August, 1942.

'Torch' was doubly impressive since it was the first time the Anglo-American alliance had operated together on such a large scale. Despite some early disagreements about strategy, and a very short time for tactical training, the two nations managed to work in close harmony. So successful was the deception plan, furthermore, that almost complete surprise was achieved. This allowed opposition to be kept to a minimum, and casualties light.

Despite all these remarkable achievements, however, two great question marks had hung over 'Torch' ever since it had first been mooted. The first of these uncertainties concerned the political attitudes of the French and Spanish, upon which much would turn. In the absence of hard intelligence, the expedition naturally had to prepare for the 'worst case' of sustained heavy fighting; and this made it a far larger and more cumbersome affair than it actually needed to be. When comparatively little French resistance was encountered, and Spain did not become involved at all, the planners were seen to have excessively over-insured. This lost them several valuable opportunities elsewhere.

The second uncertainty arose from the central question of just how Torch was supposed

to achieve grand strategic results. There was a widespread suspicion that the Allies had painstakingly provided a large tactical hat, only to draw from it a diminutive strategic rabbit.

Many Americans had hoped for an operation – codenamed 'Sledgehammer' – that would directly attack the Germans through the Cherbourg peninsula in France. They thought of the French as friends to be liberated, not enemies to be invaded. The Soviets were even more insistent that a major second front should be opened as early as possible, especially in view of the very difficult battle that was just beginning at Stalingrad. Thus, when instead the British demanded an 'indirect approach' against the French in North Africa, they were greeted with considerable incredulity from all sides. North Africa seemed a sideshow of little relevance to the main operations, and there was suspicion that Churchill was playing a deep imperial game to win back southeast Europe, using American lives and efforts merely to score postwar points against the Russians in the Mediterranean and the Balkans.

Against all this the British replied that the

military record of assault landings within Europe – which ranged from Gallipoli and Narvik to the very recent Dieppe disaster – was far from reassuring. The necessary landing craft and logistics for a D-Day in France were not yet ready; nor were the troops yet 'blooded', or Allied command structures tested. The mere threat of invasion was already enough to divert a quarter of the German field forces and half of the *Luftwaffe* to the West; but much of this would be free to return to Russia if 'Sledgehammer' should be defeated. Besides, there would be a big potential saving in shipping mileage, for if the armies in North Africa could be supplied directly through the Straits of Gibraltar instead of around the Cape, they would become a 'local' theatre to Britain, rather than the strenuously 'far distant' theatre that they had been since 1940. This could release huge shipping resources for more

important tasks, such as the sea bridge between Britain and the U.S.A. – or even the U.S.S.R. In the end, the Americans reluctantly bowed to these arguments and agreed to go ahead with 'Torch', although the closer they came to embarking upon the operation the more pessimistic their planning staff seemed to become. At one point the operation was given less than a fifty per cent chance of success.

The command team assembled for 'Torch' constituted a veritable galaxy of stars, notable among whom was Lieutenant General Dwight D. Eisenhower, the sagacious and – in the best sense – diplomatic Commander in Chief. He was seconded by Major General Mark W. Clark, who before the operation made some risky personal visits to meet Vichy moderates within Algeria itself. At a slightly less exalted level, Major General George S. Patton was to command the main U.S. assault in Morocco – his first step in a dashing 'glory ride' that would take him through Africa and Italy to France and finally the Reich. For the USAAF the command fell to yet another hero, Brigadier General James H. Doolittle, who had bombed Tokyo in April, 1942.

On the British side there was a scarcely less distinguished cast of characters, with Admiral Sir Andrew Cunningham – victor of Matapan, Taranto and many a Malta convoy – commanding the naval forces. He was supported by Vice-Admiral Sir Bertram Ramsay, who had masterminded the miracle of the little ships at Dunkirk, and who would one day preside over the D-Day landings themselves. Perhaps the British ground forces lacked an equivalently prestigious commander, since it was the relatively unknown Lieutenant General Kenneth Anderson who took command of the nascent 1st Army. He was only third choice for the appointment, however, after Alexander and Montgomery. Alas, it would also be his misfortune to be overshadowed in the history books, not entirely deservedly, by the more spectacular achievements of those two men.

The 'Torch' plan called for 24,500 American troops with 250 tanks to sail direct from the U.S.A. and land through the surf on the beaches around Casablanca. Meanwhile 18,500 more with 180 tanks would sail from Britain via Gibraltar into the more sheltered Mediterranean and land around Oran. These

Below: American generals at a North African airfield. From left to right: Major General Lloyd R. Fredendall, commander of the U.S. Central Task Force, who was later to be criticised for his role in the Kasserine battle; Lieutenant General Mark W. Clark, Eisenhower's Second in Command, who would one day liberate Rome; and Brigadier General James Doolittle, the Allied air force commander who had shaken the Japanese by bombing Tokyo.

Facing page top: Lieutenant General George S. 'Blood and Guts' Patton, photographed in Tunisia at the start of his two-and-a-half year 'glory ride'.

Facing page bottom: assault landing craft leaving their parent troop transports for the 'Torch' landings. The journey from the transports to the beaches was planned to be between six and eight miles – but 800 troops from one torpedoed transport had to sail some 150 miles in their landing craft!

U.S. infantry in the 'Torch' landings, apparently relaxed and therefore not under fire while this photograph was taken.

two U.S. forces would then combine as 5th Army and take up a defensive posture against any intervention from Spanish Morocco. A joint U.S. and British force of 20,000 men would simultaneously arrive from Britain to secure the area of Algiers. As 1st Army it would then move eastwards as rapidly as possible to capture the four key ports of Bône and Philippeville in Algeria, and Bizerta and Tunis itself in Tunisia. These ports were not deemed suitable for direct landings because they were beyond the range of Gibraltar's air cover, and too near to Axis air forces in Sicily. However, the British, at least, always believed they were really the most vital targets of all, and did not share American pessimism about venturing so far to the east.

Against such a powerful Allied assault, what was the measure of the opposition? On the French side there was plenty of infantry, some 120,000 in all, but they lacked modern equipment and their 500 aircraft were obsolete.

On the other hand, they had good coastal batteries and a very powerful Navy, based at Toulon, but with a battleship in both Casablanca and Dakar, and many smaller warships in Algerian ports. Allied planning also had to take into account the possible threat from the garrison of Spanish Morocco – some 130,000 strong – and the possibilities that the *Luftwaffe* might be invited to operate from southern Spain, or that the huge Italian battle fleet might intervene.

In their command structure the French appeared strong, and were all known to despise de Gaulle; but in reality they suffered from political divisions. Admiral Jean François Darlan commanded North Africa in the strongly anti-British spirit with which he had fought against them at Mers el Kebir in 1940. It was hoped that he would be absent at the time of the 'Torch' landings and his subordinates would be in control. Such men as General Alphonse Juin,

Riflemen filing inland from their landing craft over open beaches near Casablanca, supported by White half tracks and 'DUKWS'. Smoke in the background is from supporting naval gunfire.

and still more Major Generals Béthouart and Charles Mast, were known to be more amenable to the Allied cause, and had even been made partly aware of the plan. The last two mobilized the patriotic youth in Casablanca and Algiers to support the invasion, managing to prevent leaks to the Vichy authorities until as late as 6th November. For good measure, the Allies also hoped to use the popular General Henri Giraud, who had escaped from imprisonment in a German fortress, but in the event his inexperience and lack of formal hierarchical position in Algeria entirely negated his influence. Darlan actually turned the tables on both him and the Allied

planners by chancing to return to North Africa at the crucial moment. Receiving no clear guidelines from Pétain, he seized control of negotiations – although as a secondary surprise he proved to be considerably more flexible and less hostile than had been expected. It was largely due to his influence that a general ceasefire could be arranged within three days of the landings. Nevertheless, by his clever political footwork he continued to block the influence of de Gaulle, and to be lukewarm in active support for the Allies.

Even if peace were to be made quickly with the French, that still did not disarm the Germans. They were not initially deployed in any of the

territories under attack – nor in either Tunisia or the south of France – but they had got some inkling of the landings as early as 15th October, and were ready to move swiftly. Once the fact of the landings had become clear, from 9th November they rushed through Operation 'Anton' to completely occupy the whole of the French mainland, failing only to seize the Toulon fleet, which was scuppered. They also hastily sent troops by air to Tunisia, where a ground defence was improvised by General Walther Nehring, a tough soldier whom Hitler had just relieved of command of the *Afrika Korps*. The brilliant *Luftwaffe* Field Marshal Albert Kesselring became the overall German commander in this area and, despite some clashes with Rommel over allocations of equipment between the two North African fronts, his administrative genius went far towards consolidating Tunisia and preventing the Allies breaking out to the east.

The German reaction, although fast, was nevertheless not fast enough to prevent the Allied landings themselves. The gigantic plan swung smoothly into operation from 2nd October onwards, when the first supply convoys left Britain to begin stockpiling equipment and aircraft in Gibraltar. By the night of 7th to 8th November the attack armadas had all been assembled and were silently approaching their designated beaches. An intense reconnaissance effort and U-boat attack was mounted throughout the Mediterranean and the Central Atlantic, and the Germans were deceived into thinking that the shipping movement was nothing more than another routine convoy for Malta – or possibly an assault on Tripoli. Even when chance encounters led to sinkings by U-boats and Axis bombers, they failed to alert the German High Command that this was actually the expected invasion of French North Africa.

On arrival close to the beaches, however, a strong westerly swell disorganised and dispersed several of the assault groups. Landing was made difficult by heavy surf around Algiers and Casablanca, and many of the coastal batteries were found to be fully alert. The French navy was especially active in defence of their port at Mers el Kebir, which had already been surprised by the British in 1940, and they inflicted very heavy casualties upon U.S. *coup de main* parties trying to seize the docks at both Algiers

and Oran. Allied naval gunfire had to be widely used to suppress the shore defences and to sink several French destroyers that tried to come out and fight. Air attacks destroyed at least seventy French aircraft on the ground at the two key fields around Oran, although some of the defenders did manage to take off and shoot down Allied planes. A parachute drop designed to seize these airfields also became dispersed by bad weather in the Bay of Biscay, and failed to find its objectives. One of the airfields held out for forty hours, while the port of Oran could not be occupied before its defenders had sunk blockships to deny its use.

Even more difficult was the battle for the beaches around Casablanca, where the infantry made no progress from the shoreline until some of Patton's tanks could be landed. In this battle, the defenders' ground fire and air attacks were the heaviest of all and the weather least favourable. Some 216 out of 629 landing craft had to be written off, as compared with only 106 out of 400 at Algiers and Oran combined. Over half the 1,404 American land and air casualties suffered in the whole operation were on this front, whereas the British Army and RAF at Algiers suffered just eighty-

Below: two seriously damaged French destroyers and a light cruiser - probably *Milan*, *Albatros* and *Primauguet*, respectively - beached at Casablanca after vainly resisting the U.S. landings. At least five other French warships were badly damaged or sunk in the Casablanca battle.

Facing page top: an Algiers beach with a two-and-a-half-ton prime mover pulling a 105mm howitzer -the gun that was to remain the mainstay of U.S. field artillery from World War Two through the war in Vietnam.

Facing page bottom: a 'Priest' self-propelled M7 105mm howitzer on a Grant chassis. This was one of the earliest examples of true SP artillery, which initially suffered from mechanical unreliability.

General Lee tanks and other American equipment *en route* for Algiers in December, 1942. President Roosevelt had generously sent all supplies of the more advanced Grant tanks to the British 8th Army, leaving the growing 1st Army with the earlier, more cramped Lee.

nine losses. However, there were 662 British, 117 Dutch but only seventy U.S. naval casualties. French losses are unknown, but they must have been at least comparable in scale. A total of fifty-four Allied aircraft were lost, and perhaps a dozen ships, but in return the Allies ensured that the Vichy Navy and Air Force were no longer factors in the war, as well as destroying seven German submarines.

Despite their setbacks, by the morning of 10th November the Allies had won positions from which they were poised to make final assaults to clear all three of their main objectives. Ceasefire negotiations were already under way, however, so in most areas hostilities died down and the vital targets were secured before a final attack needed to be made. The French were satisfied that they had defended their military honour against overwhelming odds; while the Allies were relieved to have finished their long and dangerous voyage without having to face the much heavier level

A U.S. troop transport enters Algiers harbour, some time after the initial fighting has died down. Note the denseness of the buildings in the city, every block of which could have become a fearsome fortress had Algiers been stalwartly defended by the French.

of fighting they had feared as their 'worst case'.

By landing in French North Africa the Allies had indeed shortened their sea voyage to the desert theatre, and had brought the whole northern shore of the Mediterranean under threat. Despite some tactical fumbles in the landings, they had won a vast swathe of territory at relatively trivial cost and, at the same time, laid the foundations for a close, fruitful alliance with French forces. They had also unwittingly planted some fast-growing seeds of doubt in Hitler's mind that would greatly distract him – and many extra Axis resources – away from the crucial Stalingrad battle. Spain had not and would not enter the fighting, and Anglo-

American co-operation in battle had been very firmly cemented. A real step forward had thus been made in preparing for D-Day, even though it was not yet known that this would take place in 1944, rather than 1943.

One of the reasons why D-Day would be delayed was that Allied exploitation immediately after 'Torch' remained incomplete. The German footholds in Bizerta and Tunis had not been quickly stamped out by the Allied pursuit from Algiers – in the event this took almost two weeks to develop into serious tactical contact. By then it was too late to break through, and the assault soon bogged down into a wet and miserable winter

Left: U.S. infantry 'showing the flag' in Oran as they march to the front - or at least as far as their motor transport. Note the 'very French' cafe life in the background.

After advancing into Tunisia, the Americans captured this Italian 75mm cannon, which they adopted for their own use in an anti-tank role.

campaign in which the defender held all the trumps. As the 'Torch' landings had been prudently designed to cope with the 'worst case' that could be imagined, the Allies found themselves unable to switch quickly to the mobile and opportunistic form of warfare that was demanded by the actual situation. The loss of a vital week in mid-November, 1942, meant the capture of Tunisia was delayed for no less than six full months until mid-May, 1943; and this in turn threw back the timetable for the Normandy landings by a complete year. It was by no means the first occasion in the history of warfare that a great opportunity had been lost 'for the want of a nail' – but it must surely rank as one of the most striking.

# THE DAMBUSTERS

Science and technology has never played such a major part in warfare as during World War II. And no scientist or technologist had achieved such spectacular and eccentric results as Doctor Barnes Wallis, an engineer working for the Vickers Aircraft Company in Britain. Not that the projects for which he will be remembered in the history books were carried out in the course of his work for Vickers. They were projects that he dreamed up in his spare time, although the Vickers connection had its uses. 'Why on earth should we lend you a Wellinaton bomber?', said a harassed official at Bomber Command Headquarters, when Wallis wanted to test the prototype of one of his schemes. 'Well, I did design it!', retorted Wallis.

In addition to its aircraft interests, Vickers was engaged in a wide variety of heavy engineering such as steel works, and ship building. Wallis was, therefore, well aware of the huge quantities of water required by industries of this nature. Germany's heavy industry was concentrated in the Ruhr, and the vast quantities of water came from the lakes formed by four or five dams. Wallis conjectured that if some, or all, of these dams could be

For normal operations, the gigantic bomb bay of the Lancaster could accommodate both a huge 4,000 pounder and a collection of 500-pound incendiaries. This particular aircraft, 'S' for Sugar of 467 Squadron, is now on display in the Royal Air Force Museum at Hendon, London.

The Avro Lancaster seemed the obvious aircraft to select to carry the amazing weapon devised by Doctor Barnes Wallis for the attack on the Ruhr dams. The photograph shows Lancasters being assembled at a plant 'somewhere in England' - the euphemism that was used throughout the war to refer to any location.

destroyed, then for a time at least the German war effort would be disrupted. The problem was to work out how it could be done.

Conventional bombing was not going to be the answer. The dams, by their very nature, were designed to withstand great stress. A direct hit would just bounce off. The blast of a near miss on the 'dry' side would be deflected harmlessly into space by the massive structure of the dam, whilst the effect of a near miss which fell into the lake would simply be absorbed by the water. Or would it? Wallis had a theory that if the bomb were to explode flush against the wall of the dam, and close to the base, the incompressibility of millions of gallons of water in the lake would direct the whole effect of the bomb-burst into the wall itself. It was doubtful whether a single bomb, even one precisely placed, would be sufficient. But if a whole series of bombs could be delivered accurately, the battering ram effect of the explosions, all in the same place, would eventually cause the dam to give way.

The answer might be a torpedo. But torpedoes of sufficient size did not exist, and, in any case, the Germans had already thought of that one. The dams were protected by anti-torpedo nets strung across the lakes.

Wallis's eventual solution was quite simple in its scientific principle, but seemed impossible

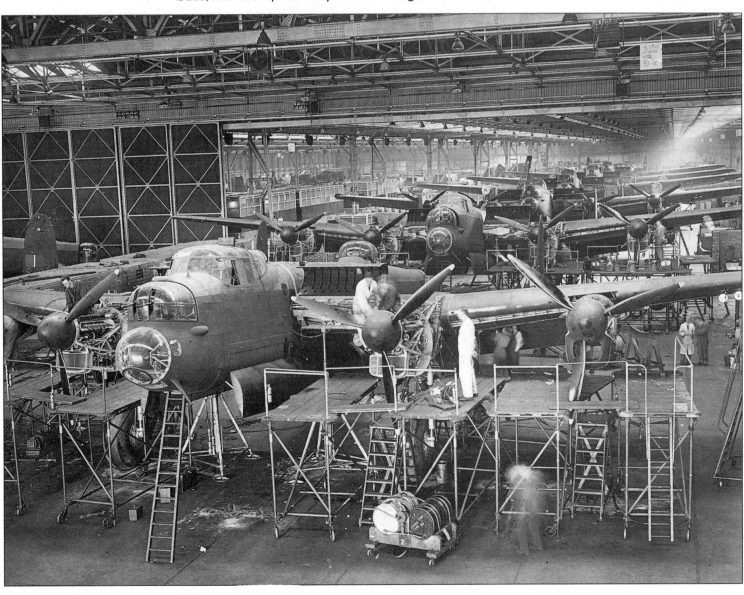

in practice. His idea was based on the childhood game of 'ducks and drakes'. A specially designed bomb would be released from low level so that it would skip along the surface of the lake, hopping over the protective torpedo nets, until it hit the dam wall. It would then sink down the face of the wall, when a delayed action fuse would detonate it in the required place.

After many weeks of experiment Wallis had produced a weapon which he believed would do the job, and he had been allowed to use one of 'his' Wellingtons to test a prototype. In fact, a series of prototypes had to be tested, because the impact with the water was so severe that the first ones disintegrated. The greater the height from which the weapon was dropped, the stronger, and therefore the heavier, it had to be. He found that, if the weight was to be kept within reasonable limits,

it had to be dropped from no higher than 60 feet.

The weapon, code named 'Upkeep', looked like a giant oil drum. To ensure that it detonated at the correct depth a hydrostatic fuse was fitted, instead of a delayed action one. In essence, it was an overgrown depth charge. Officially it was listed as a mine. The only problem now was how to deliver it.

Despite the increase in weight when it was strengthened to withstand the impact, it could still be carried by a Lancaster. (It weighed 9,250lbs, including 6,600lbs of explosive.) But carrying it was the least of the problems. As well as the need for his weapon to be dropped from precisely 60 feet above the surface of the water, Wallis required the aircraft to be travelling at exactly 220 mph. The wings had to be level at the moment of release, or the weapon would strike the water edge first, and would

**The Lancasters on the Dams Raid flew in close formation, but at tree-top height. The pilots had to remain on manual control throughout the flight, to avoid buildings, trees and electricity pylons. Maintaining strict radio silence, the wireless operators conducted conversations between the aircraft by using signalling lamps.**

Twenty Lancasters were modified to carry Wallis's 'Upkeep' weapon, and were listed as B.1 (Special). The serial number of these aircraft had a suffix 'G', which meant 'Guard', and indicated that they should be kept under strict security. For this reason there are few photographs of 617 Squadron's B.1 (Special) Lancasters.

veer off course. But perhaps most difficult of all, it had to be dropped not more than 450 yards, and not less than 400 yards, from the dam wall. At 220 mph the Lancaster would pass through the dropping zone in half a second.

All the time that Wallis had been perfecting his scheme (in his own time and at his own expense) he had been trying to convince the authorities that they should put it into action. It was early in 1943. If the attack was to take place that year, it should really happen around the end of May. At that time the lakes would be at their fullest following the spring thaw. Once May was past the water level would begin to drop, and would carry on dropping until the next year. At the end of February the go ahead was given. There were, at the most, twelve weeks left in which to find the men who could do the job, train them, and put the plan into effect.

Obviously, to achieve Wallis's parameters for delivering 'Upkeep', the training was going to be lengthy. Air Marshal Sir Arthur Harris,

Commander-in-Chief of Bomber Command, did not want to take an active squadron out of service for the time that would be necessary – the Command was already pretty busy. One way to reduce the training time would be to use only experienced crews. Harris decided to form a new squadron of hand picked aircrew, and he knew who he wanted as its leader.

On the night of 15 March 1943, Wing Commander Guy Gibson, 24 years old, flew his 173rd operation of the war, to complete his third 'tour'. He was due for a break – he had not had one since the war began three and a half years earlier. On Harris' instructions, Gibson was invited to do 'just one more trip' before taking his break. Because the operation, to be code named 'Chastise', was Top Secret, he had to make his decision with no more information than that 'it is important'. He accepted.

Within a week Gibson's crews were beginning to arrive, and 617 Squadron came into being. Everyone had completed at least two tours, or were on the verge of doing so. This

To conserve fuel for the long journey, the pilots used only the inboard engines while taxying (left) and waiting their turn to take off.

Parallel rulers and a cup of coffee (right) are two essential accessories in the Flight Planning room, as the crews study their maps, to select a route which will enable them to penetrate to the heart of Germany at low level, without crossing any major flak concentrations.

Below right: in a photograph taken five months before the Dams Raid, Wing Commander Guy Gibson poses for the camera with his pipe and the aircrew from his previous squadron.

was the cream of Bomber Command.

Training began in earnest, although even Gibson still did not know what they were training for. Within the training they had to devise ways of meeting the requirements for dropping 'Upkeep', again without knowing why they were doing it. The height was achieved by fitting spot-lights under the aircraft. One under the nose angled aft, and one under the tail angled forwards. When at the correct height, the lights on the water would align side by side, to form a figure eight. To gauge the range, the bomb aimer had a wooden isosceles triangle, with a peep-hole at the apex, and a pin at either end of the base. Spying through the hole, he waited until the pins became superimposed upon the towers on the dam,

and then pressed the bomb release. The flight engineer sat beside the pilot, calling out the speed, to maintain a constant 220 mph.

To reduce the risk of detection by radar, the trip was to be flown the whole way at low level, and either the approach or the overshoot at each dam was through a tortuous mountain valley. So the mission would need a clear sky with a fairly full moon.

Everything seemed right on 16 May, and Operation 'Chastise' took off.

Gibson led the first wave of nine aircraft, with the Möhne Dam its primary target, and the Eder as the secondary. A second wave, consisting of five aircraft, was heading for the dam at Sorpe, while a third wave, also of five aircraft, was to act as an airborne reserve,

Below: the 'bouncing bomb' in the modified bomb bay of a 617 Squadron aircraft. "'G' for George' was the personal aircraft of the squadron's commander, Wing Commander Guy Gibson.

Right: a reconnaissance shot, taken the day after the attack, of the gap in the Möhne Dam and the low water level in the reservoir.

supporting either of the other two waves as required. If not needed they were to attack minor dams independently.

After making the first run over the target himself, Gibson remained over the lake, flying in with each of the following aircraft in turn, advising the pilot over the radio, and distracting the aim of the anti-aircraft defenses. After six aircraft had bombed, the dam collapsed, and a vast torrent of water rushed down the valley. Gibson then led the remaining three Lancasters to the Eder, which was also destroyed. Meanwhile, only one aircraft of the second wave had succeeded in reaching the Sorpe, and managed to inflict only minor damage. Two of the reserve aircraft were ordered to follow up, but by the time they arrived the valley was filling with mist, which hampered their attack. The other two reserve aircraft were sent to separate alternative targets, but one was not successful, and the other was shot down before it arrived.

Eight of the nineteen aircraft which took part in Operation 'Chastise' failed to return, with the loss of 56 men. On their return to base the crews were so exhausted that they parked their aircraft in the first available dispersal. As a result, it was several days before many of the ground crews discovered whether or not the aircraft which they had dispatched had survived.

Considerable damage was caused by the raid, but without having the devastating effect which had been hoped. However, there was a considerable 'knock-on' effect. The anti-aircraft defences at the dams were immediately strengthened, the guns being committed for the rest of the war, although the dams were never attacked again. Repairs to the dams were not completed until the end of August, and to achieve this many hundreds of construction workers had to be withdrawn from work on the defences on the Channel coast in preparation for the invasion.

For his part in the raid Gibson was awarded the Victoria Cross. He turned down promotion to Group Captain (full Colonel), which would have taken him away from operational flying. He was shot down in a Mosquito during his fourth tour, and is buried in Holland.

**With smiles of relief on their faces, and loaded with equipment, a crew make their way to the transport that will take them to interrogation.**

# KURSK – THE CLASH OF STEEL

Colonel General Hermann Hoth, the commander of 4th *Panzerarmee* during the Kursk offensive. Hoth had previously commanded 4th *Panzerarmee* in the Stalingrad battles. The battle between Hoth's tanks and those of Rotmistrov's 5th Guards Tank Army at Kursk was one of the classic armoured engagements of the war.

By the summer of 1943, the German Army appeared to have recovered from the destruction of Field Marshal Paulus' 6th Army at Stalingrad. Manstein's brilliant counter-offensive at Kharkov during February and March, 1943, had brought the Soviet winter offensive to a halt and stabilised the German front. German High Command then took the decision to seize the initiative by going on the offensive. On 13th March, 1943, Operation 'Order Five' was issued. This warned that the Soviets were likely to attack during the summer months, and therefore Germany would have to make a pre-emptive strike. The chosen battleground was the Kursk salient, a sizable bulge of Soviet-held territory that jutted out from the main Soviet position.

The German Army Group South was ordered to prepare to strike north from Kharkov in April and assault the southern flank of the salient. In many ways this was a sensible decision. Kursk was the natural jumping-off point for a future Soviet offensive, but the Soviets had only recently captured the area, and were still

consolidating the 360-mile perimeter of the salient. Moreover, the Kursk operation, codenamed Operation 'Citadel', was not initially designed to be an 'all-or-nothing' attack. Rather, it was just one of a whole series of local attacks that would be carried out along the Eastern Front, including an offensive against Leningrad. In the event, 'Citadel' was to be subjected to months of delay. The offensive might have succeeded in the spring, but by the time the attack actually commenced on 5th July, 1943, the situation in the Kursk salient had changed dramatically.

'Citadel' was a controversial operation from its inception. Guderian, the Inspector General of Armoured Troops, opposed it, and Jodl, Chief of Staff at the German High Command, urged that reserves should be kept in hand to respond to any move by the Western Allies in the Mediterranean. However, Zeitzler of Army High Command, and Kluge, commander of Army Group Centre, were both in favour of 'Citadel'. Faced with contradictory advice, Hitler prevaricated, admitting that just thinking about the offensive gave him 'butterflies in his stomach'. As it was, the initial starting date of April came and went without action, as it became clear that the German forces were not ready to begin the offensive. Still no final decision was reached as Hitler considered carrying out two other subsidiary operations, 'Hawk' and 'Panther'. The fate of the offensive was not finally decided until 1st July, when Hitler finally gave the go-ahead for 'Citadel'.

The Soviets had not wasted the breathing space granted through German indecision. Stalin was receiving high-grade intelligence concerning the forthcoming German offensive at Kursk from a number of sources. 'Lucy', a Soviet spy with access to the deliberations of the German decision-making elite, forwarded invaluable information to Moscow. For some time the British had been reading German signals sent by the supposedly safe Enigma cipher machine, and Churchill passed on these 'Ultra' decrypts to the Soviets, although they were disguised as 'information from a trusted agent'. In addition, the Soviets had had an intelligence windfall by gaining possession of Enigma machines themselves. The Soviets were in much the same position as their enemies –

aware that they were about to be attacked, and forced to make a decision whether to pull back, launch a pre-emptive strike, or stand and fight. Finally, they decided on the latter course. In Zhukov's words, the Red Army would 'wear down the enemy on our defences, knock out his tanks, then bring in fresh reserves and finish off his main grouping with a general offensive'. Thus, like the Germans on the Somme in 1916, the Soviets intended to convert an enemy offensive into a defensive battle of attrition. Unlike the Germans in the earlier war, the Soviets possessed the resources to launch

a major counter-offensive once the enemy's impetus had been spent.

The success of the Soviet plan depended upon the Red Army being able to absorb the German blow without allowing the *Panzers* to make a significant penetration into Soviet positions. The Soviet answer to a German *Blitzkrieg* was to build positional defences in great depth – up to 110 miles deep in places. Some 300,000 civilians were put to work on such defences, which consisted of six belts of what the Germans called 'pakfronts' – strongpoints bristling with anti-tank guns,

A spectacular aerial view of a head-on clash between Soviet and German armour. Clouds of smoke can be observed issuing from burning vehicles. The Soviets relied mainly on the T-34 during the Kursk battle, while the Germans used five different types, including the Panther, which was probably the most effective German tank of the war.

**Operation 'Citadel' attempted to 'pinch out' the Kursk salient with assaults by 9th Army in the north and 4th *Panzerarmee* in the south. The former advanced only six miles at great loss, while the latter was initially more successful, yet still only managed a distance of some twenty-five miles before it was fought to a standstill.**

mortars and artillery. Interspersed between each belt were minefields. Beyond the main defences were the positions of Koniev's Steppe Front, the formation which was intended to deliver the *coup de grâce* to the German attackers, and some reserve positions along the bank of the River Don. The southern shoulder of the salient was held by Vatutin's Voronezh Front, the northern by Rokossovsky's Central Front, while the Southwest Front covered the southern flank of the salient, and Popov's Bryansk Front the northern. Estimates of Soviet strength at the Battle of Kursk vary. Zhukov claimed a total of 1,330,000 men and 3,600 tanks; in addition, the Soviets probably had 2,500 aircraft, while the two main fronts alone had 13,000 guns, 6,000 anti-tank guns and 1,000 rocket-launchers.

The German plan was to snip off the salient in classic fashion by simultaneously attacking the flanks. This was far from being the limited offensive which had originally been envisaged. Hitler committed a high proportion of the German Army's armour to the battle. In the words of the British military theorist and historian, Basil Liddell Hart, 'Hitler was gambling for high stakes'. Manstein's Army Group South was to use Hoth's 4th *Panzerarmee* to advance north from Belgorod against the southern flank, supported by Army Detachment Kempf. Manstein's forces consisted of six *Panzer*, five *Panzergrenadier* and eleven infantry divisions, with about 1,500 tanks and assault guns. The northern attack was to be delivered by Kluge's Army Group Centre. Model's 9th Army – which had about 900 tanks organised into six *Panzer* and one *Panzergrenadier* divisions, and fourteen infantry divisions – was to make the attack. Thus the attackers were significantly outnumbered by the defending forces.

The attack began inauspiciously for the Germans, when, forewarned by a captured German soldier of the time of the attack, Soviet guns opened up in the early hours of 5th July. At 3.30am Model's forces began their attack. As heavy rain fell on the battlefield, three *Panzer Korps* succeeded in advancing four miles. In the process they had broken through the first belt of Central Front's defences on a frontage of thirty-five miles, and had begun to make inroads into the second line of defences. Manstein's men also experienced some success – 2nd *SS Panzer Korps* and 48th *Panzer Korps*

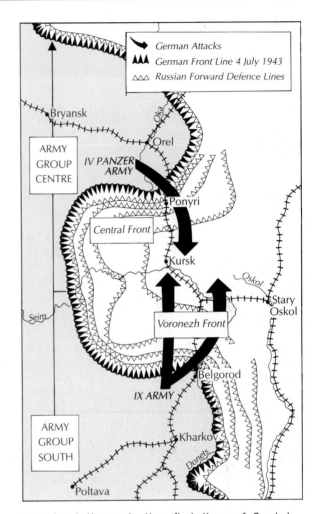

smashed through the first line of Soviet defences, forcing Vatutin to commit his reserves and to withdraw to the second line. The German assault was covered by an air umbrella of Stuka dive-bombers and fighter aircraft. The Soviets were faced with enemy formations consisting of hundreds of armoured vehicles. The new Tiger tanks and Ferdinand self-propelled guns, in which Hitler had placed so much faith, were in the vanguard, followed by Panthers, and the old workhorses of the *Panzerdivisions*, *Panzer* IIIs and IVs. The Soviets replied in kind; one German divisional commander later commented 'The Russians used aircraft in numbers as we had never yet seen in the East'. By the end of the day approximately 4,000 Soviet Armoured Fighting Vehicles (AFVs) were either engaged in the battle or preparing to join in. Both sides had suffered heavy losses of men and material, but the while the Soviets could afford to absorb

Facing page top: the price of defeat: a German tank, knocked out during the 'Citadel' offensive. While the Soviets also suffered heavy losses in their armoured formations, they, unlike the Germans, were able to replace them with relative ease.

Facing page bottom left: Stalin's 'God of War' - a Red Army mortar crew advance under fire to take up a new position. Throughout history, Russian forces have placed great emphasis on artillery, and the defenders of the Kursk salient were able to bring a massive volume of firepower to bear on the Nazi attackers.

Facing page bottom right: Soviet automatic riflemen in action. Although not as skilled as their German counterparts, the Soviet infantry were capable of performing extraordinary feats of endurance and played a major role in the Soviet victory.

Right: German troops snatch a brief rest. The German infantryman was probably the best trained and most effective soldier of the war. Each soldier was taught to be a leader, with the result that German units were still able to operate effectively even if most their officers and NCOs were killed or captured.

such losses in the long run, the Germans could not.

The struggle between Model and Rokossovsky continued on 6th July. The Soviets threw in an unsuccessful counterattack at dawn, only to see the German 9th Army continue to grind their way forward throughout the day. Rokossovsky changed his tactics, switching his tanks from an aggressive to a defensive role. The striking force of 4th *Panzerarmee*, 48th *Panzer Korps* and 2nd *SS Panzer Korps* continued to push forward, with two fresh *Panzerdivisions* also being thrown into the battle. 2nd *SS Panzer Korps* succeeded in advancing twenty-five miles. The Soviet 7th Guards Army was forced to give ground, although they repulsed twelve separate German attacks and claimed to have destroyed 332 tanks. The following day, 7th July, was a success for 4th *Panzerarmee*, who

forced the Soviets to feed in yet more reserves in an attempt to blunt the German advance. On the southern flank of the salient, 1st Tank Army was badly mauled by an attack spearheaded by 400 *Panzers*. Furthermore, Vatutin's plans for a counterblow were largely stillborn; the crisis developing on the front of 1st Tank Army and neighbouring 6th Guards Army forced him to send men and machines to stiffen the line. Army Detachment Kempf also began to make progress, although it lagged behind the two *Panzer Korps*.

Manstein's advance continued on 8th and 9th July, until by the evening of the latter the prize of the town of Oboyan, a key position in the Soviet defences, appeared within reach. But 4th *Panzerarmee*'s situation was not as healthy as it might have appeared. The impetus of the German advance was beginning to flag, and human and mechanical casualties

Far left: a tank commander's view of battle. Kursk was the largest armoured battle in history; the Soviets claimed after the war that the Germans deployed 2,000 tanks against their 3,600. A new type of German tank, the Porsche Ferdinand, proved to be unsuccessful because it lacked the secondary armament needed to keep infantrymen at bay.

Left: the infantryman's view of battle. A German soldier watches a Soviet tank from a foxhole. Infantry were not entirely defenceless against armoured vehicles; large numbers were destroyed by foot soldiers armed with bazooka-type weapons, mines and even hollow-charge grenades. Tanks were sometimes coated with anti-magnetic paste as a protection against such devices.

had been heavy. One *SS* division, which had started the battle with 300 tanks, was reduced to only eighty, and the new types of tank were not performing well. The Panther was prone to mechanical breakdown, and the Elefant, which lacked machine guns, was vulnerable to determined infantry attacks. Worse still, Model's 9th Army was ninety miles away, and the Germans had not yet broken through the Soviet defences, which were being tenaciously and skilfully defended. Finally, the strong showing of the Soviet Air Force deflected the *Luftwaffe's* attention away from the role of ground support – the role which had been so important in the German *Blitzkrieg* offensives of the early years of the war.

By 9th July Model's advance against Rokossovsky had ground to a halt. On the previous day, 9th Army had begun to crash its way through the Soviet defences on the Olkhovatka Ridge, an area of great tactical importance. The Soviet defenders fought ferociously. The Soviet 3rd Anti-Tank Brigade was almost entirely destroyed when it was attacked by a force of 300 *Panzers*, which it

engaged at ranges as small as 700 yards. On the evening of 8th July, Model, whose forces had so far lost 10,000 men, ordered the attacks to cease. In sharp contrast to the *Blitzkrieg* advances of previous campaigns, on this sector the *Panzers* had been halted within two days of the assault beginning. Two more days of attritional fighting, on 10th and 11th July, also failed to achieve a breakthrough.

On 11th July Army Group South once more renewed their offensive. The previous two days had seen both the Germans and the Red Army regroup their forces, and a furious battle develop around the town of Prokhorovka, which lies about thirty miles from Oboyan. Army Detachment Kempf advanced from the south, while the main assault was launched by three *SS* divisions (*Adolf Hitler*, *Totenkopf* and *Das Reich*) from the northeast. The Germans once again battered their way forward against tough opposition, and by the end of the day the Soviets were aware that the battle had reached its crisis. On 12th July Rotmistrov's 5th Guards Tank Army counterattacked and the greatest armoured battle in history began. About 1,500

A German Focke-Wulf 190 aircraft in action. Although at the beginning of the 'Citadel' offensive the *Luftwaffe* could put some 1,800 aircraft into the air, by the end of the battle the Red Air Force had gained air superiority. A trail of burning vehicles was the testimony to the Soviet success in the air.

AFVs – 900 Soviet, 600 German – were locked in close-range battle around Prokhorovka in area little bigger than that of a Napoleonic battlefield. By nightfall, in John Erickson's words, 'more than 300 German tanks … 88 guns and 300 lorries (lay) wrecked on the steppe: more than half the Soviet 5th Guards Tank Army lay shattered in the same area'. The battle in the Prokhorovka area continued until 15th July, but by then it was clear that Army Group South's offensive had failed.

Even before the battle for Prokhorovka had ended, Hitler had decided to bring the operation to a halt. The Anglo-American landings in Sicily on 10th July clearly influenced Hitler's decision, but other factors played their part as well. On 12th July the Soviet West Front and Bryansk Front had attacked 2nd *Panzerarmee*, which was defending the Orel area where a large German salient thrust out into Soviet-held territory. This, in turn, threatened the rear of 9th Army, which was forced to divert troops to face this new threat, and on 17th July, Model began to pull back from hard-won positions in the Kursk salient, thus nullifying the gains made in the south. The Soviets were now taking the initiative, attacking to the south as well as in the salient itself. The subsequent Soviet offensives were to carry them 250 miles from Kursk to Kiev and the River Dneiper. The fruits of Manstein's counter-offensive of March were thrown away; never again was the German army able to carry out a major offensive operation on the Eastern Front. Kursk had cost the Germans more than the initiative. They had lost about 1,000 tanks, compared with Soviets losses of about 1,500, but these lost German AFVs were virtually irreplaceable. The German *Blitzkrieg* successes of 1939-42 had been based on surprise, speed and rapid exploitation. Faced with the formidable Soviet defences in the Kursk salient, the Germans discovered that their magic formula was no longer effective.

**Soviet troops advance past a group of Russian T-34 tanks. The T-34 had features such as wide tracks, which enabled it to keep going through mud and snow, and sloping armour. Vast numbers of T-34s were built – many were used by Arab armies in the post-1948 wars with Israel.**

P.47 Thunderbolt escort fighters of the 8th Air Force Fighter Command, together with the P.38 Lightnings, could escort the bombers across occupied Europe as far as the German border. Until the long-range P.51 Mustangs came along later in the war, the bombers could carry on into Germany if they wished, but they had to take care of themselves.

By the middle of 1943 Ira C. Eaker had been been promoted to Major General, and assumed command of the whole of the 8th Air Force from Major General Carl A. Spaatz. The 8th's Bomber Command, infinitely bigger than it had been at the time of the Rouen raid just twelve months before, was now commanded by Brigadier General Frederick L. Anderson. The Air Force also had a Fighter Command now. Equipped with the Lockheed P.38 (Lightning), and the P.47 (Thunderbolt), Fighter Command could escort the B-17s to targets throughout France and Belgium. But Eaker and Anderson had plans to send the Fortresses further still. There were some juicy targets deep inside Germany, but to attack these the bombers would have to soldier on alone from the German border. The pick of these targets was Schweinfurt. A small town of some 60,000 inhabitants, in Bavaria, it occupied a

disproportionately large place in Germany's industrial war effort. Ball bearings were vital in the production of vehicles, ships and aeroplanes, and half of Germany's ball bearings were produced in five factories clustered together in Schweinfurt.

To celebrate the first anniversary of their raid on Rouen, Eaker and Anderson were planning something which would be an air battle rather than an air raid; an operation which would be of far-reaching strategic importance. The main target would be Schweinfurt. An attack on a secondary target, to be carried out a little earlier, would distract the German defences from the attack on Schweinfurt. The decoy mission would involve even deeper penetration into German territory. It was to fly right across Germany, practically to the Czechoslovakian border, to attack the Messerschmitt factory complex at Regensburg. The B-17s attacking this target would not have enough fuel to return to England, and would fly straight on to American bases in North Africa. Maybe this would confuse the German fighters. Perhaps they would be sitting on the ground waiting for the Regensburg attackers to return, while the second phase was attacking Schweinfurt. General Eaker said, 'This battlefield is going to be a thousand miles long, and five miles up in the air. It will be fought in sub-zero temperatures, and the gladiators will wear oxygen masks.'

The plan of action was that 147 B-17s of the Fourth Bombardment Wing would cross the North Sea at eight o'clock in the morning, to attack the Messerschmitt works, over three hours

flying away. Ten minutes later a further 230 bombers of the First Bombardment Wing would take off, hoping to slip through the German defences to Schweinfurt. The aircraft heading for Regensburg were expected to take the brunt of the attacks of the German fighters, so they would have the benefit of the escorts. The escorts would then return to refuel and rearm, and by the time the Schweinfurt aircraft had fought their way back from the target to the German border, they would be out again to meet them and bring them home.

The Regensburg force got airborne pretty well on time, and collected their fighter escort, augmented by several squadrons of RAF

Nicknamed 'Knockout Dropper', a Flying Fortress lines up on the runway whilst the ground crew line up on the grass beside her, waving their good wishes as she sets out on yet another mission. 'Knockout Dropper' was one of the aircraft that went to Schweinfurt – and came safely home.

The nose of this B-17G Flying Fortress tells the story of a hectic operational life. Each bomb painted on the nose represents a journey over enemy territory, but none of its operations can have been as desperate as the trip to Schweinfurt on August 17, 1943.

Spitfires. Almost as soon as they entered enemy airspace, over Holland and then Belgium, the first of the flak began to come up to meet them, and then the German fighters. From then on, until they reached Regensburg, almost two hours later, the battle was continuous. The Germans had learned that it was unprofitable to put all their eggs in one basket. There had been a time when they would have sent up all their fighters in a mass, at the outset, but they had realised that any bombers which escaped this onslaught then had a relatively unopposed journey to their targets. Their technique now was to spread out the fighters along the most likely route to be taken by the bomber stream, so that it could be subjected to continuous attacks. They had also established 'turn round' airfields, so that the fighters could land where they ran out of ammunition, and wait to have a second go at the bombers as they were on their way home.

To begin with the fighters sniped cautiously at the fringes of the bomber formations, not wishing to get themselves too involved with the fighter escorts. Their turn would come at about Aachen, when the P.47s and P.38s turned for home. Meanwhile the flak gunners could help themselves.

It was relatively uncommon for a B-17 to be shot down by flak, although spectacular direct hits were seen. With the shells fused to explode at the height at which the bombers were flying, the formations were jostled by explosions, and showered with jagged, red-hot lumps of

This patch of sky represents no more than a single tile in the whole mosaic of the massed formation of the 8th Air Force which left eastern England to attack Schweinfurt, as they had done to attack so many other targets in occupied Europe.

Right: flying so high that the sky above them seems almost black, the Fortresses are picked out by the sun, and twinkle like fireflies. Their escorts climb even higher, and begin to mark the sky above the formation with vapour trails.

The Germans protected their coastline against raiding aircraft with 'flak ships'. Inland, besides the siting of permanent flak batteries, they had mobile batteries on railway trucks. Below right: gunners run to man their weapons as an air-raid warning sounds.

Left: the formations of Flying Fortresses fly high above the cloud tops, the exhaust from their engines leaving vapour trails behind them. The bright sunlight at high level and the telltale trails made the camouflage paint jobs of the Fortresses pointless. Around the time of the Schweinfurt raid, camouflage was abandoned, and replacement aircraft were delivered with a natural metal finish.

Right: on the edge of the stratosphere the Fortresses run in to their target, their bomb doors open. Flak probes the sky around them, and punctuates the formation with the black puffs of exploding shells.

shrapnel. The shrapnel caused injuries, and often deaths, among the bomber crews, and damaged their aircraft. If the damage was sufficient to cause them to drop out of the formation they would fall prey to the fighters, who could tear them to shreds at their leisure.

Aachen passed beneath them, and as it did so the escort fighters saluted and turned for home. The bombers huddled tighter together. The German attackers became more aggressive. They had learned that the weakest point of defence of the B-17s was dead ahead. To the side and rear they could direct the fire of six, and sometimes eight, of their 0.5 in. machine guns at their attackers. Directly ahead they could defend themselves with only two guns, or at best four. Throughout the fifteen mile length of the stream of bombers, the German single engined and twin engined fighters dived head on at the formations. B-17s cartwheeled out of line, and spun down towards the earth. Sometimes parachutes blossomed behind them as they fell. Ten meant that the whole crew had escaped. Often it was less; sometimes

none at all. The remaining aircraft moved forward to fill the gaps, and keep the formation tight. One squadron commander commented, 'Our navigator has an easy job today. All he has to do is follow the burning Fortresses and the parachutes of the Group up ahead of us.'

Two and a half hours after after leaving the shores of England, the Fortresses began their run in to Regensburg. The leader, Colonel Curtis E. LeMay, was surprised that at this time the fighters seemed to leave them alone, and the anti-aircraft fire fell quiet. Over the next twenty-five minutes the formation dropped over 300 tons of bombs onto the Messerschmitt works at Regensburg. The Norden bombsight, said to be capable of putting a bomb into a barrel from 30,000 feet, did its work well. By the time the formation passed on its way, not a building remained undamaged.

As they made their way towards North Africa the fighters returned, and stayed with them until they reached the Alps. From then on their only enemy was lack of fuel, and the effects of damage that they had received getting this

A B-17 flies over its target (left), the work of its colleagues already apparent on the ground below.

One of the most frightening aspects of the daylight bombing war was the sight of comrades being anihilated. The aircraft were struck more often by shrapnel fragments from bursting shells, than by direct hits from the shells themselves. Right: when an aircraft was caught by a direct hit the result was both spectacular and horrifying.

far. When they were eventually on the ground they found that they had lost 24 of their aircraft – one aircraft out of every six that had taken off. But that was not the end of it. The facilities in North Africa were inadequate to make 55 of the badly damaged Fortresses sufficiently airworthy for the return flight to Britain.

Meanwhile, back on the airfields in Britain, the 230 bombers that should have followed LeMay's formations into Germany had been prevented from taking off by bad weather over their bases. It was not until almost midday that they eventually began to get into the air. It then took one and a half hours to assemble the formations before setting course for their target. Just as, in 1940, the RAF's radar operators had watched the Luftwaffe massing over France for their attacks on southern England, the Germans were aware of what was happening, and were ready for them even before they headed for Holland.

Because of the delay, any benefit which might have been obtained from the decoy attack on Regensburg had disappeared. If anything, it had only served to alert the German defenders. Despite the fighter escort which they had across Holland and Belgium, the German fighters weighed in with enthusiasm. As well as their machine guns and 20mm cannon, some of them carried 210mm rockets which they launched into the formations from half a mile or more away. One of the Fortresses received a direct hit, and was literally blown in half, crashing to earth in flames with the whole crew trapped on board. Other fighters trailed electrically detonated bombs, capable of severing a bomber's wing, from cables beneath their aircraft.

During the journey to Schweinfurt the First Bombardment Group lost 21 aircraft. Another was caught by flak over the target. On the return trip fourteen more were lost before the

The sky is filled from horizon to horizon with Flying Fortresses and bursting flak shells. This photograph was taken during the second attack on Schweinfurt on October 14, 1943.

'Bombs away' - the bombardiers work is done. The 'Norden' bombsight can be switched off, and control of the B-17 returns to the pilot for the journey back to England.

escort fighters returned to cover their withdrawal. The loss rate of one in six, suffered by the Regensburg attack, was repeated, and by the time aircraft damaged beyond repair were taken into account, the aggregate loss rate of the two operations amounted to one in three of the aircraft taking part.

The targets at Schweinfurt were more dispersed than at Regensburg, so much so that as the smoke from the bombs of the leading aircraft drifted across the targets, it made aiming difficult, and the accuracy and effect of the bombing suffered. Ball bearing production was restored a little over a week after the attack, although production was reduced by thirty-five percent. It was not good enough.

Bombardment crews of the 8th Air Force attended a briefing on October 14. A hush fell upon the room when the cover was drawn back from the briefing-board to reveal the target. They were going back to Schweinfurt.

It was in the Battle of the Atlantic, which was a continuous battle throughout most of the years of both world wars, that the Allies came nearest each time to suffering defeat at sea. In both wars it was a battle Britain in particular could not afford to lose.

Britain, in its role as an 'unsinkable aircraft carrier', needed food and weapons from overseas if she was to survive. Much of this food, nearly all the raw materials to make guns and tanks, and even the weapons themselves, came from across the Atlantic.

Before the Second World War, Britain had the largest merchant navy in the world; one third of the total tonnage on the high seas was British. Now Hitler held most of the continent of Europe, including the entire coastline from the Arctic waters off the North Cape of Norway down to the Bay of Biscay and Spain. All the supplies destined for Britain had, therefore, to sail through the Atlantic in order to reach the United Kingdom. Some of the supplies would then go on to the Soviet Union, to sustain her too in the war against fascism.

In the Atlantic, and also on the route north to the Arctic ports of the USSR, the merchant ships and their escorts faced German surface raiders and U-boats. Furthermore, they had to battle against the weather, often as dangerous as the enemy itself.

In the Second World War the Battle of the Atlantic proper began with the defeat of France in July 1940, and the German occupation of the French west-coast ports of Brest, La Pallice, St. Nazaire, Lorient, and Bordeaux. The Battle of the Atlantic would continue for nearly six years, and would be fiercely fought, with the advantage continually passing from one side to the other.

The flag officer commanding the German U-boats, Admiral Donitz, moved his headquarters from Berlin to Lorient to be near his submarines. The U-boats would be Germany's main weapon in this battle for, after the sinking of the *Bismarck*, surface raiding in the Atlantic virtually ended. It nonetheless always remained a potential threat to the Arctic convoys.

For most of the War the main British headquarters for the Battle of the Atlantic were in Liverpool. From here the admiral in charge of

the western approaches was responsible for the convoys and their escorts. With London's docks virtually closed by bombing and Britain's North Sea ports often endangered by mines, the ports on the west coast became the centre for most merchant shipping.

The importance of the battle was underlined by Churchill's setting-up of a special cabinet committee to meet the challenges to Britain's supply lifeline. A series of distinguished British admirals commanded the western approaches. These included such dignitaries as Sir Martin Dunbar-Nasmith, who won the Victoria Cross as a submariner in the Dardanelles in 1915, Sir Percy Noble and, perhaps the greatest of them all, Sir Max Horton. Each lobbied throughout his period in office for more resources for the vital Atlantic battle zone.

For, in addition to the actual fighting, this was to be a battle of resources. The Allies had to build ships faster than the German U-boats could sink them. They had to find escorts, and the crews to man them, in the face of dozens of other demands on the naval services. The air-force commanders had to be persuaded to divert much needed aircraft to Coastal Command rather than to the bombing campaign in Germany. The arguments, like the fighting out in the Atlantic, swayed back and forth, and with equal ferocity.

It is beyond the scope of this chapter to analyse the many occasions upon which policy or strategy influenced the course of the Battle of the Atlantic. John Terraine's account in *Business in Great Waters* is required reading for any serious student of the U-Boat wars.

It is, however, worth reminding ourselves of a few of the key factors. The assembly-line construction of all-welded American Liberty ships was crucial. These were coming on-stream so magnificently fast that they were keeping up with the losses being suffered at sea.

The provision of escorts was haphazard at times, and resulted in the use of a broad mix of vessels, manned by crews of very varying abilities. American assistance, even before the U.S.A. was involved in the War, was a determining factor. The provision of the fifty lend-lease destroyers in exchange for naval bases on British and Commonwealth territory was more than a token gesture. The repair

The key to winning the Battle of the Atlantic was air power. Whilst there was still a gap between the area which could be covered by U.S. Coast Guard aircraft (top right) and by the aircraft meeting convoys from airfields in Britain or Iceland, U-boats reigned supreme. Providing aircraft with a longer range became a priority for Allied chiefs, one that was eventually realised.

One extremely effective way of providing air cover for convoys was by using aircraft from escort carriers. Grumman Avengers (bottom right) could cover thousands of miles of sea in searching for threats to a convoy.

Left: a German U-boat under final attack from a long-range Liberator. Three U.S. Navy aircraft and two army bombers have successfully attacked the U-boat and smoke is coming from the conning tower. Strafing attacks have kept the U-boat crew from their guns. The circular splashes in the water mark cannon fire from the attacking plane.

facilities available in the U.S.A. were equally important.

For the Germans, the War had come too soon for the building plans which Donitz had counted on, and this meant that he always had less U-boats than he required. He started the War with only twenty-four U-boats ready for active service. Nevertheless, and despite RAF and U.S.AAF bombing, U-boat production never really faltered. Even in 1943 and 1944, the years of their greatest losses, U-boats were still being built faster than they were being sunk.

In strategic terms, the Allies' greatest missed opportunity was probably their failure to bomb the underground U-boat pens as these were being constructed. Once they were built, the pens provided an invulnerable haven for U-boats in port, for the Germans were masters in

the use of concrete. Losses in harbour were minimal for most of the War; U-boats had to be caught and sunk at sea.

Including some two dozen U-boats lost in collision or scuttled when Allied troops captured their home bases, out of the total 1,162 U-boats built, 791 were sunk in the Second World War.

After resources, politics also played its part in influencing the course of the Battle of the Atlantic. In the summer of 1941, Hitler took a decision which hindered Admiral Donitz's campaign against the supply ships travelling to Britain. He gave orders for six U-boats to go to the Mediterranean, to be followed by another six.

Rommel was doing well against the British in the desert, but his supplies from Italy were under constant attack from the Royal Navy.

A U-boat survivor is about to be taken aboard the Free French corvette *Aconit*. Note the breathing tube from the German seaman's escape gear around his neck. In an Atlantic convoy battle on 10 March, 1943, the *Aconit* helped sink both U-432 and U-444 either by gunfire or ramming.

Although Hitler and Mussolini controlled the whole of the northern coastline of the Mediterranean, the British had naval bases at either end, plus the beleaguered island fortress of Malta in the middle.

Hitler wanted these twelve U-boats to help a reinforced *Luftwaffe* protect the supply lines to Africa. The first six hardly accomplished anything. Two of the second group did not even reach the Mediterranean, and a third was sunk soon after. Later, however, the U-boats would score two important successes. The aircraft carrier HMS *Ark Royal* and the battleship HMS *Barham* were sunk within a few days of each other, the latter with heavy loss of life.

However, Hitler's diversion of twelve U-boats from the Atlantic effectively gave Allied shipping almost a two-month 'holiday' there at a time when the merchant ships and their escorts badly needed the break. As 1941 drew to an end, Britain was stocked up with supplies and in a stronger psychological position to continue waging the Battle of the Atlantic.

In 1942 Hitler would once again intervene directly in U-boat warfare, insisting on the deployment of more submarines in Norwegian waters. Against most of the evidence he was convinced Churchill was planning to make an attack on Norway. These submarines at least saw action against those convoys going to Russia. They also proved useful as scouts and scavengers when surface raiders were employed against the merchantmen.

After the Battle of the Bismarck Sea, Hitler's rage at the failure of his surface ships resulted in the loss of Admiral Erich Raeder as commander in chief of the German Navy. Raeder was succeeded by Admiral Donitz in January 1943. Donitz would retain his responsibility for U-boats, correctly believing that nobody else had the same knowledge and experience of U-boat warfare as he did.

U-boat headquarters were moved to Berlin, and integrated into the German Admiralty. Things would not be the same, even though Donitz's long-standing chief of staff, Rear Admiral Godt, succeeded him as Flag Officer, U-boats, and Godt's former position was filled by Gunther Hessler, Donitz's son-in-law, and himself a U-boat ace.

Donitz could no longer influence detailed events nor direct the actual battles as he had done in the past. He also had many other

naval preoccupations besides U-boats. In fact, he was to find himself at variance with Hitler, defending the very surface-ship policies over which his predecessor Raeder had lost his job.

Tactics, merging with strategy, also greatly influenced the Battle of the Atlantic. In 1943, tactics altered considerably as new forces were brought to bear. These included the introduction of small aircraft carriers into convoy escort duty, and a determined campaign by Coastal Command to sink the U-boats as they travelled through the Bay of Biscay.

The escort carriers were ships that weighed not much than 10,000 tons and could be built in less than a year. They would account for twenty-six U-boats. While Coastal Command waited to get aircraft that could cover the air 'gap' over the Atlantic, it waged a determined war in the Bay of Biscay. This was almost a private battle between the huge Sunderland flying boats, the Catalinas and Liberators provided by the U.S. and the U-boats. The battle is excellently described in *Conflict Over The Bay*, by Norman Franks (William Kimber, 1986).

Another of its aspects can be studied in Kenneth Poolman's *Focke-Wulf Condor – Scourge* of the Atlantic (MacDonald & Jane's, 1978).

Other tactics are also worthy of separate study in book-length histories. These include the use of 'wolf-packs' of U-boats working together in ocean-wide ambushes, and the countermeasures of the Allied 'hunter-killer' Escort Groups. These special groups, trained to work together, operated directly against the U-boats. They would pursue and and trap them in complex depth charge attacks, leaving the smaller warships of the close escort to stay and protect the merchant ships.

Another factor worth considering is that of morale, in this case that of the U-boat crews. These men were extremely well trained. Even towards the end, when fresh crews were desperately needed, cutbacks in the length and intensity of their training were seldom allowed. If they were not strictly volunteers in the most democratic meaning of the word, they did feel themselves to be a chosen breed. They enjoyed privileges in terms of leave and

**Left: the crew of the 4,793-ton German blockade runner *Silvaplane* are about to be taken aboard HMS *Adventure*, under Captain Bowes Lyon. Intercepted by the British warship 200 miles off Brest, the *Silvaplane* was scuttled and blown up by her crew, all of whom were rescued.**

**Despite the successes of aircraft in attacking U-boats, the main weapon in the Battle of the Atlantic was always the depth charge. Depth charges are ready to be dropped over the stern of a corvette (right), whilst an RAF Coastal Command aircraft arrives to escort the convoy into a British port.**

It cannot be repeated often enough that the object of all convoy work (left) in the Battle of the Atlantic was 'the safe and timely arrival' of the merchant ships. Sinking U-boats was an incidental bonus, and each success facilitiated future passages, but it was getting the ships through that really mattered.

It was always important to the morale of merchant seamen in the Battle of the Atlantic to know they had a good chance of being rescued. This picture of survivors from the torpedoed British freighter *Blairlogie*, sitting in a ship's lifeboat aboard a still-neutral U.S. merchantman, the *American Shipper* (right), is clearly posed, but the overall impression is reassuring.

shore comforts not bestowed on many others in the German forces.

This was perhaps deservedly so, for the crews faced real danger and the likelihood of a terrible fate, crushed and suffocated at the bottom of the sea. There was seldom hope of escape – over half the U-boats sunk left no survivors. Where there were survivors they usually numbered only a handful from each submarine, out of a crew of between forty and fifty.

In 1940, there were no survivors at all from eleven of the twenty-three U-boats sunk. In 1941 there were no survivors from fifteen out of thirty-five; and in 1942, fifty-nine of the eighty-five U-boats that went down did so without a single man escaping. In 1943, the year in which the Battle of the Atlantic was finally won, 154 U-boats out of the 238 sunk had no survivors. At the time, most U-boat crews were probably not wholly aware of the odds against them. Whereas they might hear of the loss of an individual boat, full details were seldom announced publicly. Where possible the extent

of such losses were also kept from the submariners.

Another instance where morale was decisive was among merchant seamen, who were so often passive targets. Professional seamen have always had to contend with the perils of the deep and the possibility of death, but not so the younger, wartime-only recruits. Faced with the thought of death by drowning or, more likely, from exposure, they showed considerable courage. Though inevitably there were instances of panic, fear and selfishness when a ship was torpedoed.

A boost for the morale of the merchant seamen came with the advent of rescue ships, merchantmen specially equipped to pick up survivors. Sailing in the 'tail-end charlie' position of a convoy, these would drop back when ships were hit and take the survivors aboard, despite the risk of becoming victims themselves. When no rescue ships were available, or if they had been sunk, the convoy commodore would invite the last ship in each column to take over

The men (right) rescued after eighty-three days in the Atlantic on a raft (left) were a U.S. gunner and two Dutch seamen. Two other crewmen, who were on the raft with them after the ship sank, died during this ordeal. The men lived on rainwater, and such fish as they could catch. They drifted 1,000 miles before being picked up.

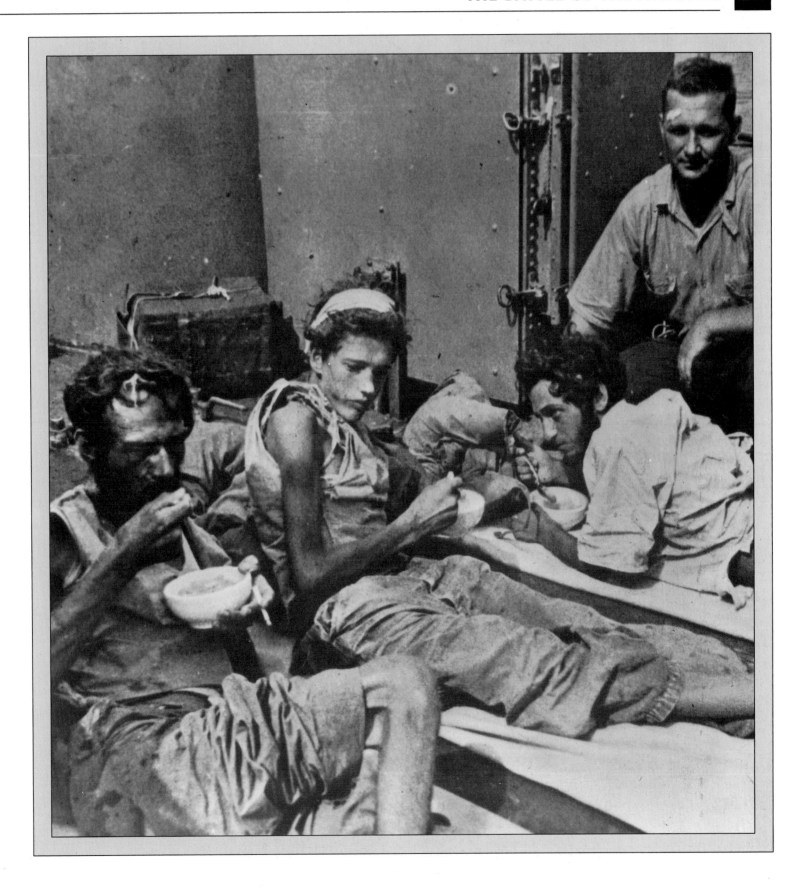

this function. Some coped admirably, despite the extra risk; others declined the invitation and steamed on.

Escort commanders were not supposed to detach warships for rescue work. The escorts were too badly needed to be put at risk by stopping to pick up survivors. Many escort commanders broke these rules, arguing that, if crews were simply abandoned, the morale of the merchant seamen would suffer. They had to be made to feel that they stood at least a fighting chance of survival if they were sunk.

There was no easy solution to this problem. Nor was there any relief from the even more distressing thought that 'total war' could mean machine-gunning survivors in the water. In World War I, Admiral Fisher had said 'the essence of war is violence, and moderation in war is imbecility'. This view would seem to suggest that it would be reasonable for U-boats to kill survivors rather than to let them reach safety and sail again. Similarly, the RAF could stop dropping life rafts to U-boat men struggling in the waters of the Bay of Biscay.

Luckily, few of those in the Battle of the Atlantic subscribed to Admiral Fisher's opinion. There were reports of boats overturned by submarines travelling fast on the surface that had not seen them. Equally there were times when U-boats were shelled after surfacing to surrender. However, on the whole all seamen were felt to deserve a chance of rescue.

It was, nonetheless, a ruthless, bitter battle, one that was often fought in those appalling weather conditions that have been stressed again and again. Many of those involved had seen their fellows killed, or lost loved ones in enemy bombing raids at home. Generally, however, those thrown into the treacherous waters were regarded not as friend or foe, but merely as 'survivors' who were to be rescued or helped towards safety whenever possible. There is a camaraderie of the sea which transcends even wartime conditions.

**Left: the 10,000-ton British motor vessel *Dunbar Castle* hit a mine on 9 January, 1940 – a reminder that U-boats, surface raiders and German long-range Condor aircraft were not the only hazards faced by ships crossing the Atlantic.**

**Right: eight identical ships being built at shipyards in Los Angeles. The place where the Battle of the Atlantic was really won was in the shipyards of America on both the east and west coasts. Revolutionary assembly-line procedures for building liberty ships and other merchant vessels ensured that ships were being completed quicker than U-boats could sink them.**

# BURMA – FROM IMPHAL TO KOHIMA

Troops of Lieutenant General Motozo Yanagida's 33rd Division pass through a Burmese village on their way to the Chindwin in February, 1944. The Japanese were still confident of victory, while the Burmese, who less than two years earlier had greeted the Japanese as liberators, were now disillusioned and apathetic.

At the beginning of 1944 the war on the Indian-Burmese frontier was at a stalemate. Neither the British on the Arakan and Assam fronts, or their American and Chinese allies to the north, had been able to launch a successful offensive. For their part, the Japanese had been content to remain on the defensive, holding the line their invading forces had first reached in May, 1942. But the stagnation which had characterised this 'forgotten' war was about to come to an end. Since the autumn of 1943 new spirit had been breathed into British Far Eastern forces: a new command headed by Lord Louis Mountbatten – South East Asia Command (SEAC) – had been established and a brilliant trainer and logistics expert, General George 'Pop' Giffard, had been appointed to command SEAC's land forces. The 'forgotten' Far Eastern army also received a new commander – Lieutenant General William ('Uncle Bill') Slim – and, reinforced, retrained and rebuilt, had been reborn as 14th Army.

Since October 1943, 5th and 7th Indian divisions of 14th Army's XV Corps had been advancing slowly and methodically down the Arakan Front against increasing Japanese resistance. In the far north another offensive was in preparation – a glider-borne assault by five brigades of Major General Orde Wingate's Chindits, designed to support a drive southward by General 'Vinegar Joe' Stilwell's Sino-American forces. But for Slim these operations were diversions from where he intended to fight the main battle and launch his offensive for the reconquest of Burma. Forty miles west of the Japanese front on the Chindwin River, beyond the jungle-clad mountains along which ran the Indian-Burmese border, lay a 700-square-mile plain. At its centre was Imphal, a small town which served as the capital of the Indian border district of Manipur. A single road linked Imphal with the outside world. It meandered eighty miles north through mountains to the hill station of Kohima, from where it swung fifty miles northwest to a railhead at Dimapur. Throughout 1943, troops and supplies had poured in through this railhead from India – Slim had concentrated the three

Moving secretly on Kohima, heavily laden troops of the Japanese 33rd Division, accompanied by pack animals and bullocks, ford a tributary of the Chindwin at Marcy in 1944. Supply lines in this area were so bad that once these troops had consumed the supplies they carried with them they starved.

Despite the thick jungle and rough terrain the Japanese 14th Tank Regiment was able to get a number of tanks (below) through the Kebaw Valley and onto the Imphal-Tiddim Road in an attempt to cut off the retreat of 17th Indian Division. The effort was unsuccessful - on the night of 22nd March six of these tanks were destroyed by British mines.

divisions of 14th Army's IV Corps on this plain, and had transformed it into a springboard for his offensive. It now contained 100,000 troops, 50,000 Indian labourers, six airfields and several vast depots, the largest of which, at Dimapur, was a mile wide and eleven miles long.

In preparation for the offensive, two roads had been built from Imphal to the Chindwin River. One ran seventy miles southwest via the villages of Palel and Tamu to the river at Sittaung, and here IV Corps' commander Lieutenant General Geoffrey Scoones had deployed Major General Douglas Gracey's 20th Indian Division. The other ran 130 miles directly south to Tiddim, before swinging west to Fort White and the Chindwin at Kalewa. Here Scoones had positioned Major General 'Punch' Cowan's 17th Indian Division. The remaining division, 23rd Indian, he held in reserve at Imphal. Scoone's deployments were designed for the offensive. During January,

however, British intelligence began piecing together indications that the Japanese were preparing to launch their own offensive towards Imphal. Slim hoped very much that such was the case – it would be much easier to destroy the Japanese in a battle on the Imphal Plain, where British superiority in armour and air power could be brought to bear, than to fight them beyond the Chindwin.

The Japanese were indeed preparing to attack, but in numbers much greater than the British believed possible. Burma Area commander Lieutenant General Masakazu Kawabe believed a successful assault on Imphal would have a profound effect on Japan's strategic situation. Not only would it disrupt Slim's preparations for the reconquest of Burma, but if Dimapur were taken, the Sino-American and Chindit operations, supplied almost entirely from this depot, would be seriously inconvenienced and Stilwell's efforts to reopen a land route to China would end forever. Moreover, there remained a possibility that a successful Japanese invasion of India – albeit an invasion of a remote border territory – would spark off an explosion of anti-British nationalism throughout the sub-continent, with incalculable consequences for the Allied cause in the Far East.

To ensure the success of 'U-Go' – the Japanese codename for the offensive – Kawabe planned to divert Slim's attention. On 4th February, 54th and 55th divisions struck into the Arakan where, by 12th February, they had surrounded XV Corps. The situation was serious, but Slim refused to take Kawabe's bait; instead he ordered XV Corps to stand firm, and supplied it by air. Kawabe had not yet fought against a general of Slim's calibre and assumed that his deception had been successful. On the night of 6th March he set the first stage of 'U-Go' in motion. Lieutenant General Renya Mutaguchi, commander of 15th Army, now in operational control, sent his 33rd Division across the Chindwin near Kalew. Avoiding contact with British patrols, the Division infiltrated through the Chin Hills. It then split into two columns. The bulk of the Division under Lieutenant General Motozo Yanagida marched due west and, by 12th March, established roadblocks on the Imphal-Tiddim road, which cut 17th Indian Division off from its base. Meanwhile, a powerful detached column, including a regiment of light tanks under Major General Tsunoru Yamamoto, moved due north to cut the Imphal-Sittaung road and isolate 20th Indian Division. Mutaguchi made his next move on the night of 15th March, when Lieutenant General Masafumi Yamauchi's 15th Division crossed the Chindwin River at a point a hundred miles north of Kalewa. They then struck northwest for Sangshak, a small town thirty

miles northeast of Imphal, from where Yamauchi intended to drive due west and cut the Imphal-Kohima road. Further upriver on the same night Lieutenant General Kotoku Sato's 31st Division crossed at two points forty miles apart and moved in three columns towards Kohima, its ultimate objective being the huge supply depot at Dimapur.

In all, Mutaguchi had sent 100,000 men across the Chindwin, a force so large that he estimated the conquest of Manipur would take only three weeks. It had to. The logistics of 15th Army were primitive in the extreme – large herds of cattle were driven in the wake of the advancing columns, but even with these Mutaguchi knew that his army could not be fed much after the beginning of April unless it captured British supply depots. Another factor also loomed large in his calculations. His meteorologists had forecast that the monsoon would break early in May, which would turn the dirt roads and tracks of Manipur to quagmires and reduce resupply to a trickle. Against a determined enemy an operation of this sort would have been folly, but Mutaguchi had fought Eastern Army before and held it in profound contempt. He did not know of the transformation Giffard and Slim had effected.

Having been warned well in advance of Operation 'U-Go', Slim and Scoones had prepared a defence plan; rather than resisting the Japanese when they crossed the Chindwin, 17th and 20th Indian divisions were to fall back and form a tight defensive perimeter around Imphal. Unfortunately, Slim's intelligence had been inaccurate in one crucial detail. The predicted date for the attack was 15th March, nine days later than 33rd Division's actual crossing of the Chindwin. It was not just the timing of the attack which surprised the British commanders, but also its sheer scale. Cowan's 17th Indian Division, its 16,000 men, 2,500 vehicles and 3,000 mules strung out along twenty miles of highway, did not begin its withdrawal until late on the afternoon of 14th March. A few hours later, Yanagida's troops were pressing all along Cowan's right flank, and in many places Japanese battalions managed to position themselves between the widely spaced British units. The withdrawal slowed to a crawl, Cowan's men fighting a series of desperate clearing operations.

Realizing he was presiding over a disaster,

**Winding like a giant white snake through the jungle, the Imphal-Tiddim Road was the scene of 17th Indian Division's epic struggle with the Japanese 33rd Division.**

Scoones rushed two brigades of 23rd Division south. These struck Yanagida's troops in the rear and enabled 17th Indian Division to fight free of the Japanese grip. On 26th March the British and Indians reached Bishenpur, twenty miles south of Imphal, and turned to face their enemy. Meanwhile, Yamamoto's force was approaching the Palel-Sittaung road and threatening 20th Indian Division's communications. After reluctantly destroying his depots, Gracey ordered a withdrawal to a line of hills, the Shenan Saddle, some ten miles to the east of Palel. With the completion of these withdrawals, the perimeter around Imphal was secure. Slim had acted just in time, for on 29th March, Yamauchi's 15th Division reached a point only fifteen miles north of Imphal on the Imphal-Kohima road and IV Corps was now cut off.

Although the attack was both heavier and more rapid than expected, Slim and Scoones were still confident, as thus far Japanese moves had more or less conformed with intelligence appreciations. But on 27th March 14th Army HQ received news of a potential catastrophe. Six days earlier, 50th Indian Paratroop Brigade had been attacked by a strong Japanese force (part of 31st Division) at Sangshak thirty miles northeast of Imphal. The paratroopers were quickly surrounded, but after a week long battle had been able to fight their way back to Imphal. They had discovered on a dead Japanese officer a map which showed clearly

that an entire division was advancing towards undefended Dimapur. Slim now moved rapidly and decisively. By 2nd April he had appointed Lieutenant General Montagu Stopford to the command of a new formation, XXXIII Corps, tasked specifically with the defence of the railhead. Already the first elements of 7th Indian Division had been flown in from the Arakan, followed closely by the highly trained and well-equipped 2nd British Division. For Slim, Dimapur was all important – a scratch garrison of 1,500 commanded by a Chindit officer, Colonel Richards, already in Kohima, was ordered to hold for as long as possible, while Stopford prepared for a defensive battle around Dimapur.

But there was to be no Battle of Dimapur, for against all expectations Richards' men held Kohima. The odds were incredible. By 5th April 12,000 of Sato's men had surrounded the garrison and moved in for the kill. From their dugouts on Kohima Ridge – a series of hogs' backs and hills a mile long and a half mile wide that dominated the road to Dimapur – Richards' men bloodily repulsed assault after assault. By sheer weight of numbers, the Japanese gradually inched forward and on 17th April stormed Garrison Hill, a feature in the centre of the ridge, which cut Richards' force into two pockets. At dawn on 18th April few amongst the garrison believed they would live to see the sun set.

In fact help was close at hand. Since 5th April 7th Division's 161st Brigade had been fighting its way to the garrison, but had itself been surrounded by Jotsoma, a few miles west of Kohima. By 11th April the airlift of troops had transformed the situation at Dimapur, and

Facing page top: men of 2nd Battalion Dorsetshire Regiment drag a dead Japanese from a foxhole on Kohima Ridge, 13th May, 1944. The Dorset's capture of the ridge marked the turning point of the battle, although the Japanese fought on from other positions for nearly another two months.

Facing page bottom: British soldiers advance cautiously through elephant grass towards the Chindwin in July, 1944. Although the Japanese were ill and emaciated by this time, their rearguards put up tenacious resistance and delayed the British advance in hundreds of small actions.

While the major battles raged around Imphal and Kohima, 'Vinegar Joe' Stilwell's Sino-American forces (right), supported by British Chindits, closed on Myitkyna in northern Burma. Despite being greatly outnumbered, the Japanese held on until 3rd August.

Stopford now ordered 2nd British Division to strike towards Kohima. Seven days later, with the garrison on its last legs, 1st Royal Berkshires, 2nd Division's spearhead, broke through the Japanese cordon.

Slim now received another piece of valuable intelligence. A signal had been found on the body of a Japanese sergeant major ordering Sato to send one third of his troops to support the attack on Imphal. Slim knew that this move had to be prevented at all costs and ordered 2nd Division to keep up the pressure on the Japanese. Major General J.H. Grover, 2nd Division's commander, was reluctant to put in costly frontal attacks on the now heavily entrenched Japanese positions on Kohima Ridge and the surrounding hills. Attempting to outflank Sato, he sent two of his brigades to strike the Japanese simultaneously from the north and south, but progress was slow and casualties heavy. The battle dragged on into May, the British and Japanese hammering away at each other from positions which were often only a few yards apart. Fighting was most furious in Kohima village itself, where a tennis court in front of the Japanese-held District Commissioner's bungalow had become the front line, over which the opposing sides lobbed showers of grenades. Slowly, British material

superiority began to tell. By 13th May 2nd Division's artillery had pumped 11,500 round into Japanese positions, and under cover of this fire bulldozers had cleared a precipitous track to the tennis court, up which engineers now winched a Lee-Grant tank. At dawn on 13th May it rolled forward to the edge of a terrace overlooking the tennis court, and hurtled down an almost sheer slope. Miraculously the tank landed upright in the middle of the court, its crew shaken but uninjured. The gunner traversed the turret and fired at point-blank range through the weapons slits in the Japanese bunkers. Then 2nd Battalion Dorsetshire Regiment charged forward, and within minutes the last Japanese position on Kohima Ridge was in British hands.

Meanwhile, a much larger battle was raging around besieged Imphal. Yamauchi's 15th Division had taken Nungshigum Hill only ten miles north of Imphal on 6th April. A week later, under the cover of RAF dive-bombers, British tanks rolled up a narrow ridge in single file to Nungshigum's summit. Yamauchi had thought an armoured attack impossible, and his division had no anti-tank guns. Even so, the Japanese fought back desperately with small arms and mountain guns. The Lee-Grants and their supporting infantry pulverised the defenders, but at an enormous cost – every British officer was either killed or wounded. To the west, Yamamoto's force, reinforced by units of the Indian National Army, struck at 20th Indian Division's positions on the Shenan Saddle. The Japanese captured a key feature (which both British and Japanese were to name Nippon Hill) on 8th April. Two days later, the Gurkhas put in a counterattack and were cut to pieces. On 11th April swarms of Hurribombers and the concentrated fire of 20th Indian Division's artillery turned the once jungle-clad summit into a ploughed field. After storming up Nippon's slopes, 1st Battalion Devonshires wiped out the dazed survivors. But the following day the Japanese counterattacked and, securing the eastern side of the hill, dug in only yards from the British.

And so it went on – day after day. To the south, Yanigida's 33rd Division took Torbung and struck north to Bishenpur. Infiltrating through thick jungle, Japanese units clashed bloodily with the defenders in scores of platoon-size actions. By the end of April Yanagida's attack had broken down – the once-despised British and Indians had proved themselves the equals of the Japanese in jungle fighting. Mutaguchi's three-week offensive had turned into an attritional struggle in which the side best able to feed the battle was bound to win. This was the British. As early as 18th March SEAC

commander, Lord Louis Mountbatten, had diverted American transport aircraft from their supply operation to China, and together the USAAF and RAF flew in 18,000 tons of supplies, one million gallons of fuel and the entire 5th Indian Division from Arakan, as well as evacuating 13,000 wounded and 43,000 non-combatants. As Slim's army waxed, Mutaguchi's waned. The monsoon broke on 27th April, earlier than Japanese meteorologists had forecast, and from that time forth an already inadequate flow of supplies dwindled to a trickle. Weak with starvation and riddled with disease, nevertheless the Japanese fought on. A desperate Mutaguchi began blaming his generals for the failure – he sacked Yanagida from command of 33rd Division, but the new commander, Major General Nobuo Tanaka, could do no better. On 2nd June, two weeks after he had taken over, he confided to his diary: 'The officers and men look dreadful. They've let their hair and beards grow and look just like wild men of the mountains. More than a hundred days have passed since the operation began and in all that time there's been almost nothing to eat and there's not an ounce of fat left on any of them. They all look pale and skinny from undernourishment.'

To the north at Kohima, Sato's men were in an even worse condition. By 31st May Sato had had enough. He ignored instructions from Mutaguchi to stay put and fell back with the remnant of his division towards Imphal. The British harried them all the way. On 22nd June, the eighty-eighth day of the siege, XXXIII Corps' troops broke through the last remaining Japanese roadblock and reached Imphal. Mutaguchi tried to cling on for a few more weeks, but on 8th July he, too, broke and so began the dreadful retreat to the Chindwin. A Japanese historian has summarised what now took place: '15th Army, once released from battle, was no longer a body of soldiers, but a herd of exhausted men.' Weeks later the pathetic survivors crossed the Chindwin – they had left 65,000 dead behind. The total British and Indian casualties, 18,000, had not been light, but of these only 5,000 had been killed. Thanks to rapid aerial evacuation, the majority of the wounded would live to fight again. It could not be denied that 14th Army had won a great defensive battle – the road to the reconquest of Burma was now open.

Showing the strain of months of continuous combat a Chindit column withdraws to India in August, 1944. Slim had deep misgivings about their operation but the Chindits countered, claiming that they had held down two Japanese divisions which otherwise would have been sent to Imphal-Kohima.

# D-DAY – THE INVASION OF EUROPE

General Field Marshal Erwin Rommel with his staff inspecting the 'Atlantic Wall', the German defences against Allied invasion which stretched from the Netherlands to the Spanish border. Despite Rommel's efforts, this Wall was not complete by the time of the D-Day invasion, and was weak at the Normandy coast.

There is probably no date in the Second World War as famous as D-Day. On 6th June, 1944, the Allies returned to the continent of Europe in Operation 'Overlord', the greatest amphibious invasion ever mounted – 156,000 American, British and Canadian troops went ashore in twenty-four hours, the precursors of an army of over two million men. It was the decisive moment for which both the Allies and the Germans had long prepared. The man entrusted by Adolf Hitler with stopping the invasion, Field Marshal Erwin Rommel, believed that his only hope of success was to defeat the Allies on the beaches on D-Day itself. As early as April, Rommel observed, in a phrase that became history, that 'for the Allies, as well as for Germany, it will be the longest day'.

Rommel's command of Army Group B consisted of 15th Army, defending the Pas de Calais and Belgium, and 7th Army under Colonel General Friedrich Dollmann, defending Normandy and Brittany. Rommel had direct access to Hitler over the head of his immediate superior, Field Marshal Gerd von Rundstedt

commanding OB West, but Hitler gave neither of them complete control over his crucial reserve of armoured divisions in France, *Panzergruppe West*. Rommel wanted this armour as close to the beaches as possible, while von Rundstedt wanted it held back to counterattack the Allies as they came inland. The result was a compromise which pleased neither. Yet Hitler, von Rundstedt and Rommel all believed the Pas de Calais area to be the probable invasion site, a belief encouraged by the Allies with their deception plan, Operation 'Fortitude', which created the illusion of strong American forces in southeast England opposite the German 15th Army.

The Allied Supreme Commander for Operation 'Overlord' was General Dwight D. Eisenhower, whose staff at SHAEF (Supreme Headquarters Allied Expeditionary Force) devised the landing plan for D-Day. Since not all the Allied troops could land at once, however, the commander for the invasion was General Bernard Montgomery, commanding 21st Army Group (U.S. 1st Army and British 2nd

Army). This was the first time in history that a defended coastal position like the German Atlantic Wall had been stormed from the seaward side, and in order to succeed, the Allies needed both air superiority over northern France, which had been achieved by D-Day, and the element of surprise, which they obtained through Operation 'Fortitude' and through attacking in bad weather. They were so successful that, although the Germans received some warnings of the invasion, on D-Day itself both Rommel and Dollmann were away from their headquarters.

The first American and British paratroopers landed in Normandy at about 12.20am on D-Day. Montgomery had elected to assault on a five-division front along the sandy, shelving beaches of the Normandy resorts, from the base of the Cotentin peninsula eastwards to the regional capital of Caen and the River Orne. The Americans took the two western landing beaches, codenamed 'Utah' and 'Omaha', and the British and Canadians the eastern beaches, codenamed 'Gold', 'Juno' and 'Sword'. To secure the flanks of these landings, the American 82nd Airborne Division and 101st Airborne Division were dropped inland west of 'Utah' Beach, and British 6th Airborne Division east of the River Orne, capturing the vital river crossings. The surprise of mounting a parachute assault by night was offset by the wild scattering of all three divisions in the dark, contributing to their 3,000 casualties.

The invasion area was defended by German 7th Army's LXXXIV *Panzer Korps* under General Erich Marcks, with 709th Static Division opposite the American landing beaches and 716th Static Division opposite the British beaches. These static divisions had no transport, were weak in numbers and of poor fighting quality. The Allies had, however, failed to locate the veteran 352nd Division opposite 'Omaha'

**General Montgomery ashore from an amphibious DUKW craft in Normandy on D-Day Plus One, 7th June, to set up his 21st Army Group headquarters. Although responsible for the planning beforehand, Montgomery, like all senior commanders, had little direct role in the events of D-Day.**

Operation 'Overlord'. Going ashore on D-Day from the sea were 57,500 American and over 75,000 British and Canadian troops, plus 900 armoured vehicles and 600 guns. Omaha Beach met with the stiffest opposition - nearly 4,000 men were casualties there by the end of the 'longest day'.

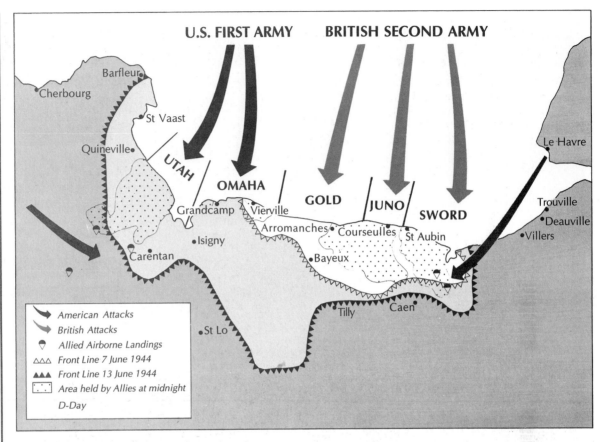

**U.S. FIRST ARMY**

**BRITISH SECOND ARMY**

Barfleur

Cherbourg

St Vaast

Quineville

Le Havre

UTAH

OMAHA

GOLD

JUNO

SWORD

Trouville

Grandcamp · Vierville

Arromanches · Courseulles · St Aubin

Deauville

Villers

Isigny

Bayeux

Carentan

Tilly    Caen

St Lo

↘ American Attacks
↘ British Attacks
⛟ Allied Airborne Landings
△△△ Front Line 7 June 1944
▲▲▲ Front Line 13 June 1944
▢ Area held by Allies at midnight D-Day

Beach and 21st *Panzerdivision*, part of the German armoured reserve, just south of Caen itself. By 2.15am 7th Army was on the alert, ready for the invasion.

At about 3.00am, as the parachutists were securing their objectives, the first of the Allied warships began to arrive off the Normandy coast. About 2,000 medium and heavy bombers joined with battleships, cruisers, and lighter vessels in a bombardment of the German positions. Before dawn, at 5.00am, von Rundstedt's headquarters ordered two armoured divisions held in reserve near Paris, 12th *SS Panzer* and *Panzer 'Lehr'*, towards Normandy, and sent a formal request to Hitler's headquarters at Berchtesgaden in southern Bavaria for their release. However, no-one was willing to wake Hitler with the still-confused news of the fighting, and the order to move the divisions was revoked until 4.00pm. Both divisions lost heavily to Allied ground-attack aircraft in moving up, and neither reached the battlefields before the end of D-Day. Rommel, also in southern Germany, was not told of the invasion until about 10.15am. Driving flat out, the

German commander reached Army Group B headquarters that evening.

U.S. 1st Army opted to land an hour before the British, taking advantage of the higher tide. At 6.30am, with supporting fire from the ships out to sea, the first American troops reached their beaches. The assault was made by three specially trained Regimental Combat Teams, or RCTs, each made up of a regiment of three battalions of infantry, plus supporting armour, artillery and engineers, and which amounted to no more than 9,000 men in total. The rough weather chosen for the assault meant that tides were higher and beaches narrower than had been expected. Landing craft and amphibious tanks were swamped in the two-hour trip from the Allied ships to the shore. At 'Utah', 8th Regimental Combat Team of 4th Division landed almost quietly to discover that, in the confusion, it had come ashore on the wrong beach, about 2,000 yards south of where it should have been and away from the main German defences. Rather than move position, the landing force linked up with the paratroopers inland and waited while the rest

Facing page: an American paratrooper of 82nd Airborne Division resting beside the signpost of Saint Mere-Eglise, scene for his division of some of the strongest resistance during the night airborne assault at the start of the D-Day invasion. The village was eventually captured by the Americans after heavy fighting.

Below: American troops of 1st Infantry Division in their landing craft approaching 'Omaha' Beach on the morning of D-Day. The line of the 'Omaha' bluff can be seen rising up from the beach, already under fire from naval support gunnery out at sea.

of the Division arrived. Meanwhile, east of 'Utah' across the estuary of the River Vire, men of 2nd U.S. Rangers scaled sheer cliffs at Pointe du Hoc in order to capture a crucial German battery. This bold exploit became an anticlimax when the battery turned out to have no mounted guns.

The force allotted to 'Omaha' Beach was 16th RCT of 1st Division – the famous 'Big Red One' division – and 116th RCT of 29th Division, under 1st Division command for the assault. Almost from the start, this landing went wrong. Of the thirty-two amphibious tanks launched in support of 16th RCT, only two reached the beach, the rest being swamped in rough seas. Underwater obstacles, concealed by the high tide, ripped the bottoms out of landing craft. Once ashore, the Americans were confronted with a high bluff dominating the beach about 2,000 yards inland, fiercely held by the unexpected 352nd Division. Within minutes of landing, the two RCTs were pinned down and taking heavy casualties. It took the whole day for 1st Division and 29th Division to fight their way off the beaches and onto the bluff, leaving 2,500 casualties behind them on 'Bloody Omaha'. Apart from the airborne divisions, total American casualties for the day were about 4,000 men.

The British landings began at 7.25am, subjecting the defenders to an extra hour's bombardment from the warships. Like the Americans, British 2nd Army based its assaulting forces on units of three battalions, but under the British system these came from different regiments and combined into brigades, not regiments. The addition of engineers,

amphibious tanks and artillery made these into brigade groups, of which the British supplied three and the Canadians two. Wide use was made of the 'funnies', specially designed armoured assault vehicles supplied by 79th Armoured Division. In addition, two brigades of Commandos also came ashore with the first wave.

In the centre at 'Gold' Beach, the landing force was 231st Brigade Group and 69th Brigade Group of 50th (Northumbrian) Division, attacking with two battalions leading and one in support. The westernmost edge of the British landing overlapped with 352nd Division's easternmost defences, and like the Americans on 'Omaha', 231st Brigade Group took the rest of the day to chop its way through. In the centre, though, the British and Canadians were facing only 716th Static Division, which could not hold them. The landing of 7th Brigade Group and 8th Brigade Group of 3rd Canadian Division on 'Juno' Beach at 7.35am made steady progress inland and secured its D-Day objectives by mid-morning. Late in the day the first elements of 51st (Highland) Division and 7th Armoured Division ('The Desert Rats') were able to land in Normandy.

The most ambitious of the D-Day objectives was given to 8th Brigade Group of British 3rd Division on 'Sword' Beach, opposite the city of Caen itself. With 1st Special Service (Commando) Brigade covering its flank and linking up with 6th Airborne Division, this force of about 3,000 men was to spearhead the advance ten miles inland and secure the whole of Caen within the first day, to prevent the Germans using the city as a defensive strongpoint. Like the Americans at 'Omaha,' nothing went right for the British at 'Sword'. Unsupported infantry could not overcome the German strongpoints, while the narrow beaches and wild seas delayed or prevented the landing of heavier equipment. When they did manage to advance, 3rd Division ran into the arriving tanks and infantry of 21st *Panzerdivision*, and could make no further progress. On the credit side, they also stopped the crucial attempt by the German armour late in the day to drive them back to the beaches. On 'Gold', 'Juno' and 'Sword', the British and Canadians suffered about 3,500 casualties, bringing the Allied total to about 10,000. Under the battering that they had

**Facing page top left:** American troops descending a scrambling net into a landing craft. In the heavy seas off Normandy the trip from ship to shore in the landing craft could take as long as three hours, and many troops drowned when their crafts were swamped or hit underwater obstacles.

**Facing page top right:** British troops of 3rd Division coming ashore on Sword Beach early on D-Day. The soldiers in the foreground are members of the Beach Party, a specialist group set up to control movement and landing on the beach, which is still under fire from German troops.

**Facing page bottom:** men of 3rd Canadian Division coming ashore at 'Juno' Beach, at the holiday resort of Besnieres, during the late morning of D-Day. The very narrow strips of beach, due to the high tide resulting from bad weather, caused considerable landing problems for all the Allies. As the day drew on and the beaches were secured, more Allied troops were able to land unhindered.

**Right:** Allied air superiority ensured that German armour and transport was destroyed as soon as it appeared on the roads.

received, 709th Static Division, 716th Static Division and 352nd Division were reduced to almost battalion strength, although as the day ended, 91st Air-Landing Division arrived from the West to support them. Estimates of German losses reach as high as 9,000 men.

Inevitably, more thought had been spent by the Allies on making their landings a success than on deciding what was to happen afterwards. On 7th June, Montgomery came ashore from his floating headquarters to take command of the land battle. All five beaches were securely held, and the Germans had lost their first chance to push the Allies back into the sea. The crucial 'longest day' was over and won by the Allies. It would take until 12th June, however, before the five beaches were linked together into a defensive perimeter. In this period the Germans came to realise the impossibility of conducting offensive operations in the face of Allied air power and artillery, including the warships still out at sea. The longer the fighting in Normandy lasted, the more Rommel's assessment that the Germans' only chance was to win in the first twenty-four hours appeared correct.

Also on 7th June the first elements of 12th *SS Panzerdivision* joined 21st *Panzerdivision* in front of Caen. Although the British and Canadians held off the German armour's attempts to break through to the beaches, the presence of these powerful armoured divisions ruled out the early capture of the city. Instead, Montgomery played brilliantly on the German fears for Caen by threatening to envelop it with his British forces, pulling more and more of the German armour towards Caen and away from U.S. 1st Army. The city finally fell to the Canadians on 18th July. On the previous day, Rommel was wounded when attacked in his staff car by an Allied fighter-bomber, and relieved of command of Army Group B. On 25th July, U.S. 1st Army broke through the weak German forces opposing it, and moved out of Normandy towards the interior of France. Exactly a month later, on 25th August, Army Group B had been wiped out and Paris was liberated by the Allies. With most of France recaptured and the Germans in full retreat, the end of the war was, for the first time, clearly in sight.

# THE BATTLE OF THE PHILIPPINE SEA

In August 1944, President Roosevelt met his two Pacific commanders in chief, General Douglas MacArthur and Admiral Chester W. Nimitz, aboard a U.S. cruiser in Pearl Harbo, to discuss the next steps in the war in the Pacific.

One of the biggest developments in warfare at sea during the Second World War was this use of amphibious forces for island hopping.

World War I had been almost entirely a matter of giant armies fighting it out on land. Apart from the original Battle of the Atlantic and one major naval engagement, Jutland, all the conclusive fighting between 1914 and 1918 took place on the continent of Europe.

By the Second World War the situation had completely changed. The Allies had to fight their way back onto that very continent. They also had to defeat the Japanese in fighting for hundreds of islands scattered across the whole length and breadth of the Pacific Ocean.

In the course of doing so, they had to develop a new dimension of sea warfare: the amphibious assault. This required almost a new science of warfare, with skills and techniques all of its own.

The Japanese, in their successful sweep through the southwest Pacific, never needed to develop such techniques. Instead, they specialised in landing small parties from destroyers and cruisers. These parties would then make their way through generally undefended jungle and attack where least expected. The Germans, however, were never to launch Operation 'Sealion', their planned cross-Channel invasion of Britain, and their attack on Crete relied heavily on parachute troops and command of the air. Amphibious

**A Japanese aircraft is hit on 10 October, 1944. It was later sunk. As the War moved northwards towards Japan, carrier-borne aircraft from Admiral Halsey's Third Fleet began removing the remnants of Japanese shipping from the Pacific.**

warfare needed new types of vessel, new types of forces.

Once again, it was American production methods that held the key to success. Over three years, the U.S.A. produced 45,000 vessels of varying design, and 56,000 amphibious vehicles. The Allies found new specialists to man the landing craft and to build and maintain the beachheads that had to serve as ports.

The British used mainly Royal Marines and 'hostilities only' sailors from the Royal Naval Volunteer Reserve for their landing craft. The Americans relied on the U.S. Marines, who were traditionally responsible for amphibious operations. Added to these, however, were many Navy men, Coast Guards, and Army engineers, to create a fully integrated force.

The British had had some limited experience in amphibious assault both raiding against the Lofoten Islands and Vaagso in 1941, and in the attack on Dieppe in 1942. The North African landings of Operation Torch, though this was anything but a copybook exercise, gave the Allies further experience, as did the landings in Sicily and Italy.

However, it would be in the Pacific, from 1942, that the real art of amphibious warfare would be developed. After Guadalcanal, there were American assaults in support of the Australians fighting in New Guinea. The Americans would progress up the Solomons, into the Bismarck Archipelago and New Britain, and thence on to Guam, the Philippines, Iwo Jima and Okinawa.

Hindsight enables historians to discern patterns and make judgements that are not always so obvious at the time. Most historians appear to agree that the U.S. seemed almost to be fighting two separate campaigns in the

**Top left:** an aerial view of Iwo Jima gives an idea of the minute size of the island, despite which it saw some of the fiercest fighting of the Pacific war. The American invasion armada can be seen offshore.

**Bottom left:** rockets from a U.S. rocket ship hurtle towards the Japanese defences. Okinawa suffered some of the fiercest pre-invasion bombardment of any island during the Pacific war.

**Right:** 16-inch shells from a U.S. battleship can be clearly seen in the top left-hand corner of the picture as they are fired towards Okinawa.

Pacific: the Army game and the Navy game.

Each campaign involved amphibious warfare and inter-service cooperation, but the overall strategies were not always as well coordinated as they should have been. Whether this resulted from the absence of one overall supreme commander or from the singularly strong personality of General MacArthur will probably never be satisfactorily resolved.

In his drive from the southwest into the central Pacific, MacArthur appeared to see things differently from those planning the Navy game to the north. There were occasions when his promise to the Philippines: 'I will return', seemed to take precedence over the main strategy of defeating Japan and occupying Tokyo.

It seems cruel perhaps to leapfrog quickly over the thirty months of bitter fighting that took place between the battles of Guadalcanal and Iwo Jima. The names of the islands that saw action during this period will for ever be imprinted upon the American consciousness, but, American success in mastering the practice of amphibious warfare meant that, after Guadalcanal, nobody doubted that each successive landing would succeed. These landings included Tarawa in the Gilbert Islands in 1943, Eniwetok in the Marshalls and Saipan in the Marianas in 1944, the Philippines from October 1944 onwards, and then Iwo Jima and Okinawa in 1945.

From the navy's point of view, its involvement did not differ greatly from island to island. The U.S. Task Forces had to prevent the Japanese interfering with the troop landings, and ensure the safe arrival of supplies and reinforcements. They carried out preliminary bombardments, and were often involved later in providing close supporting fire. They also had to intercept any attempt by the Japanese to send reinforcements to their own island garrisons and, where possible, prevent supplies getting through.

Admiral William F. Halsey was another naval officer who qualified as an aviator. From early 1942, he was involved in almost every action in the Pacific that included aircraft carriers, and he was in command of the American force that won the Battle of Cape Engano on 25 October, 1944. He later commanded the Third Fleet at Okinawa, and in attacks on Japan itself.

A fleet of U.S. aircraft carriers at sea in 1945.

In this latter task the U.S. forces were greatly helped by the way in which their submarines had come to dominate the waters of the Pacific. A good example of this came in the southwest Pacific in April/May 1944. The Japanese were trying to run a convoy of reinforcements to positions in the Halmahera islands of the Dutch East Indies.

A convoy carrying 20,000 Japanese troops left Shanghai in China, travelling through Philippine waters towards Halmahera. On 26 April, 1944 the USS *Jack* sank the transport *Yoshida Maru* off Manila Bay. Ten days later three more ships fell to the USS *Gurnard*. Nearly half that force of 20,000 men never arrived.

What the island battles *did* prove was that the Japanese would not surrender. Most of their garrisons died fighting, and only miniscule numbers were prepared to become prisoners of war. At Kwajelein Atoll, the Americans lost

372 dead and, 1,582 wounded. Of the Japanese garrison of 8,675, only 265 surrendered. Similarly, Eniwetok cost the Americans 195 dead, and 521 wounded but of the 3,431 strong Japanese garrison, only sixty-four surrendered.

Figures such as these made it clear that the more islands that could safely be bypassed the better. They also confirmed that the final invasion of Japan would be just as costly as the planners had feared.

Before passing on to the only significant naval battle before the Battles of the Leyte Gulf, it is perhaps appropriate to pay tribute to those who manned the landing craft in these island landings. Their key contribution should never be dismissed lightly. A good analysis of the craft used and their development during the War is contained in *Assault from the Sea* by J.W. Land. From the merchant seamen aboard

An aerial view of an assembled task force. At least one example of just about every vessel in front-line service in the U.S. Navy at the time is included somewhere.

an LSS (Landing Ship, Stern-chute) to the men who manned an LBK (Landing Barge, Kitchen), we should remember the crews who were the heart of each operation's success, and the men who sailed the first waves of assault craft onto the beach.

British craft were generally manned by a coxswain, a gunner/bowman, and a mechanic/engine-man who would also help with ropes at the rear of the craft. They were at the 'sharp end' of each and every amphibious operation in Europe, and suffered casualties accordingly. They and their American brethren in the Pacific deserve greater attention in books about naval warfare than they have on the whole been accorded to date.

A naval battle that illustrates the new role the submarine played in the Pacific is the Battle of the Philippine Sea, 19/21 June, 1944. To support the Marianas operation some nineteen American submarines were placed

in position off Formosa, the Philippines and the Marianas. Another nine submarines from the U.S. Seventh Fleet provided reinforcements.

No sooner had the Japanese begun preparing their fleet for action than the submarines began to take their toll. The USS *Harder* sank the destroyers *Minatsuki, Hayanami* and *Tanikaze* off Tawi-Tawi. As the very strong Japanese force moved off, it was reported by one U.S. submarine; then, as the carriers went through the San Bernardino Strait, they were reported by another; and the presence of battleships east of Mindanao was reported by yet another submarine.

These warnings gave Admiral Spruance time to assemble the full body of Task Force 58 west of the Marianas to cover the American landing operations. Spruance faced a main force, under Vice Admiral Takao Kurita, of four Japanese battleships, three carriers, five cruisers and eight destroyers; and two separate carrier forces:

**The apparently haphazard formation of an assembled task force.**

Carrier Force 'A', under Vice Admiral Jisaburo Ozawa, had the brand-new *Taiho*, the sturdy faithfuls *Shokaku* and *Zuikaku*; three cruisers and six destroyers; Carrier Force 'B', under Rear Admiral Joshima, had three more aircraft carriers, the *Junyo*, the *Hiyo* and the *Ryuho*, plus a battleship, cruisers and destroyers.

The Japanese located various elements of TF58, and, on the morning of 19th June, 1944, sent off 372 aircraft in four waves. The advance warning given by the submarines and the American advantage of radar, however, allowed their fighters to intercept quickly. Supported by anti-aircraft fire from the U.S. battleships and their escorts, the fighters enjoyed the greatest air victory of the War. It came to be known as 'The Great Marianas Turkey Shoot'.

242 of the Japanese aircraft were shot down. Others were destroyed when they landed on Guam to refuel. Although they scored a hit on the USS *South Dakota*, none of the strikes really threatened the U.S. aircraft carriers.

Meanwhile, the U.S. submarine *Albacore* torpedoed the aircraft carrier *Taiho*, which later exploded and sank, taking three quarters of her crew with her. In her turn the USS *Cavalla* torpedoed and sank the *Shokaku*. Next day, American aircraft caught the Japanese refuelling, and a third carrier, the *Hiyo*, was sunk, together with two tankers. Three further carriers, including the *Zuikaku*, and a battleship were damaged.

Twenty U.S. aircraft were lost. However, despite the carriers turning on their lights, the main American losses came when their planes returned. Seventy-two were lost in crashes on deck or had to crash-land in the sea alongside. Out of 209 crews, 160 survived.

The Japanese withdrew and, though tempted to pursue them with his battleships, Admiral Spruance stayed to fulfil his primary task of protecting the Marianas landings. It was a great American victory, and an indication of things to come in the carrier battles that would follow in the following months.

# THE MARIANAS TURKEY SHOOT

In the air battle, a form of warfare unique to the 20th century, success or failure has always been dependent upon the finely balanced combination of the men and machines sent into battle by the antagonists. The balance has seldom been simply a matter of weight of numbers, but of a combination of the expertise of the men and the technical superiority of the machines. A single factor has often been sufficient to swing the balance, when in all other respects the two sides have been equal. In World War I such an event was the introduction of guns synchronised to fire through the arc of the propeller.

At the time of Pearl Harbor the Japanese had the ascendancy over America because their airmen had the advantage of experience in their war with the Chinese, whilst the American

airmen were untried in combat. Also the American air forces were surprised by the capabilities of the Japanese aircraft. The American pilots, in their P.40s, and with no combat experience, were no match for the seasoned Japanese in their A6Ms, the redoubtable Zeros.

By 1944 the balance had swung the other way. The Japanese expansion through the Pacific and Indian Oceans had been extravagant in its wastage of aircraft and aircrews, while America had been learning from experience. The United States Navy Air Force now had a wealth of experienced aircrew, and aircraft which were well tried and at least a match for the latest version of the Zero. The majority of the Japanese aircrews were novice replacements.

From an all-time low after Pearl Harbor, the U.S. Navy's strength in the Pacific increased steadily. Two aircraft carriers, one an Independence Class, and one an Essex Class, both their decks crammed with aircraft, lead a Task Force unit of the Third Fleet.

In 1941 the Japanese had both experienced pilots and superior aircraft. However, by 1944 most of the Japanese veterans had been lost, and their aircraft outclassed. The novice Japanese fighter pilots fell in waves, so that any of the land-based bombers which tried to attack were unescorted and vulnerable.

America was anxious to begin B-29 raids on the Japanese homeland. As they progressively recaptured the Pacific islands, they decided to bypass Truk and the Carolines, and leap forward to the Marianas, from where they would be able to begin those operations. At the same time, the Japanese had devised a plan to lure the American Fleet into the area of the Carolines, where it would be trapped between their fleet and their shore-based aircraft. The scene was set for a showdown.

The overall command of the American plan was in the hands of Admiral Raymond Spruance, commanding the US Fifth Fleet. The Fifth Fleet was the largest and most powerful fleet in naval history, and depended heavily on the use of air power. Here the aircraft carrier had already become the capital ship of the 20th century. The fleet's striking force was Task Force 58, commanded by Rear Admiral Marc Mitscher.

Mitscher's force was divided into five elements. Task Groups 58.1 to 58.4 were carrier task groups with up to two fleet carriers and two light carriers each, and Task Group 58.7 was based around a group of seven fast battleships. The elements of TF. 58 could be used either as a unified Task Force, or as separate entities, allowing for groups to be detached to refuel and replenish without interrupting operations.

On June 11, 1944, TF 58 began to wear down the defences of the Marianas, in preparation for the landings. Their four Carrier Task Groups carried over 450 Hellcat fighters, and large formations of these were despatched over the islands to draw the Japanese aircraft into combat. By the end of the day they had destroyed 80 aircraft in combat and a further 30 on the ground. Their own losses had been only 21 Hellcats. By June 15 TF 58 had achieved sufficient air supremacy to launch the invasion, and 140,000 troops were landed by the Fifth Fleet on the islands of Saipan and Guam.

On the same day the Japanese main fleet sailed from the Suli Archipelago and joined up with the Mobile Fleet, under Vice Admiral Jisaburo Ozawa. Ozawa detached a force, under Vice-Admiral Kurita, with three light carriers, four battleships, five cruisers and eight destroyers. This fleet was the bait which, it was

Left: a Grumman Avenger torpedo bomber on the flight deck of the USS *Lexington*. The Avenger had entered service in 1942 and by June 1944 it had an established reputation with both the U.S. Navy and the Fleet Air Arm of the British Navy.

The anti-aircraft gunners (below left) of the Third Fleet had learned to give a good account of themselves by the last year of the war. Any bomber that broke through the screen of defensive fighters still had the Fleet's barrage to contend with.

The men on board the USS *Birmingham* (right) have not bothered to don their steel helmets, as they watch their fighter pilots have a field day 30,000 feet above, turning the sky into a reproduction of the skies over London four years earlier.

Below right: almost obscured by smoke and flame, a Japanese 'Betty' sinks off Saipan. This was one of fourteen Japanese planes brought down by anti-aircraft fire during the battle.

Left: a striking picture of a Helldiver (SB2C) peeling off to come in for a landing on its carrier's flight deck.

Below left: the Grumman Hellcat became the mainstay of the carrier-based fighters in the Pacific, beginning to replace the Wildcat during 1943. The *Essex* and the *Independence* were the first two carriers to embark the Hellcat.

Landing accidents on the carriers were often spectacular. A damaged and weakened Hellcat (below far right) has been ripped apart as its hook engaged the arrester wire. The pilot is being rescued from his cockpit, and the wreckage bulldozed over the side before the next aircraft can come home to roost.

One Helldiver (below right, top and bottom) has missed the arrester wires altogether, and has been brought to a halt by the wire barrier. The whirling propeller hurls splinters of wood from the flight deck and, as the engine is wrenched from its mountings, the broken fuel lines spray burning fuel back over the cockpits.

hoped, would lure the Americans within range of the main fleet, poised 100 miles behind it.

The two fleets jockeyed for position, and tried to keep track of the enemy force's movements. TF 58 made some use of reconnaissance aircraft, but relied mainly on reports from submarines and the direction finders at Pearl Harbor. These reports suggested that the Japanese were about 400 miles west-southwest of where TF 58 lay, off the Marianas. Mitscher wished to steam in that direction, to be better placed for an attack, but Spruance decided that his primary function was to protect the landings at Saipan and Guam, so they did not fall into the Japanese trap.

Early in the morning of June 19, Ozawa began flying off search aircraft, and by 8.30 a.m. he had enough information to launch his first strike. By 10 a.m. he had launched three strikes, totalling over 250 aircraft, of which about half were Zeros. The radar on board the American ships detected the approach of the strikes at 150 miles range, giving them plenty of time to get their fighters into the air. Most of the Hellcat pilots had been with the fleet for two years or more and were experienced veterans;

the majority of the Japanese were new to combat and proved to be no opposition for the TF 58 men. At debriefing one of them remarked, 'It's as easy as shooting turkeys.' The idea stuck. The battle became known as 'The Great Marianas Turkey Shoot'.

Those Japanese aircraft not shot down over the fleet went on to land at Guam or Tinian, in the Marianas, to refuel to return to their ships. TF 58's aircraft, patrolling over the islands, caught them as they were landing. Ozawa lost 218 aircraft, and finished the day with no more than 100 serviceable aircraft at his disposal. He had also had other problems while his strike aircraft had been away. The Japanese fleet had been attacked by submarines, which had sunk two of his carrier, including the *Taiho*, his flagship. He had been obliged to transfer his flag to the cruiser *Haguro*.

Returning to their carriers, the Japanese pilots made exaggerated claims of their successes, which left Ozawa with a picture more optimistic than the situation justified. He therefore hoped that he might still achieve a victory, and remained within reach of the

American fleet. He was found by Mitscher's searching aircraft the following afternoon. There would not be time to launch a strike and recover the aircraft before darkness fell over the carriers, but Mitscher was not prepared to risk losing his quarry. Over 200 aircraft were launched. A mixture of Hellcats, Helldivers and torpedo-carrying Avengers. Without the means to fight them off, Ozawa lost one of his remaining carriers and two of his refuellers. Two other carriers were severely damaged.

It was getting on for midnight before the strike returned to the fleet. Mitscher decided to take the risk of his fleet being within sight of any prowling Japanese craft, and ordered the whole fleet to light up. This enabled many of the aircraft to get down safely, but eighty or more of them either put down in the sea, or were destroyed in landing accidents. Thirteen aircrew were lost in landing or ditching.

At last Ozawa was convinced that he was beaten, and withdrew towards Okinawa.

The last great carrier battle of World War II was over.

**Damage control and fire fighting were vital on a carrier, where thousands of gallons of aviation fuel were carried in tanks beneath the flight deck. Whether a fire was caused by enemy action or by a crashing plane, it had to be controlled at once.**

# BAGRATION – SOVIET SLEDGEHAMMER

**Rescued! A child is lifted out of her underground hiding place by Soviet troops who have just liberated her hometown. The sufferings of the Soviet civilian population during the war were immense. Regarded as sub-human by the Nazis, many were sent to Germany as slave labour.**

At the end of June, 1944, the attention of both Hitler and the West was focused on Normandy. On the Eastern Front, however, the Red Army was preparing to launch Operation 'Bagration', an offensive that dwarfed that of Montgomery's 21st Army Group in France. Four Soviet Fronts (army groups), totalling 1.2 million men organised into 166 divisions, with 5,200 tanks and self-propelled guns and 6,000 aircraft were to attack on a 450-mile front. In the event, Soviet forces smashed through the German Army Group Centre, commanded by Field Marshal Ernst von Busch, and all but destroyed it. It was the greatest *Blitzkrieg* in history.

The Soviets began planning for Operation 'Bagration' in April, 1944. Stalin personally chose the name of the operation to liberate Belorussia – Bagration was one of the Russian generals of the War of 1812 against Napoleon. In line with their concept of 'operational art', *Stavka* (the Soviet High Command) saw the struggle against Germany as one huge campaign. The first six months of 1944 had already seen the Red Army win significant victories. In the north, the siege of Leningrad was raised in January; in the south, an offensive in the Ukraine had

ruptured the front of Army Group South in February and by the end of April the Soviets had cleared the Crimean peninsula and were rolling across the frontier into Germany's increasingly half-hearted ally, Roumania. Belorussia was chosen as the site of the next Soviet offensive, in part because it would have been dangerous to begin the advance from the Ukraine into the Balkans with Army Group Centre poised to fall across the Soviet lines of communication.

The objective of the Soviet forces was a German salient which protruded into Soviet-held territory. Busch's forces had a perimeter of some 650 miles to defend. The core of Army Group Centre's resistance was located in four areas, at Vitebsk, Orsha, Mogilev and Bobruysk. Once these positions had been eliminated, it was believed that the German defensive crust would have been broken, and the rest of the Army Group Centre could be destroyed at the Red Army's leisure. Six axes of advance were to be used. General Bagramyan's 1st Baltic Front was to attack north of Vitebsk against Reinhardt's 3rd *Panzerarmee*, and in co-operation with the northern portion of

Left: German troops manhandle munition carts bogged down in the Don Delta. The Russian climate was one of the principal problems facing German troops on the Eastern Front. Frequently, wheeled motor vehicles were unusable, and Russian horse drawn *panje* wagons or human muscle power had to be used instead.

Facing page top: Red Army artillery and tanks cross a river during the advance towards Lvov. The scale of the Soviet victory in Belorussia in the summer of 1944 is frequently underestimated by Westerners, who usually pay more attention to the Anglo-American offensive in France during the same period.

Facing page bottom: the fruits of lend-lease: Soviet motorized infantry move up in American-built vehicles. American equipment made a vital contribution to the Soviet war effort.

Chernyakhovsky's 3rd Belorussian Front, Vitebsk was to be encircled. Bagramyan's Front was then to provide a flank guard against a southward push by Army Group North, while 3rd Belorussian Front formed the northern arm of a pincer movement on Minsk; the other part of 3rd Belorussian Front was to also to drive north of Minsk, via Orcha. Zakharov's 2nd Belorussian Front was to move through Mogilev and launch a frontal pinning attack on Minsk, the most important communications centre in Belorussia. Rokossovski's 1st Belorussian Front was to surround Bobruysk, and then unite with Chernyakhovsky in destroying enemy forces in the Minsk area. Further advances were planned after the huge salient was snipped off, including an advance by 1st Belorussian Front (which had a frontage of no less than 670 kilometres) towards the extreme southwestern corner of the salient, towards Kovel, Lublin and ultimately Warsaw.

By early June, 1944, Busch was becoming increasingly disturbed by the evidence that clearly pointed towards a major enemy offensive in Belorussia. However, the Soviets had put into execution a highly successful programme of *maskirovka* – a term which literally means 'masking' and encompasses diversionary and deceptive moves – and, as a result, the Germans failed to detect the presence of three entire armies with 3rd Belorussian Front before the day of the assault. The principal victims of the *maskirovka* programme were Adolf Hitler and the German High Command, who became convinced that the Soviets would strike at German forces in Roumania. Hitler's reasoning was guided by a certain amount of logic, as the Roumanian oilfields were vital to the German war economy. Hitler thus took the decision to deploy the bulk of his reserves, which included 18th *Panzer* and *Panzergrenadier* divisions, in the south. Thus, on the eve of the Soviet offensive, Army Group Centre could field only thirty-two infantry and two *Panzerdivisions* – about 700,000 men – against the Soviet hordes.

At 4.00am on 22nd June, 1944, the third anniversary of Operation 'Barbarossa', the Russian attack began. Two hours of preliminary bombardment heralded the start of the attack. The Soviets amassed overwhelming superiority of numbers in the key break-through sectors. General Chernyakhovsky's 3rd Belorussian Front had an average of no less than 178 artillery pieces per kilometre in their attack sectors and 142nd Rifle Corps had the advantage of 166 aircraft sorties made against the Germans at the beginning of the attack. The Soviets also

had a still more precious asset: surprise. However, German formations, despite being desperately short of reserves, struggled to stem the Soviet advance. Even Rokossovsky, commander of 1st Belorussian Front, paid tribute to German tenaciousness in the defence: 'By eight o'clock in the morning the Nazis had recovered from the blows. The telephones at our observation post were ringing constantly: one army commander after another reported new counterattacks launched by tactical enemy reserves. A stubborn battle ensued for the first defence position. Here and there it turned into violent hand-to-hand fighting'.

The overwhelming numbers of Soviet troops, skilfully handled by their commanders, had broken the back of 3rd *Panzerarmee*'s resistance within forty-eight hours of the offensive's start. Busch, who shared Hitler's belief in positional, rather than mobile defence, refused to allow Reinhardt to abandon Vitebsk, and thus sacrificed 30,000 men in the defence of the town, which fell to the Soviets on 27th June. The news of Vitebsk's liberation resounded around the world. On 28th June President Roosevelt sent a message to Stalin conveying 'my congratulations to you personally and to your gallant army'.

Zakharov's 2nd and Chernyakhovsky's 3rd Belorussian fronts were also making excellent progress against German 4th Army based around Orcha and Mogilev. Orcha fell to 11th Guards and 31st Army on 27th June, although German 9th Army, covering Bobruysk, succeeded in slowing the advance of 3rd and 48th armies of 1st Belorussian Front north of the town. This ray of hope for the Germans

disappeared when Rokossovsky threw 9th Tank Corps into the fray. On 27th June, six German divisions were encircled at Bobruysk. Rokossovsky did not pause to eliminate the Bobruysk pocket. To pin von Vormann's 9th Army in Bobruysk until the second echelon arrived, massive airstrikes were made by 16th Air Army on the city. By 28th June two German corps had been destroyed at Mogilev; the following day, Bobruysk was taken by the Red Army. One week after 'Bagration' started, the four key bastions of the German defence had been eliminated, and Soviet forces had driven ninety-five miles into the rear of Army Group Centre.

Gradually awakening to the full extent of the catastrophe unfolding in Belorussia, Hitler replaced Busch with Field Marshal Model on 28th June. Hitler accompanied this command change with the issue of Operational 'Order 8', which gave unrealistic orders to continue with static defence. Meanwhile, *Stavka* attempted to capitalise on their victories by using 2nd Belorussian Front and elements of 1st and 3rd Belorussian fronts to achieve a massive encirclement in the area of Minsk. On 3rd July, 5th Guards Tank, 11th Guards and 31st Army captured the ancient city. Five corps of 4th and 9th German armies were caught in a pocket east of Minsk and 33rd, 50th and 49th Soviet armies moved in to annihilate them. Although elements of 9th Army did break out, some 35,000 Germans surrendered on 12th July.

As Army Group Centre reeled under the blows delivered in Belorussia, neighbouring German formations were also coming under pressure. To the south, the Soviets attacked on

**A Red Army scouting party creeps towards the German positions, grenades in hand. The Soviets made highly effective use of deception measures in the run-up to Operation 'Bagration', a factor which contributed substantially to their success.**

**Right: Soviet infantry advance under the covering fire of a tank. The Soviets massed their troops on selected breakthrough sectors along the length of Belorussian salient, achieving overwhelming local superiority in infantry, armour, aircraft and artillery.**

**Below: Soviet fighter aircraft of Third Belorussian Front. The figure in the foreground is Captain Mayorov, who was awarded the decoration of Hero of the Soviet Union. By the time of 'Bagration' the Soviets could field a formidable force of some 8,500 front-line aircraft.**

13th July against Army Group North Ukraine. Although the Germans fell back to a prepared position – the 'Prinz Eugen Line' – they were outflanked, and were forced to retreat to the line of the River Bug. On 18th July Soviet tanks of Koniev's 1st Ukrainian Front surrounded and then liquidated German XIII Corps at Brody, east of the great city of Lvov. Lvov itself fell nine days later. In the Baltic states, too, Soviet forces took the offensive. The Soviets completed another major encirclement at Vilna, which fell on 13th July, and by the end of the month General Schorner's Army Group North had been isolated from both Army Group Centre and East Prussia, although the Soviets delayed a full scale assault on Army Group North until later in the year. Although Hitler agreed to evacuate part of Estonia, he would have been better advised to cut his losses entirely and use the *Kriegsmarine* to evacuate Schorner's men by sea to defend the Reich itself. On 5th October the Soviets wrenched the German positions apart. Russian tanks poured through the gap, and Army Group North was pinned against the coast.

However, the main battlefield remained Belorussia, where a further stage of the operation began on 18th July. Once again, the Soviets achieved surprise when 1st Belorussian Front attacked and drove deep into German positions. By 25th July Soviet troops had reached the River Vistula, the river that runs through Warsaw. Having advanced such vast distances since June, the Soviets were beginning to outrun their supply lines, and sharp German counterattacks further limited the Soviet advance. By the end of August, as the doomed

Warsaw Uprising raged, major offensive moves had ended.

Operation 'Bagration' had destroyed most of Army Group Centre, thirty German divisions had been annihilated, and Soviet forces had moved 300 miles nearer to Germany. The Red Army had demonstrated in the most convincing way possible just how much it had learned from its mistakes in the first years of the war. The Soviet successes were not merely the product of overwhelming numbers and brute force. By

Warsaw in flames: the destruction of the Warsaw Ghetto, 1943. Similar scenes were enacted during the uprising of the Polish Home Army in the autumn of 1944. In both cases, the Nazis suppressed the insurrections with considerable savagery. In 1944, some of the worst atrocities were committed by the notorious Dirlewanger Penal Brigade.

the successful use of *maskirovka*, the Red Army had succeeded in achieving surprise on a number of levels, and had ensured that they had significant numerical superiority on the decisive axes of advance. Once they had broken into the German defences, they ruthlessly and efficiently exploited their successes, using armoured and mechanised formations to penetrate deep into the enemy rear and disrupt and disorient the German forces. Furthermore, the Soviet offensives came as a series of hammer blows; the German forces were never allowed the luxury of catching their breath. The flexibility of the Red Army stands out in sharp contrast to the rigidity of the German defenders, who were out-thought, as well as out-fought, in the summer of 1944.

There is a sad footnote to Operation 'Bagration'. As the spearheads of the Soviet 2nd Tank Army approached to within eight miles of Warsaw, the underground Polish Home Army rose to liberate their capital. Only about 30,000 of the 250,000 strong Home Army were armed. The insurrection began on 1st August. The Germans, under the command of SS

General von dem Bach-Zelewski, committed tanks, artillery and aircraft to the battle in a savage attempt to crush the uprising. The Soviets gave the insurgents little help. Most of the Home Army was anti-Communist, and it would certainly have been politically inconvenient for Stalin to contend with a large, non-communist Polish force in Warsaw; memories of the Russian invasion in 1939 were still fresh. But it is also clear that Rokossovski's 1st Belorussian Front could not have attacked Warsaw in early August because of logistic problems. It would seem that, in military terms, the Uprising was launched prematurely. However, Stalin did nothing to aid the Poles in the early, critical stages of the battle. The Soviets began to advance on 10th September, but on 2nd October Bor-Komorowski capitulated. In all, 200,000 Poles had died, including 15,000 members of the Home Army. Hitler ordered Warsaw to be razed to the ground, but there was little left to destroy. Bor-Komorowski accurately described Warsaw as an empty shell of a city, where the 'dead are buried inside the ruins or alongside them.'

# ARNHEM – THE BRIDGE TOO FAR

Operation 'Market-Garden' is launched on 17th September. Although they succeeded in capturing the bridge at Arnhem, ultimately 1st Airborne Division could not hold it against two *Waffen-SS Panzerdivisions*.

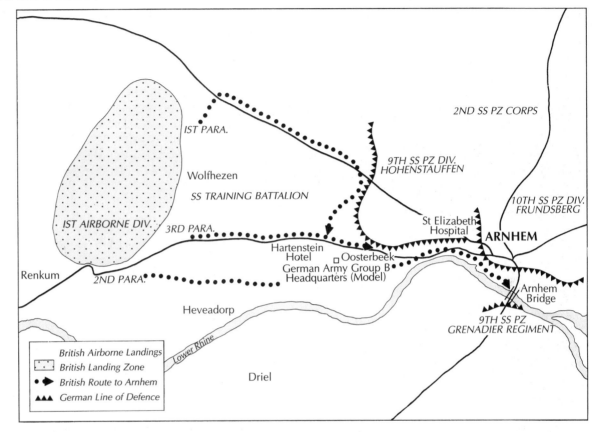

On 1st September, 1944, General Dwight D. Eisenhower, as Supreme Allied Commander, assumed direct command of the Allied land forces in Europe from General Bernard Montgomery, who reverted to the command of his own 21st Army Group and was promoted to field marshal in compensation. On that date, Montgomery's forces, together with Lieutenant General Omar Bradley's 12th Army Group and 6th Army Group under Lieutenant General Jake Devers, were driving flat out across France and the Low Countries towards the German border, with the Germans in full retreat before them. On 4th September, Adolf Hitler recalled from enforced retirement the elderly Field Marshal Gerd von Rundstedt to command all German forces on the Western Front in place of Field Marshal Walter Model, who himself reverted to command of Army Group B, covering Holland and northern Germany. The prospects for Germany were grim. After its mauling in France, Army Group B barely existed, the Western Front was wide open, and total

defeat seemed only a matter of weeks. On the day von Rundstedt was appointed, British 2nd Army under General Sir Miles Dempsey, part of Montgomery's command, liberated Brussels, and, a day later, Antwerp. After coming 250 miles in five days, the British only had to advance another sixty-five miles to the River Rhine – and the German industrial heartland of the Ruhr – to end the war.

Months before the D-Day invasion, the Allied strategy for this phase of the campaign had been agreed. Canadian, British and American armies would advance on a broad front like the outspread fingers of a hand, giving the Germans no chance to counterattack in a single thrust, and letting all share equally in the glory of victory. Yet with German garrisons still holding the Channel ports and main river estuaries, all Allied supplies were coming from Normandy alone, along an ever-lengthening supply line. Eisenhower's staff advised him that such a rate of advance could not be maintained – his three army groups were simply

running out of fuel and ammunition as they moved.

Montgomery's solution to Eisenhower's dilemma required a major change in Allied strategy. While Canadian 1st Army dealt with the Channel ports, British 2nd Army would drive on a narrow front northwards through Holland to the Rhine; U.S. 1st Army covering its flank. All other American forces would halt and give up their supplies to support this drive. Eisenhower, however, refused to change from the broad-front strategy, arguing that American public opinion would not stand for British troops under Montgomery appearing to win the war. Convinced he was right, although in danger of insubordination for his insistance, Montgomery continued to press Eisenhower on this point. Finally, on 10th September, Eisenhower compromised. Montgomery could try for a bridgehead over the Rhine, using Eisenhower's strategic reserve, 1st Allied Airborne Army, which had been sitting unused in Britain since its formation in July.

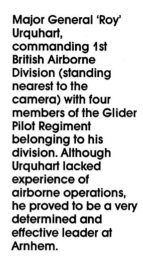

**Major General 'Roy' Urquhart, commanding 1st British Airborne Division (standing nearest to the camera) with four members of the Glider Pilot Regiment belonging to his division. Although Urquhart lacked experience of airborne operations, he proved to be a very determined and effective leader at Arnhem.**

**Below: the main road bridge over the Lower Rhine at Arnhem, the chief prize of Operation 'Market-Garden'. This view from the north shows how built-up areas ruled out any glider landing close to the bridge itself. The flat area south of the bridge was also considered unsuitable for gliders.**

British paratroopers on the ground at Arnhem, with supplies still coming in. Jeeps were flown in by glider to make ground movement easier, but a plan to seize Arnhem Bridge with a sudden dash by a special jeep squadron came to nothing when the jeeps were ambushed by German troops.

The new 1st Allied Airborne Army was commanded by the American Lieutenant General Lewis Brereton, a pilot and former commander of 9th U.S. Air Force, with the British Lieutenant General Frederick 'Boy' Browning as his deputy and ground commander. Browning also commanded 1st British Airborne Corps, consisting of 1st Airborne Division and 1st Polish Parachute Brigade (6th Airborne Division was still refitting after its role in Normandy).

Lieutenant General Matthew Ridgeway commanded XVIII U.S. Airborne Corps, consisting of 82nd and 101st airborne divisions. These forces would be dropped by air to seize key bridges behind the German lines across which Lieutenant General Brian Horrocks' British XXX Corps, led by the Guards Armoured Division, would advance. The final bridge across the Rhine at Arnhem was the target of British 1st Airborne Division under Major General 'Roy' Urquhart. According to Montgomery's plan, Urquhart's Division would hold Arnhem bridge for two days before the Guards arrived and established themselves on the north bank of the Rhine. Then, 52nd (Lowland) Division, would be flown in to improvised airstrips near Arnhem and secure the bridgehead. The plan was codenamed Operation 'Market-Garden', with 1st Allied Airborne Army as 'Market' and British 2nd Army as 'Garden'. Never before had airborne forces been used to secure a deep strategic penetration in this manner. It was a considerable risk, but Montgomery was gambling to end the war before Christmas, and Browning advised him that, if necessary, 1st Airborne Division could hold Arnhem bridge for four days instead of two.

From Eisenhower's approval to the start of 'Market-Garden' was only seven days. The airborne forces, however, were well trained and had already seen seventeen plans made and cancelled at the last minute – they were anxious to get into the war before it ended. After the experience of a night drop on D-Day, their commanders agreed to go by daylight, but not even the Allied air forces had enough transport aircraft to move three and a half divisions at once. An airborne division was two parachute regiments (brigades in the British Army) and one air-landing regiment in gliders. The two American divisions opted to use all their paratroops on the first drop, with the glider regiments joining them on the following day.

Major General Urquhart chose a single parachute brigade, plus his air-landing brigade with its heavier weapons. The only landing zone suitable for gliders turned out to be eight miles northwest of Arnhem bridge – a long walk for troops who relied on surprise for their success. The big problems for all airborne forces was their lack of armour and anti-armour weapons should they encounter tanks, and the difficulties of supply. Some intelligence reports suggested German armoured forces at Arnhem, but in the general rush and euphoria of battle these reports were not considered sufficient reason to cancel the operation.

At 2.00pm on Sunday, 17th September, all along the line of the planned XXX Corps advance, airborne soldiers jumped from their aircraft into battle and gliders skidded down onto their landing zones. Nearest to the British line, 101st Airborne began to secure the bridges in the area of Eindhoven. Fifteen minutes later, the Guards Armoured Division began its attack through the defences of German 15th Army to link up with the paratroops. In the centre, 82nd Airborne Division dropped near the town of Nijmegen, itself the site of one of the crucial

Left: British paratroopers pressing forward through the built-up areas of Arnhem, unable to reach the bridge due to the unexpected *Waffen-SS* presence. The battle brought serious destruction to the town of Arnhem, which until then had escaped the worst ravages of the war.

Right: the men who made it - members of 1st Airborne Division who swam or rowed back across the Rhine after the decision to evacuate 1st Airborne Division from Arnhem. A few have kept their famous red berets, now the international hallmark of airborne forces.

The British were surprised to find *Waffen-SS* armoured troops (below) among the first of their prisoners at Arnhem. Later it would be the turn of 1st Airborne Division's men to surrender. Treatment of prisoners on both sides was very good, each respecting the other's high fighting ability.

river bridges. Neither the Guards nor the American paratroops, however, found German resistance as light as they had expected on the flat, open heathland that characterised much of the terrain for the advance.

In just a few days, Field Marshal Model had performed miracles in putting back together formations that the Allies believed they had wiped out, and even his most improvised defence imposed a crucial delay on the Allied advance. It was also too much to hope that all the twelve bridges over the rivers and canals needed for 'Market-Garden' could be captured intact. The bridge at Son, just north of Eindhoven, was blown by the Germans just before its capture, and the main bridge at Nijmegen, in the centre of the advance, was too strongly held for the paratroops to take it. As bridging equipment and boats were rushed up behind the armoured spearhead, 'Market-Garden' began to slip badly behind schedule. None of this was known, however, at Arnhem, where Urquhart's forces had landed safely and set off for their objective – the main bridge across the Rhine in the centre of the town.

The chief reason for 1st Airborne Division's ignorance was that in the wooded, flooded and low-lying Dutch countryside, their radios would not function properly. Urquhart had no contact with higher formations, nor with his own paratroop battalions, which were being dispatched down the road to Arnhem as rapidly as possible. By mid-afternoon, frustrated at finding his Division slipping away from him, the General set off down the main route towards Arnhem to link up with his advancing men. There he found out what they had already discovered. By chance, the British Division had

dropped practically next door to Field Marshal Model's headquarters at Oosterbeek, while nearby, north of Arnhem, resting and refitting from its near destruction in Normandy, was General Wilhelm Bittrich's II *SS Panzer Korps*, comprising of two *Panzerdivisions*, 9th *SS Panzerdivision 'Hohenstauffen'* and 10th *SS Panzerdivision 'Frundsberg'*. Although well below strength, these elite armoured divisions were far too strong for airborne troops to overcome. As the German pressure increased and the radios remained uncooperative, Major General Urquhart decided to stay with 1st Parachute Brigade on the road to Arnhem. He had no control over the rest of his Division, and no indication of whether his troops had reached the bridge. He would remain out of contact with the rest of his Division for the next thirty-six hours.

In fact, a single British battalion, 2nd Battalion of 1st Parachute Brigade under Lieutenant Colonel John Frost, reached Arnhem bridge on the evening of 17th September and took up defensive positions in the houses on the northern side of the bridge. So began what Lieutenant General Ridgeway would later call 'the outstanding small unit action of the war'. Arnhem bridge, the objective an entire Division was to hold for two days against light opposition, was held by Frost's battalion – with a few more troops who also made it through to the bridge, including the division's anti-tank gunners – against the tanks and infantry of 9th *SS Panzerdivision* for three days and nights. On

the morning of Wednesday, 20th September, Frost was able to speak to Urquhart by radio, only to find that the rest of the Division was itself being surrounded by the Germans. Finally, that afternoon, Frost was himself wounded and the battalion, out of food and ammunition, was overwhelmed. To their surprise, the surviving paratroops, nearly all of them wounded, found that the *Waffen-SS* men treated them well, showing respect for an enemy that had more than lived up to their own standards of bravery. It was not until midnight that night that the first tanks of XXX Corps got across Nijmegen bridge, the last obstacle before Arnhem.

The only remaining question was whether anything could be salvaged from 'Market-Garden'. Without a good bridge, armoured troops could not cross the Rhine. The rest of Urquhart's Division had arrived at Arnhem, but its supply zones had been overrun by the *Waffen-SS*, and the entire Division was fighting at Oosterbeek with its back to the river. The Polish brigade, dropped according to plan on the south side of the Rhine, was unable to help. Although the distance from Nijmegen was less than ten miles, it was across the flattest of the Dutch heathland, in the face of increasing German opposition. It took until 22nd September for the first units of the Guards Armoured Division to reach the south bank of the Rhine, to be separated by 400 yards of river

from Urquhart's men. On the evening of 24th September Urquhart, now in radio communication with Browning's headquarters, reported that his Division was out of supplies and ammunition – it would either need to be supported or withdrawn. In the early hours of 26th September, after volunteers had agreed to stay with the wounded, the men of 1st Airborne Division, abandoning their equipment, piloted small boats or swam across the Rhine to safety. Horrocks then pulled his forces back towards Nijmegen. 'Market-Garden' was a failure.

Of 10,000 men of 1st Airborne Division and 1st Polish Parachute Brigade who fought at Arnhem, Major General Urquhart took 2,163 men back across the Rhine with him. The German casualties were 3,300 dead and wounded. The result was a fifty-mile salient into Holland leading nowhere. Montgomery's first gamble was also his only defeat in a major battle. Characteristically, he refused to admit this, calling 'Market-Garden' ninety per cent successful. Whether, if the operation had worked, Eisenhower would have agreed to Montgomery's change of strategy is a matter of speculation. As it was, the broad-front strategy continued and the Allied armies, all short of supplies, slowed their advance before the German frontier. The war would *not* be over by Christmas.

**Some who did not make it. German soldiers and British dead in the streets of Arnhem after the battle. About 8,000 British soldiers were killed or taken prisoner in the course of the battle. Some men remained in hiding for months. After Arnhem, 1st Airborne Division was not re-formed.**

# THE BATTLES OF LEYTE GULF

**A giant amphibious force steams towards the Philippines - Transports, LSTs and smaller vessels cover the water.**

Four separate battles are generally grouped together under the overall title of Leyte Gulf. These are the battles of the Sibuyan Sea, the Surigao Strait, Samar and Cape Engano.

Each was a very different engagement from the others, and each provides important lessons to be learned. Together they marked a last desperate attempt on the part of the Japanese to halt the now unstoppable American advance on their country. The Leyte battles did not end the war in the Pacific, which continued for almost a year. However, each battle, as a conclusive American victory, indicated the way fortunes were inevitably turning.

Assembled for the battles were the largest fleets either side had ever produced. The D-day armada invading Normandy probably involved slightly larger numbers, but the U.S. Third and Seventh Fleets added together formed the most powerful naval force of all time.

The invasion of the Philippines, originally planned for December 1944, was brought forward to October. The United States 6th Army would land on the eastern side of Leyte, just south of Samar. Air support was to come from land-based U.S.AAF aircraft operating from nearby islands and from the main American carrier force, a part of the U.S. Third Fleet, under Admiral W.F. Halsey. Added to this there were three task forces, consisting of six escort carriers each and forming part of the U.S. Seventh Fleet, under Vice Admiral Kinkaid. Vice Admiral Kinkaid also had a fire support and bombardment force of six battleships, three heavy cruisers, two light cruisers and sixteen destroyers.

The problem of the difference between the navy and the army approach has been mentioned elsewhere and is exemplified here. Vice Admiral Kinkaid took his orders from General MacArthur, whilst Admiral Halsey was directly responsible to Admiral Nimitz. At one stage this nearly spelled disaster. Halsey stuck to what he had been told was his overriding task, to destroy the Japanese carrier force, and

A U.S. battleship, screened by fleet destroyers, steams into position (top left) to begin a bombardment of the Japanese in the Philippines.

A close-up of battleships of the U.S. Seventh Fleet in formation (bottom left) in Lingayen Gulf prior to bombarding Luzon. Some of the ships were amongst those salvaged from Pearl Harbor.

General MacArthur returns to the Philippines. On 20 October, 1944, landings began on Leyte Island (right) and over the following three days a total of 200,000 troups came ashore.

incorrectly assumed that Kinkaid had taken precautions to stop the Japanese coming through the Surigao Strait and getting at the landing force.

However, all that came later. Air attacks and bombardments preceded the landing on 20 October and, as soon as the Japanese were sure where the U.S. attack was aimed, they began moving in their forces in strength from Brunei, in Borneo, and elsewhere. Halsey's Third Fleet was guarding the north, and Kinkaid's Seventh Fleet, in particular the escort carriers, was closely involved in the landings.

The first Japanese force under Vice Admiral Kurita was extremely strong, but had no aircraft carriers with it. It *did* have two giant battleships, the *Yamato* and the *Musashi*, three other battleships, ten heavy cruisers, two light cruisers acting as destroyer leaders, and fifteen destroyers. The Japanese southern force, under Vice Admiral Nishimura, had another two battleships, a heavy cruiser and four destroyers. The second striking force, under Vice Admiral Shima, added three cruisers and another six destroyers. The Japanese aircraft-carrier force, under Vice Admiral Ozawa, was coming down from the north with four aircraft carriers, two converted carrier/battleships, three more

cruisers and eight destroyers and destroyer escorts. There were also transport groups and supply forces. In addition there were submarines, both American and Japanese, everywhere.

First reports that the Japanese were on the move came from the submarines USS *Darter* and USS *Dace*, operating together. After sending off a sighting report, the *Darter* duly sank the cruiser *Atago*, and the *Dace* sank the *Maya*. The *Darter* torpedoed another cruiser, but ran onto a reef and was lost – though her crew were rescued by the *Dace*.

As a result of the submarines' report, Admiral Halsey brought up three of his task groups, a total of eleven carriers, five fleet and six light fleet. The fourth of his carrier task groups was attacked by Japanese planes, and the USS *Princeton* was hit and had to be abandoned. The cruiser USS *Birmingham* was also badly damaged by explosions whilst trying to help the aircraft carrier.

The Battle of the Sibuyan Sea began on 24 October when four waves of American carrier aircraft attacked the Japanese Centre Force. This was a straightforward carrier-versus-battleship battle, in which the Japanese came off badly. The *Musashi* was sunk after suffering

Left: a coast guard manned LST (Landing Ship, Tank), loaded with troops and vehicles and on its way to reinforce General MacArthur's forces on Leyte, in the Philippines.

Crowded scenes on the beach at Leyte (right) as troops, following on after the first wave of landings, unload supplies and equipment for the campaign against the Japanese occupiers of the Philippines.

some ten bomb and six torpedo hits. Most of the other battleships were hit, but none of them were put out of action. Kurita withdrew west.

The Battle of Surigao Strait began when the two other Japanese forces came in from the south, and plans were made to intercept them. Initially thirteen groups of three PT-boats each tried to interrupt their passage, and one Japanese cruiser, the *Abukuma*, was torpedoed. A series of torpedo attacks by destroyers followed, and these proved even more successful than the PT-boats. Torpedo hits were scored on the battleship *Fuso*, which later sank, together with three Japanese destroyers

What distinguished this battle from the others was that it was the last time battleships fought in classic line-of-battle style. It also demonstrated that centimetric radar now allowed those U.S. battleships equipped with it to fight a night engagement, and to do so at ranges that had never even been contemplated before.

As the remnants of Nishimura's striking force made its way up the Surigao Strait, Admiral Kinkaid gave Rear Admiral Oldendorf the order

to deploy the six battleships, the *Mississippi*, the *Maryland*, the *West Virginia*, the *Tennessee*, the *California* and the *Pennsylvania*, so that they could prevent the Japanese reaching the Leyte landings.

Protected by both a left- and a right-flank cruiser squadron, this would have been a formidable force for Nishimura to tackle with just one battleship, a cruiser and a single surviving destroyer, even if he had been expecting reinforcement from the cruisers and destroyers of the second striking force coming up behind.

So indeed it proved. First the cruisers, and then the three battleships with centimetric radar opened fire, the *West Virginia* firing her first salvo at 22,800 yards. Between them the *West Virginia*, the *Tennessee* and the *California* fired over two hundred large-calibre armour-piercing shells. Nishimura's flagship, the battleship Yamashiro took a terrible hammering, as did the heavy cruiser *Mogami*. Ablaze, the *Yamashiro*, turned away, only to be torpedoed by the destroyer USS *Smoot*. She sank in about eight minutes, taking Admiral

Nishimura and most of her crew down with her.

The second Japanese striking force, under Vice Admiral Shima, and consisting of three cruisers and seven destroyers, still intended coming to support Admiral Nishimura's force. However, there was virtually nothing left of it. The destroyer *Shigure* and the completely disabled cruiser *Mogami* were all that remained. In fact, in her eagerness, Shima's flagship cruiser, the *Nachi*, collided with *Mogami*, thereby greatly reducing her speed. The cruiser *Abukuma*, torpedoed by PT-137, would be finished off the following day by land-based U.S.AAF planes. Admiral Shima finally withdrew his much depleted force of two cruisers and four destroyers. The two-stage Battle of the Surigao Strait was over.

The Battle of Samar was very nearly an American disaster. But for some luck, and some excellent ship handling by Rear Admiral Clifton Sprague, the Battles of the Leyte Gulf might have had a different significance for us today.

The main problem was that the split command between Admiral Halsey and Vice Admiral Kinkaid had resulted in neither guarding the San Bernardino Strait against Vice Admiral Kurita's first striking force. Halsey had been told that his primary task was the destruction of the major portion of the enemy fleet, and assumed this took precedence over supporting the Seventh Fleet at Leyte.

The portion of the enemy fleet Halsey set out to destroy was the Japanese carrier force to the north, and not the still very strong surface fleet of battleships and cruisers now heading for Leyte. In a sense, Halsey fell for the very lure that Admiral Toyoda, directing the overall Japanese strategy from afar, had intended.

Halsey also thought that the first Japanese striking force had been considerably weakened by the previous day's fighting. Exaggerated air reports had claimed at least four of its battleships as 'torpedoed and bombed', with one sunk, and heavy cruiser losses.

Certainly the 70,000-ton *Musashi* had gone down, but most of the force was intact and heading through the San Barnardino Strait, which each of the two American admirals thought the other was covering. Neither was, and so the Japanese striking force headed straight for the landing area, protected only by the three task force groupings of six escort carriers each. These were slow moving, lightly armed and almost unarmoured, and were never intended for fighting a fleet action.

The three groups, nicknamed Taffy One, Two and Three from their official nomenclatures TG 77.4.1, TG 77.4.2 and TG 77.4.3, were ranged in this numerical order, from south to north. Thus it was Rear Admiral Clifton Sprague's northerly Task Force, Taffy Three, that suffered the main brunt of Kurita's attack.

One of his planes spotted the Japanese bearing down like a wolf on the fold. At 0638 hours on 25th October the 18-inch guns of the *Yamato* opened up at 37,000 yards. By this time Admiral Clifton Sprague had organised his small carrier fleet into an almost wagon-train-like circle. He got his planes airborne and called desperately for help to his fellow

commanders, Rear Admirals Felix Stump and Thomas Sprague. They too launched their planes, but were respectively sixty and 130 miles away. Rear Admiral Oldendorf's battleships were three hours sailing away.

Just when it looked as though Taffy Three would be obliterated there was a sudden rain squall, which hid the American force for a vital half-hour. It was now that Admiral Kurita, who fought the battle extremely badly, made his first mistake. He assumed that all American aircraft carriers had speeds of around 30 knots, whereas the escort carriers only did about 18 knots, and ordered his ships into a top-speed 'general chase'.

A gallant destroyer attack caused the *Yamato* to turn away and saw two cruisers hit, one by torpedoes and one by bombs. Three of the attacking ships were lost along with the escort carrier *Gambier Bay*. Revenge came when aircraft from Taffy One sank the cruiser *Chokai*, and aircraft from Taffy Two sank the *Chikuma*.

Still convinced that the escort carriers could do 30 knots, the Japanese admiral called off his pursuing ships. Harrassed by further aircraft attacks, he then decided to withdraw back through the San Barnardino Strait.

A final novelty in this battle that so often verged on disaster was the use of kamikaze bombers. These scored hits on several escort carriers: the *Santee* and the *Suwanee* from Taffy One, and the *Kitkun Bay*, the *Kalinin Bay* and the *St. Lo*, from Taffy Three. The escort carriers proved to be tough little ships, and most managed both to keep going and to continue operating aircraft, although the kamikaze bomber that went through the *St. Lo*'s flight deck caused explosions in her hangar below, and thus sank her.

Off Samar the Americans lost two escort carriers, two destroyers and a destroyer escort. The Japanese lost three 8-inch gun cruisers. Both sides had several ships damaged. It was an unlikely victory; a fleet of escort carriers and their destroyers had caused a main battleship and cruiser fleet to withdraw.

The final battle, that of Cape Engano on 25 October, 1944, was won by the biggest battalion in keeping with the more usual Pacific tradition. The Japanese *did* achieve their purpose in luring Halsey away, but, with his blood up, he saw to it that their success cost them dearly.

Cape Engano was also a fairly one-sided battle, as by then the four Japanese aircraft carriers and two converted battleship/carriers were almost denuded of planes. Many of these had been forced to land ashore after flying to the limit of their range without finding targets. This left about seventy-six planes at the disposal of the Japanese. Halsey's combined aircraft force was ten times greater.

When Halsey's planes found Vice Admiral Ozawa's ships, the results were fairly conclusive. Four aircraft carriers, including the Pearl Harbor veteran *Zuikaku* were sunk. The other casualties were the lighter fleet carriers *Chitose*, *Chiyoda* and *Zuiho*. The two converted battleship/carriers escaped, as did the cruisers and all but one destroyer. The cruiser *Tama* had been damaged, however, and was later sunk by the submarine USS *Jallao*. *Jallao* was one of a five-submarine patrol waiting across the path of Admiral Ozawa's withdrawal.

Fighting would continue around Leyte for several more weeks, and kamikaze attacks would claim several more American lives. However, there is no doubt that the Americans eventually emerged victorious from all the very varied naval engagements that group together to form the Battles of the Leyte Gulf.

**Left: the USS *Princetown*, hit amidships by Japanese bombs, burns fiercely. Eventually she had to be abandoned and was sunk by other U.S. warships.**

**Top right: U.S. Carrier Division 25 undergoing a two-and-a-half hour attack by Japanese forces off the Leyte Gulf. The photograph was taken from the USS *White Plains*.**

**Bottom right: the wakes of Japanese ships under attack in Tables Strait during the Battle of Leyte Gulf show the evasive action taken during a bombing attack.**

# THE BATTLE OF THE BULGE

The German offensive in the Ardennes, often called 'The Battle of the Bulge', began on 16th December, 1944, and was the last great gamble of the Third Reich. By late 1944, Soviet troops were pushing the Germans steadily back on the Eastern Front, German cities were being destroyed round the clock by the Allied strategic bombing offensive, the Italian peninsula had been liberated, and Allied ground forces were advancing virtually unopposed through France and the Low Countries – being stopped only by their own supply difficulties and the German frontier defences, the *Westwall* (known to the Allies as the Siegfried Line). On 20th July, 1944, Adolf Hitler survived an assassination attempt by members of the German Army who had hoped to negotiate peace after his death. Thereafter, Hitler relied less on the Army and more on the Nazi Party's own forces, the *Waffen-SS*, as well as upon his own increasingly erratic judgement. It seemed that nothing could save Germany from being crushed on all sides.

Hitler decided that there was one chance. The alliance between the Soviet Union, the United States and the British Empire was, he argued, inherently unstable and would collapse under a sufficient shock. As Germany moved at last to a 'total war' footing, enough troops could still be scraped together to mount one last offensive on the Western Front through the thinly held line of the Ardennes forest, towards the port of Antwerp. By attacking through the

bad going of the Ardennes, in bad weather and close to Christmas, the Germans could achieve surprise and reduce the massive Allied air superiority that had so hampered their previous armoured operations. By taking Antwerp, they would cut off the main Allied supply base for the Western Front, surrounding Canadian 1st Army and British 2nd Army, as well as 9th and 1st U.S. armies, leaving them with no choice but to surrender or evacuate in another Dunkirk. The British would blame the Americans for the loss of their troops, and the Anglo-American alliance might well break down altogether. Even at worst, there could be no attack from the West for at least six months, in which time Germany would develop its 'wonder weapons' and be free to concentrate on defeating the Soviet Union.

The problem with Hitler's plan was that it needed everything to go right at once. It needed German troops to advance in fog and snow at high speed through hills and forests along dirt roads, reaching the River Meuse in two days and Antwerp in four, before the Allies could respond. It needed the British and Americans to quarrel and collapse in the face of the German offensive. It needed a small German armoured force to out-fight three or four times its own number of troops, showing a superiority over the Americans that – for a scratch force in the fifth year of the war – was scarcely to be expected. None of Hitler's generals had any faith in his plan, and only loyalty and fear compelled them to carry it out. This was very much Hitler's personal battle.

Originally codenamed 'Watch on the Rhine' but later renamed 'Autumn Mist', the German attack was made by Army Group B under Field Marshal Walter Model. Eight armoured and thirteen infantry divisions assembled in secret against the five southernmost divisions of U.S. 1st Army under Lieutenant General Courtney Hodges. At 7.30am on 16th December, after a two-hour artillery bombardment, the five infantry divisions of 6th *Panzerarmee* attacked the two southernmost divisions of U.S. V Corps positioned in front of the Elsenborn Ridge. Behind the infantry waited four powerful *Waffen-SS* armoured divisions, the force expected to reach Antwerp in four days. The remaining forces were German Army rather

Adolf Hitler at his headquarters at Rastenburg with Joseph Goebbels, his Reich Plenipotentiary for Total War, shortly after the unsuccessful bomb plot against Hitler's life. It was Goebbels who scraped together a last reserve of German troops for the Ardennes offensive.

The formidable 88mm KwK43 anti-tank gun fitted to a Wespe assault gun, and also the main armament of the *Panzer* VI 'Tiger' and 'King Tiger.' Although few in number and slow in movement, these 'wonder weapons' caused much trouble for the Americans during the Ardennes offensive.

than *Waffen-SS*. The original plan called for 5th *Panzerarmee* of four infantry and three armoured divisions to cover 6th *Panzerarmee's* flank and for 7th Army of four infantry divisions to secure the flank against American interference from the south. Hitler also held one armoured division in reserve. From the start, however, 6th *Panzerarmee's* attack against the veteran troops of V Corps made little progress. In contrast, U.S. VIII Corps, holding a line of more than a hundred miles with inadequate troops further south, was burst upon by 5th *Panzerarmee*, and its least experienced division totally surrounded. Even so, the rest of VIII Corps put up a tough defence. Small forces of English-speaking German troops in American uniforms, driving behind the Allied lines, produced much confusion but no major results. After two hard days' fighting, the Germans were clearly making progress too slowly, and in the wrong places. They were still nowhere in sight of the Meuse.

Lieutenant General Omar Bradley, commanding 12th Army Group, of which 1st Army was a part, assumed at first that he was facing a small German spoiling attack, but nevertheless began to move armoured divisions from the north and south in support of VIII Corps. Using the two days bought by their front-line troops, the Americans, although they had no clear picture of what was happening, secured the crucial road junctions at Saint Vith in the north and Bastogne in the south against the German advance. Short of engineers, and unable to move easily across country in the snow and mud, the Germans were heavily dependent on these roads. The only formation of 6th *Panzerarmee* making progress was 'Kampfgruppe Peiper', a force of a hundred tanks and 4,000 infantry belonging to 1st *SS Panzerdivision*, which had broken through the Losheim Gap and was driving on, unsupported, towards the Meuse, unaware that the rest of the Division had failed to follow it. Meanwhile, on 19th December, the lead elements of 5th *Panzerarmee* reached the outskirts of Bastogne, only to find a solid defence based on newly arrived 101st Airborne Division and armoured support. Unable to take Bastogne and maintain their advance, the Germans by-passed the town, leaving it for their arriving infantry.

Despite the initial shock, the Americans recovered well from the surprise of 'Autumn

Mist'. Indeed, the reaction of Allied higher commanders was the same as that of their German enemies – that the offensive could not possibly succeed. Nevertheless, on first hearing of the attack on 16th December, both Field Marshal Montgomery commanding 21st Army Group to the north, and Lieutenant General Patton, commanding U.S. 3rd Army to the south of U.S. 1st Army, ordered their staffs to draw up plans in case what appeared to be a spoiling attack was something more. On 19th December, with the picture much clearer, General Dwight D. Eisenhower called a major conference for his commanders at Verdun to decide the next move. The German attack had failed to take St Vith or Bastogne, and, although the Americans were still retreating, there was no panic and the initial surprise had now gone. Lieutenant General Hodges was to continue his defence, moving the powerful U.S. VII Corps down from the north to extend his line against *Kampfgruppe Peiper*. While this line held, the crucial counterattack would be made from the south by Patton's U.S. 3rd Army, which would relieve Bastogne and smash through the flank protection provided by 7th Army to roll up the German line. Patton decided that his first attack would come in three days with at least three divisions.

This made two separate battles, one in the north, the other in the south. Eisenhower needed someone to co-ordinate the northern battle, and also some reserves on the line of the Meuse, just in case the Germans broke through. On the following day he telephoned 21st Army Group and, drawing a line through the centre of the battlefield, placed Montgomery in charge of all troops north of that line. Montgomery at once set British XXX Corps in motion towards the Meuse, and his presence did much to restore calm and order in the northern part of the battlefield. His actual command function, however, consisted largely

in agreeing to the shape of the battle which circumstances, and his American subordinates, had already dictated.

These Allied command decisions doomed Hitler's offensive. Although the Germans were able to find another eight divisions to add to the battle, they could not match the growing Allied strength – the equivalent of thirty-five divisions before the battle ended. By 21st December repeated attempts by 6th *Panzerarmee* to break through on the Elsenborn Ridge had come to nothing. Bastogne, although surrounded and under heavy pressure, refused to surrender. On 23rd December Montgomery, reluctant to incur heavy casualties now that his line was secure, authorised an American retreat from St Vith, but so great were German traffic problems that they were at first unable to advance. Also, on 23rd December the bad weather, which the Germans had regarded as crucial, lifted and the Allies were able to deploy their full air power to attack the Germans on the ground and to supply their own troops by air. By 24th December *Kampfgruppe Peiper*, the last German hope in the north, was surrounded, cut off and out of fuel miles in front of friendly troops. Nevertheless, a few hundred of its members escaped on foot back to the German lines. Finally, after a three-day offensive, III Corps of Patton's U.S. 3rd Army broke through from the south to link up with the troops in Bastogne on 26th December.

The last German effort on 26th December produced the limit of their advance, resulting in a long, narrow salient, 'the Bulge', pointing towards the River Meuse. A few tanks of 5th *Panzerarmee* actually reached the Meuse at Dinant on Christmas Day, only to turn back after a skirmish with tanks of British XXX Corps. By this time most of the German forces were seriously low on fuel. There simply were not the troops to maintain the offensive, or even to hold position. An attempt by 5th *Panzerarmee* to secure the southern flank by capturing Bastogne on 30th December stalled against a further attack by U.S. 3rd Army. It was the end for 'Autumn Mist'. Hitler, however, would not concede defeat. He insisted that the 'Bulge' should be held as the starting point for yet another planned offensive.

Against the overwhelming land and air power that the Allies could now deploy, the

German Attacks 16-20 Dec. 1944
German Attacks 21-25 Dec. 1944
German Front Line 16 Dec. 1944
German Front Line 25 Dec. 1944
Extent of "Battlegroup Peiper" penetration
U.S. Petrol Dumps

**Below:** Operation 'Autumn Mist', the last German offensive of the war, saw Hitler's forces push west as far as Celles. Ironically, the petrol-starved German army came within a few miles of a crucial U.S. fuel dump, but were unaware of its existence.

**Facing page top left:** a soldier of a *Volksgrenadier* division, which was largely made up of children, the sick, and the elderly, with little enthusiasm for the fight. Such troops were typical of the German forces in the Ardennes.

**Facing page top right:** twenty-nine-year old Lieutenant Colonel Joachim 'Jochen' Peiper of 1st *SS Panzerdivision*, one of the outstanding German armoured commanders of the war. A shadow was cast over his *Waffen-SS* division's achievements in the Ardennes since it was also responsible for the 'Malmedy Massacre' of nearly a hundred American prisoners.

**Facing page bottom:** small, improvised American ambush points like this one were crucial in slowing the German advance and buying time for the arriving reinforcements.

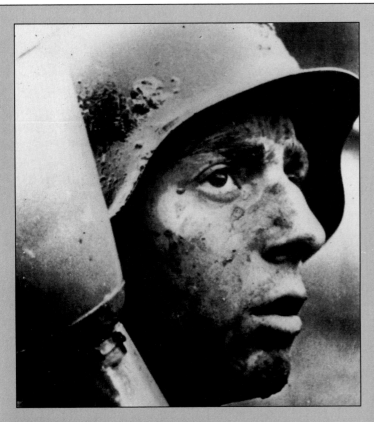

Improvisation and flexibility were the keynotes of the American defence. Facing page top: paratroopers of 82nd Airborne Division on the march in the northern part of the Bulge early in the battle. Further south at Bastogne, 101st Airborne Division played a crucial role as infantry in the defence.

Facing page bottom left: a *Panzer* V 'Panther' of an *SS Panzerdivision* knocked out in a street at Manhay, just south of Liege, on 30th December. By this time the German offensive had largely spent itself, and this tank marks one of the furthest German advances before the Allied counterattack.

Facing page bottom right: tank tracks in the snow. Once the weather improved the German columns were at the mercy of Allied aircraft. Here an advancing German force has been attacked from the air and suffered heavy casualties. Such use of air power was crucial in winning the battle.

Right: the end of Hitler's dream – American paratroopers take prisoner the first of four German soldiers hiding in a barn near Henumont, Belgium in January, 1945. The losses of the Ardennes offensive left the German Army entirely without reserves.

'Bulge' could not be held. But, made cautious by the surprise that they had received from 'Autumn Mist', the Allies were content to push the Germans back slowly, having themselves the same difficulty attacking through the snow. Renewed offensives in January by Montgomery and Patton drove the Germans, harassed by aircraft, back to their starting lines, and on 28th January the Americans pronounced the battle officially over. Army Group B, not for the first time in the Second World War, had been effectively wiped out, losing between 100,000 and 120,000 men and about 1,000 of its 1,500 tanks. On 31st December Hitler launched a much smaller offensive of ten divisions, Operation 'Nordwind', against American forces in Alsace, which achieved little. Undaunted, he ordered Operation 'Bodenplatte' a day later, which was designed as a low-level attack by virtually the whole German operational strength – more than 1,000 fighters and fighter-bombers – against the Allied air forces. Its only result was their own virtual self-destruction.

The elimination of these last German reserves meant that they had nothing to stop the Soviet Vistula-Oder offensive on the Eastern Front, which began on 12th January and advanced to within fifty miles of Berlin in three weeks. American losses in 'Autumn Mist' were between 75,000 and 80,000. The British were not seriously engaged in the battle, losing fewer than 1,400 men. Although not taken lightly, these losses had little or no effect on the Allied ability to conduct offensive operations in the following spring, whereas the failure of Hitler's last offensive guaranteed the defeat of Nazi Germany.

# MANDALAY AND MEIKTILA

Throughout the late summer and autumn of 1944, the Allied forces of 14th Army pursued Japanese General Mutaguchi's shattered forces across the Chin Hills and down the Kebaw valley to the Chindwin River. It was a slow business. Monsoon rain sheeted down, converting the dirt roads to quagmires. Vehicles became bogged up to their axles and sometimes the army made as little as three miles a day. Mutaguchi's rearguards, although ill and starving, put up tenacious resistance – each one had to be wiped out in costly, time-consuming, small-unit actions. It was not until early December that IV Corps reached Sittaung and XXXIII Corps arrived at Mawlaik and Kalewa. Although exhausted, the British did not rest – IV Corps' engineers quickly constructed a 1,150-foot long Bailey Bridge across the Chindwin, the longest ever built. Operation 'Capital', the Allied codename for the reconquest of central Burma, could now begin.

Lieutenant General William Slim, the 14th Army commander, was convinced that the Japanese would meet his advance as close to the Chindwin as possible, probably in the Taungdan Range, a long line of rugged, jungle-clad hills that rose some twenty miles east of the Chindwin and ran parallel to it. His forces were now between a hundred and 150 miles from the railhead at Dimapur. Although 14th Army was a half million strong, he knew that even with lavish aerial resupply he would be unable to maintain more than about five divisions beyond the Chindwin. The Taungdan barrier had to be pierced as quickly as possible and the Japanese driven southeast into the flat savannah country of the Shwebo Plain, the heart of Burma's dry belt. Here conditions

resembled those of the Western Desert. Slim's armoured brigades and fighter-bombers would make short work of the Japanese divisions, no matter how numerous they might be, for the latter had few tanks and virtually no air support.

On 4th December IV Corps, which since August had been commanded by Lieutenant General Frank Messervy, broke out of its bridgehead at Sittaung. With a new commander had come a reorganisation – IV Corps now comprised 7th and 19th Indian divisions and two tank brigades. In the lead was 19th Indian Division, its commander Major General 'Pete' Rees driving with the advance guard. It swept through the Taungdan Range and headed due east for Indaw, from where it was to swing south for Shwebo. Meanwhile, at Kalewa, Lieutenant General Montagu Stopford's XXXIII Corps, now comprising British 2nd Division, 20th Indian Division and 254 Tank Brigade, prepared to strike towards Japanese airfields at Yeu, seventy miles to the southeast, and at Monywa, a hundred miles due south on the Chindwin. On 15th December, only eleven days after leaving Sittaung, 19th Indian Division rolled into Indaw – it had cut through the apparently formidable Taundan Range and had encountered little resistance. The advance was going well – too well. Slim was perturbed and doubts began to crowd in.

The 14th Army commander was right to be worried. Slim had based his appreciation of Japanese strategy on what he knew about Kawabe and Mutaguchi, both tenacious but none too bright. They had demonstrated in the Imphal-Kohima battle a marked reluctance to give ground, even when the situation was hopeless. What Slim did not know was that, in

Slim's plans for the reconquest of Burma depended on maintaining complete aerial supremacy over the northern and central regions of the country. By January, 1945 British bombers ranged at will, destroying railway bridges (below) and disrupting the flow of supplies to Japanese divisions preparing for the 'Battle of the Irrawaddy Shore'.

Lieutenant General F.W. Messervy played a key role in dislodging the Japanese from their strong positions behind the Irrawaddy. Undetected by the Japanese, his IV Corps advanced 300 miles down a jungle track, and then stormed across the Irrawaddy to capture the Japanese supply depot at Meiktila.

the aftermath of the Imphal-Kohima debacle, Tokyo had instituted a thorough shake up of Burma Area Army's High Command. Kawabe had been replaced by Lieutenant General Hyotaro Kimura, a wily and intelligent soldier, who was prepared to withdraw in order to destroy his enemy. In a remarkable effort, Japanese reinforcements had poured into Burma in the autumn of 1944, and Kimura now commanded 250,000 men, organized in eleven divisions. A new commander, Lieutenant General Shihachi Katamura, had taken over 15th Army, its shattered 15th, 31st, and 33rd divisions had been rebuilt, and a new division, the 53rd, had been attached to it. Once more it was a formidable force.

Kimura had no intention of fighting a battle on the Shwebo Plain where Slim would hold all the cards. He left only light covering forces to the west of the Chindwin and ordered a general withdrawal to the eastern bank of the Irrawaddy. Here, behind the hundred-mile bend in the river that extended from Mandalay to Pakokku, Kimura instructed Katamura to deploy his 15th, 31st and 33rd divisions. It was a formidable defensive position. Along this stretch, the Irrawaddy was one-and-a-half-miles wide and banked by bluffs and cliffs, some of which were as high as the cliffs of Dover. Katamura stationed 53rd Division on the extreme left flank where it could reinforce Pakokku and cover Meiktila. The latter was the road and rail junction of central Burma, as well as the site of four airfields and a vast depot from which Japanese forces in central and northern Burma drew most of their supplies. Further south, between Meiktila and Rangoon, Kimura stationed 18th and 2nd divisions to act as a reserve. Finally, he ordered 28th Army, whose area of responsibility covered the Arakan and the Yenangyaung oilfields, to take over the defence of the area from Pakokku westwards.

Kimura had placed Katamura's 15th Army in a strong situation. If Slim wanted to take Rangoon he would have to fight his way across the Irrawaddy at the very limit of his logistic chain, whereas Katamura would be able to feed his battle from Meiktila. Kimura believed this encounter would be decisive and referred to it as the 'Battle of the Irrawaddy Shore' – in short, he intended to impose on Slim the same sort of battle that Slim had imposed on the hapless Mutaguchi and Kawabe at Imphal

and Kohima.

Kimura was a competent general – Slim was a military genius. Twenty-four hours after Rees had reached Indaw, Slim's misgivings crystalised into certainty. Reports from reconnaissance flights and documents captured during 19th Division's advance indicated a major Japanese withdrawal behind the Irrawaddy – it was clear that a gigantic trap was being prepared for 14th Army. Having divined Kimura's plan, Slim prepared to turn the tables on him. During the retreat of 1942, one of Slim's units had withdrawn through Pakokku and then along a bullock-cart track which ran due north to the west of the Chindwin all the way to Kalewa. It had served as a secure avenue for the retreat and he now intended to use this track to outflank Kimura's carefully contrived positions. Although it was 150 miles long and dirt surfaced, Slim's engineers estimated they could convert it to an all-weather road in about six weeks by laying along its length strips of bitumen coated hessian – 'bithess'. Slim proposed to send an entire corps down this road to Pakokku on Kurasaka's left flank – it would then cross the Irrawaddy and dash a further ninety miles to the southeast to capture Meiktila.

Operation 'Extended Capital', the codename Slim gave his scheme, was a design

Major General 'Punch' Cowan, C.O. of 17th Indian Division, confers with Messervy before the assault on Meiktila. Cowan's division spearheaded the crossing of the Irrawaddy and played a leading role in the capture of the depot.

An Indian MP halts traffic to allow men of the 4th Battalion 4th Gurkhas to cross a Bailey bridge on their way to assault Mandalay Hill. The Gurkha's seizure of the hill cleared the way for other elements of 19th Indian Division to move on Mandalay.

worthy of Napoleon – it has never been surpassed and only rarely equalled. It involved a massive redeployment which few armies could have carried out in less than a month; Slim's army did it in twenty-four hours! Slim ordered the establishment of a dummy headquarters for IV Corps at Indaw, which he tasked with maintaining radio traffic at existing levels. Rees' 19th Indian Division was transferred to XXXIII Corps, and the 19th and 2nd British divisions were then to advance to Shwebo, after which Rees' Division would swing east and cross the Irrawaddy at a point some forty miles north of Mandalay, while British 2nd Division was to advance due south to cross the Irrawaddy twenty miles west of the city. Meanwhile, 20th Indian Division was to advance south east along the left bank of the Chindwin to Monywa, and then strike due east to the Irrawaddy, crossing the river some ten miles to the west of 2nd Division's bridgehead. Slim reasoned that these movements would so absorb Japanese attention they would fail to detect the simultaneous advance of Scoone's reconstituted IV Corps, now composed of 7th and 17th Indian divisions and two tank brigades, down the track to Pakokku. Once IV Corps had taken Meiktila, the Japanese would have no

option other than to withdraw troops from their Irrawaddy defences and concentrate on recapturing their depots. The battle for Meiktila would then become a replay of Imphal-Kohima, while to the north XXXIII Corps broke through the Irrawaddy defences and captured Mandalay.

On 16th December 19th Indian Division began its advance on Shwebo. Eight days later, British 2nd Division struck southeast in a converging attack. Japanese resistance was slight, and on 5th January both divisions reached their objective. In accordance with Slim's plan, 19th Division now swung east and, between 11th and 17th January, managed to cross the Irrawaddy and establish bridgeheads at Singu and Thabeikkyin – villages between forty and fifty miles north of Mandalay. Rees' role now was to isolate Mandalay from the north and draw off the Japanese from the city and from the Irrawaddy bend. He succeeded brilliantly. An alarmed Katamura pulled 53rd Division away from Pakokku, thereby exposing Meiktila, and withdrew 15th Division from its positions on the Irrawaddy and rushed them north to nip out 19th Indian Division's bridgeheads. For the time being, Rees stayed on the defensive, allowing the Japanese to

waste themselves in desperate attacks against his perimeters.

Meanwhile, British 2nd Division had advanced slowly south from Shwebo and 20th Indian Division had struck south east from Kalewa. On 20th February both divisions reached the Irrawaddy some twenty miles west of Mandalay and launched their first assault crossings. Although Katamura's withdrawal of 15th Division had weakened the defences, the British and Indians suffered heavy casualties. In many places attempts to cross were abandoned. By 24th February small bridgeheads had been established, but it took another three weeks of bloody assaults, supported by 'cab-ranks' of fighter-bombers, to convert these scattered pockets into a secure lodgement.

Now came Slim's masterstroke. As he had surmised, Japanese attention was fully occupied by the fighting on the Irrawaddy. In mid-January Katamura received a report from a reconnaissance flight (the only one which managed to penetrate a dense RAF fighter screen) that a column of at least 2,000 tanks and trucks was moving south along the Kalewa-Pauk track. He dismissed the report as incredible

– if the pilot had seen anything at all, which he very much doubted, it was probably a lightly equipped Chindit raiding column. Undetected, IV Corps' advance guard reached Pauk on 26th January. Training his binoculars to the southeast, Indian 17th Division's commander Major General 'Punch' Cowan caught his first sight of the Irrawaddy's cliffs, still some thirty miles distant. Nearly a month was to pass before the bulk of IV Corps arrived at Pauk, though the delay was in part intentional, for it allowed time for the battles to the northeast to develop. On 21st February IV Corps surged across the Irrawaddy at Nyaungu, a village twenty miles down river from Pakokku. A better place could not have been chosen – it was on the boundary between 20th Army's and 15th Army's areas of responsibility, and was lightly held by troops of the Indian National Army, who fled at the first shot.

Three days later, Brigadier Miles Smeeton's 255th Tank Brigade burst out of the bridgehead and, scattering bewildered Japanese rear area troops, raced twenty miles to Oyin. Lone Japanese, boxes of explosives strapped to their chests, hurled themselves between tank tracks, but they were too few to halt the advance. On 22nd February Smeeton's tanks rolled into Taungtha only forty-three miles from Meiktila. Even now Katamura still believed that his depot was threatened by nothing more than a raiding column which could be handled by the 4,000 soldiers in Meiktila, though they were mainly lines-of-communication troops and convalescents in the hospital. On 26th February the Deccan Horse, the leading regiment of 255th Brigade, reached Thabuktong, fifteen miles from Meiktila and overran an airstrip. Within hours, petrol, ammunition and the fresh 99th Brigade of 5th Indian Division had been flown in. Three days later, the tank brigades supported by 17th Indian Division hooked north and south of Meiktila and closed in for the kill.

It was not an easy battle. Although rear area troops, the Japanese fought desperately from hastily dug bunkers. Some squatted in foxholes, 250lbs aerial bombs clasped tightly between their knees and stones in their hands, waiting to strike the detonator when tanks passed overhead. The Gurkhas, advancing in a protective screen before the armour, killed them all. Slim, who had flown to Thabuktong to confer with Cowan, demanded to be driven to

The little village of Ywathitgyi on the Irrawady basin road. Troops of 19th Indian Division fought their way along this road into the northeastern outskirts of Mandalay in the face of fanatical Japanese resistance. The sudden emergence of this threat to Mandalay caused the Japanese to pull reserves to the northeast, thereby exposing Meiktila.

Right: an RAF bomber circles the massive walls of Fort Differin, the last major Japanese position inside Mandalay. When the fifty-foot-thick walls proved impervious to artillery fire, low flying aircraft lobbed 2,000lb bombs onto them.

Below: a 3' mortar of 17th Indian Division gives support to infantry attacking the outskirts of Meiktila. The heavily outnumbered Japanese fought desperately from hastily constructed bunkers, and each one had to be destroyed in set piece attacks.

the front, and could not resist joining his old unit, 1st Battalion 7th Gurkhas, in one bloodily resisted assault. By 3rd March Meiktila was in Cowan's hands – Indian 17th Division's soldiers counted 2,000 Japanese bodies, though many more lay buried in bunkers and tunnels.

Katamura finally realized the true nature of the threat to Meiktila on 25th February. In a frenzy, he withdrew 18th Division from northern Burma, ordered 49th Division north from Rangoon, stripped 31st Division of its heavy guns, detached regiments from 33rd and 15th divisions and ordered the lot to converge on the town. The response was vigorous but uncoordinated. A local counterattack recaptured Taungtha on 5th March, cutting Meiktila's road link to the Irrawaddy, but it would be another five days before major Japanese units could be in position to launch a full-scale assault.

For Cowan, the loss of Taungtha was a setback but not a serious one. His 17th Division had been besieged before and Cowan knew that, as long as he held even one of Meiktila's airfields, aerial resupply would suffice. Cowan did not wait for the Japanese to come to him. Leaving 99th Brigade to hold the town, he sent his armoured forces out in five directions along the roads radiating from Meiktila to intercept the Japanese advance, and by 11th March his tanks were skirmishing with the enemy on the open plains.

Since 25th February Meiktila had absorbed Katamura's attention. On 6th March, however, a new threat materialised. Rees had formed Stiletto Forces, an armoured column which burst out of 19th Division's bridgehead and headed south for Mandalay. Rees tore along with Stiletto's spearhead, behaving with the panache and ruthlessness of an *SS Panzer*

commander. When a deep *chaung* (dry water course) halted the column, Rees ordered three three-ton trucks rolled into it on their sides, and the tanks rolled over them. Infantry clinging to their superstructures, the tanks pressed on through the night of 6th March, and by the following afternoon 1,000-foot high Mandalay Hill was in sight. During the night of 7th March 4th Battalion of 4th Gurkha Regiment crept up the northeastern side of the hill and at dawn stormed the summit. Within forty-eight hours 19th Division was in the northern suburbs of Mandalay – within another twenty-four hours it had fought its way to Fort Dufferin, a massive 2,000-square-yard cantonment protected by a moat seventy-five-yards wide and walls thirty-feet thick. The battle for Mandalay now resembled a mediaeval siege – 6" howitzers battered the walls from point-blank range and B-25s skipped 2,000lbs bombs into them. On 20th March the Japanese abandoned Dufferin and withdrew from the remainder of the city, their retreat impelled not only by the ferocity of 19th Division's assault, but also because British 2nd Division had broken out of its bridgehead at Ngazun eight days earlier and was now attacking Mandalay from the south.

Due to the deteriorating situation in Mandalay, on 12th March Kimura removed the conduct of the Meiktila battle from Katamura and placed it under the control of Lieutenant General Masaki Honda, commander of 23rd Army. Honda now designated the heterogeneous units closing around Meiktila the 'Army of the Decisive Battle', but it was an army in name only. The regiments from 15th Army, and 18th and 49th Divisions were all on different radio nets and used different frequencies. Instead of a massed onslaught,

the attempts to take Meiktila degenerated into a series of uncoordinated thrusts. Even so, the Japanese fought well. They managed to get within small-arms' range of one of Meiktila's airfields and fire along the runway, but the aircraft kept coming. With virtually no armour they wheeled their 75mm field guns forward and fired Ta Dam shells (an early form of shaped charge) at tanks from ranges of less than 250 yards. By 22nd March Honda's gunners had destroyed fifty British tanks for the loss of fifty guns. The 'Army of the Decisive Battle' had only twenty guns left, while the British had many more tanks – it was clear who was going to win.

Yet by this time the recapture of Meiktila had become irrelevant. Withdrawn from Mandalay, 15th Army was streaming to the southeast. Having broken out of its bridgehead on 8th March, 20th Indian Division now rampaged across 15th Army's line of retreat, cutting off and wiping out entire battalions. The object of the Army of the Decisive Battle

was no longer to take Meiktila, but to prevent Cowan's force from also striking southeast and turning the withdrawal into a rout. Honda held on just long enough to allow the remnant of 15th Army to pass through Thazi, ten miles east of Meiktila, and then on 31st March he too pulled south.

Unlike the bloodbath at Imphal-Kohima, the Japanese suffered only 13,000 casualties at Mandalay-Meiktila, although the majority of these were dead. The British had fewer killed (2,300), but many wounded (15,700). The infliction of heavy casualties had not been part of Slim's plan. His skilfully handled divisions had forced a numerically superior Japanese army to abandon a formidable defensive position, and had smashed the cohesion of seven Japanese divisions, sending them fleeing south. Slim did not give them time to regroup. His armoured columns sped after them, and now the retreat became a rout. The Burma campaign was all but over.

**Troops of Cowan's 17th Division enter the ruined city of Pegu, only fifty miles north of Rangoon, on 1st May, 1945. Three days of bitter fighting had delayed Cowan's advance, and the onset of the monsoon that very afternoon brought the advance to a stop. Rangoon was liberated two days later by a seaborne landing.**

# KAMIKAZE – THE DIVINE WIND

**The kamikaze pilots of the Japanese Navy, and their tokkatai counterparts of the Army Air Force, were treated with great ceremony. This was no undercover operation and numerous photographs such as this exist. The pilots parade to receive their final instructions.**

In the 13th Century, a Mongol horde, led by Kublai Khan, was invading Japan supported by a vast fleet. Just as the defeat of the Japanese seemed certain, a typhoon sprang up. The Mongol fleet was scattered, and Japan was saved. The salvation was attributed to *Kamikaze*, the Divine Wind, sent by the Sun Goddess, Amaterasu Omikami. In 1944 Japan was outnumbered in both ships and aircraft; the American fleet and their allies were massing for the final series of assaults. Could Kamikaze blow once again, and stave off the inevitable?

It was becoming obvious that a major action in the Leyte Gulf, in the Philippines, was imminent. The part to be played by American carrier aircraft would be crucial, and Vice-Admiral Takijiro Ohnishi, Commander of the Japanese Naval Air Force's First Air Fleet, had the problem of neutralising the threat. The enemy's carrier task group had to be rendered ineffective for at least a week, to give the Japanese Second Fleet, a fleet without a single carrier of its own, a chance to get through to the Gulf to prey upon the American troop transports.

There was a high attrition rate among Japanese torpedo bombers and high-level bombers, and their success rate was minimal. Ohnishi had a plan to improve the return he was getting in exchange for his own losses. He paid a visit to the 201st Air Group, on the island of Luzon, to seek volunteers for a 'Special Attack Group'. The 201st, equipped with Zeros, had been practicing the technique of 'skip bombing' – approaching an enemy ship at high speed and low level – to launch a 250kg bomb which would bounce off the water and bury itself in the side of the ship, above its armour plating. The Special Attack Group would modify the technique slightly. They would not release their bomb, but would fly with it, to plunge both themselves and their bomb into the side of their target. This would greatly increase their accuracy. Most air forces could cite examples, in both World Wars, of airmen making the supreme sacrifice at a crucial moment in an air battle, but this had always been a spur of the moment action, in the heat of battle. Ohnishi's pilot sacrifice was to be premeditated and organised.

Some of the deficiencies of the first 'Zeros' were corrected in the ultimate version, the A6M5 (left), but it still did not achieve superiority over the Hellcats. It was, however, still a formidable weapon in the hands of a pilot who was committed to the death.

The Japanese planned to replace the 'Zero' with the A7M Reppu (Hurricane) (below left), code-named 'Sam' by the Allies. Fortunately it did not emerge from the production line in time to join the onslaught of the Divine Wind. With a planned diving speed of 550 mph, it would have been difficult to stop either by fighter interception or by anti-aircraft gunfire.

Right: another flattop, the USS *Kitkun Bay*, receives the attention of the kamikazes. This time the suicide plane has received a direct hit, and appears to be diving into the sea alongside its intended target.

There was no shortage of volunteers from the pilots of 201st Air Group. They went to work almost immediately. From 20 October their aircraft ranged the Philippines, seeking the elusive American carriers. Their first success came on October 25. Five Zeros carrying bombs, with four others flying escort, located a carrier group, and attacked. All five Kamikazes were successful in hitting carriers. The escort carrier *St. Lo* received hits from two of the Zeros and sank, earning the doubtful privilege of becoming the first victim of the new 'Divine Wind' which had begun to blow.

Other units were added to 201st, to form the 'Special Attack Corps', and from then on the American fleet was subjected to daily Kamikaze attacks. By the end of January 1945 the Kamikazes operating out of the Philippines had made over 400 sorties, and had lost 380 aircraft. In the process they had sunk 16 more ships, including another carrier, and had damaged almost 90 others, 17 of them capital

The crewmen on the bridge of an attacked ship stare anxiously into the smoke, hoping to spot the next kamikaze in time either to engage it or to take avoiding action.

Before a mission, the suicide squads went through a ceremony based on the rites of the ancient samurai. After receiving a final libation, the pilot was helped by a comrade to don the samurai headband symbolizing courage and composure.

ships – battleships, carriers or cruisers. Ohnishi became so convinced of the comparative effectiveness of the 'special attack' technique that he extended it to all the aircraft of the First Air Fleet; bombers and torpedo bombers, as well as the 'Zeros. He also preached the doctrine to the commander of the Second Air Fleet, Vice-Admiral Shigeru Fukudome. Eventually Fukudome reluctantly agreed, and the Second Air Fleet was added to the Special Attack Corps.

Vice-Admiral Ohnishi was not the only one who had had the idea of suicide missions. During the summer of 1944 a junior officer, Ensign Ohta, an air transport pilot flying out of Rabaul, had drawn up plans for a piloted rocket-propelled bomb. His idea was considered by Navy High Command and the Aeronautics Department. Experiments were carried out with all speed, and by the end of 1944 the Yokosuka MXY 7, the Okha (Cherry Blossom) had been put into production. Built

principally of wood, the Ohka carried a warhead of 1,800kg of explosive, and was powered by five rocket motors, which would hurl it towards its target at over 600 mph. It was to be carried, beneath a Mitsubishi G4M 'Betty' land bomber to within twenty miles of its target, when the pilot would operate the release and fire the engines for the final approach. The Americans called the Ohka the 'Baka' (foolish) bomb. It first appeared during operations in the Okinawa area, during the summer of 1945. Fortunately for the fleet, the Betty, with its flying bomb on board, was very slow and unmanoeuverable, and vulnerable to the American carrier fighters. The Japanese did not have the resources in fighter aircraft to provide the Bettys with sufficient escorts to make certain that they could deliver their Baka safely to the release point.

The techniques of the 'special attack' were studied, and a training programme was instituted for the volunteer pilots. The flight was divided into three phases, and training was given to prepare the pilot for the particular demands of each phase. The main problem during the takeoff phase was the need for it to be carried out as quickly as possible. Since the plan to prevent the Allied landings at Leyte had failed, the Kamikaze bases were now within range of American land based bombers. The Special Attack aircraft were dispersed around the airfields, and camouflaged, to minimise the risk of them being destroyed on the ground. The first two days of the training programme were devoted to the practice of getting quickly and safely from the hide and into the air. This was followed by two days of intensive training in formation flying. It was obvious that if the Kamikazes and their escorts arrived over the target area en masse, the defenders would have much greater difficulty in dealing with them than if they arrived piecemeal. Finally, the trainees spent three days studying the problems of the approach to the target, angle of attack, and target selection.

In the spring and early summer of 1945, by which time operations had moved to the Okinawa area, both Navy and Army Air Forces were carrying out suicide missions. It was decided that their efforts should be coordinated. This resulted in a series of mass attacks, designated 'Kikusui' (floating chrysanthemum) operations. The first and biggest of these, on April 6/7, put 355 Kamikazes

Right: there can be no doubt as to the intention of the pilot of this Aichi D3A 'Val' dive bomber as it hurtles towards a U.S. cruiser. Unless a lucky last-second direct hit explodes the 'Val' in mid air, there is now no way that the ship can avoid serious damage.

Overleaf: a kamikaze 'Zero' about to plunge into the side of a U.S. capital ship. The photograph is believed to have been taken from the bridge of the battleship USS *Missouri*, which was damaged by kamikaze attacks in the Okinawa area on April 11 and 16, 1945.

into the air. Although more than 200 were shot down before reaching the fleet, those that got through inflicted considerable damage. Four ships were sunk, and twenty-five more, including a battleship and a carrier, were damaged.

There was, by now, a change in the attitude of the pilots. In the early days the Special Attack Corps had been made up entirely of volunteers, filled with a spirit of spontaneous enthusiasm. Now the enthusiasm was beginning to wane, and pressure was having to be brought to encourage 'volunteers'. This meant that the flying training period had to be preceded by a period of indoctrination.

All was to no avail. The Divine Wind had not prevented the landings at Leyte, and it did not prevent the defeat of the defenders of Okinawa. Now the American forces had moved to within reach of the Japanese homeland. Japan braced itself for invasion, but it was not to come. American B-29s could now fly missions over Japan with much less risk than their soldiers and marines would face storming the beaches. The Allies believed that the end was in sight, and at the end of July an ultimatum was published, demanding immediate unconditional surrender of the armed forces of Japan. The demand was rejected. Leaflets were dropped on eleven Japanese cities, telling them that they were in danger of intensive aerial bombardment, and on July 28 six of them were bombed. Twelve more cities were

The Yokosuka MXY7 Ohka, a piloted flying bomb, the ultimate weapon of the kamikaze pilot, code-named 'Baka' by the Allies. The Ohka had a range of little more than twenty miles, and was carried to within range of its target by a 'mother aircraft', usually a Mitsubishi G4M 'Betty'.

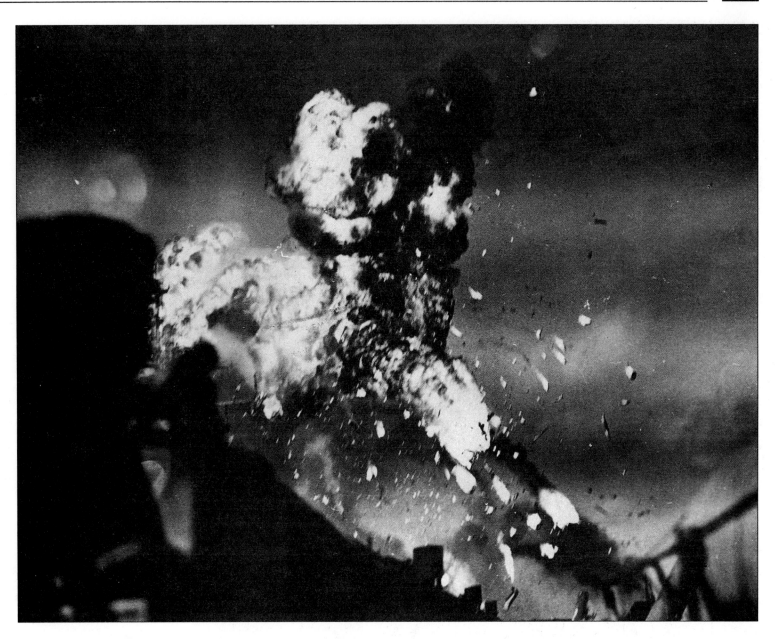

**Besides the damage inflicted by the war load of the suicide aircraft, its fuel tanks acted as an enormous incendiary device. This gasoline-fired inferno was photographed during an attack on the USS Intrepid.**

warned on July 31, and, as the ultimatum was still not accepted, four of them were bombed on August 1. The final warning was given on August 5. The U.S. Army Air Force had dropped a million and a half leaflets each day, and three million copies of the ultimatum. Then came America's own Divine Wind; on August 6 at Hiroshima, and again on the 9th at Nagasaki.

On August 15 a public announcement was made of Japan's acceptance of the ultimatum. That evening, in the study on the second floor of his residence, Vice-Admiral Takijiro Ohnishi joined the men of his Special Attack Corps, performing *hara-kiri* – ritual suicide – with his ceremonial sword. His Divine Wind had not prevented his nation's defeat, and the Allies victory in Japan was added to their victory in Europe, three months earlier.

World War II was over. It had begun with a German air raid on Poland; it ended with an American air raid on Japan. The prophesy made by Britain's Winston Churchill had come true. There had been many disasters, there had been immeasurable cost and tribulation, but in the end there had been Victory.

By the time the kamikaze battle was launched, it was already too late for it to alter the outcome of the war, which came to a violent end with the entry of the 'Enola Gay'. This B-29 bomber carried 'Little Boy', the atomic bomb which was dropped on Hiroshima on August 6, 1945.

The mushroom cloud which resulted from the explosion of 'Fat Boy', the second atomic weapon, dropped on Nagasaki three days after the explosion in Hiroshima.

The total devastation (overleaf) created by the atomic explosions convinced the Japanese civil power to overrule the military authorities and accept the unconditional surrender demanded by the Allies to bring World War II to an end.

# MANCHURIA – FORGOTTEN VICTORY

Red Army troops boarding the Trans-Siberian train for the Manchurian front. A massive logistical effort was needed to make the campaign possible, but despite the immensity of the build-up, the Soviets still achieved surprise.

In August, 1945, one of the least-studied but most spectacular campaigns of the war was fought in Manchuria. In just two weeks, the Soviet Red Army overwhelmed Japan's Kwantung Army and advanced up to 900 kilometres into enemy territory. Far from the popular myth of a bludgeon-like Red Army, in this campaign the Soviets demonstrated the impressive skills they had learnt fighting the *Wehrmacht*, and earned themselves a share in the spoils of the Asian victory.

The Kwantung Army had been a crack force, but by 1945 it had fallen on hard times. Over three-quarters of its troops were raw conscripts, while its 'Manchuko Empire' auxiliaries were useless. The Army's small number of tanks were merely thinly armoured vehicles with one 57mm gun, unable to successfully engage Soviet tanks in combat. Similarly, the Japanese 37mm anti-tank gun would only

stop a Soviet tank in exceptional circumstances. Two divisions lacked anti-tank guns, transport or artillery and none had heavy artillery. Completing this picture of weakness, their planes were trainers with virtually no combat capability.

Despite these weaknesses, attacking Manchuria should not be dismissed as an easy task; after all, the Japanese did not have a reputation for tame surrenders. Manchuria was 1,200 kilometres from east to west, and mountains, desert and major rivers all hindered Soviet access to the region. The Japanese planned to make Manchuria's geography work for them by delaying the enemy in frontier fortifications, and then withdrawing hundreds of kilometres to the south where the pursuing, but hopefully exhausted Soviets could be counterattacked.

A tremendous logistical effort enabled Soviet

Far Eastern Command to deploy numerically superior forces against Japan. Entire armies had travelled 12,000 kilometres, over a million railway wagons had made the long journey on the Trans-Siberian and thousand of new tanks were delivered to the front. The U.S.S.R. enjoyed a qualitative advantage as well as a numerical one; Soviet guns, planes and tanks were better than anything the Japanese possessed. The Soviet 'workhorse' tank, the T34, with a 76mm or 85mm gun, was superior to Japanese tanks, while the JS2, with its 122mm gun, had no Japanese rivals.

Needing a rapid victory to establish the U.S.S.R.'s credibility as a Far Eastern victor, Stalin imposed commanders who had succeeded against the *Wehrmacht*, thus passing over men on the spot who doubted that speedy victory was possible. Far Eastern Commander Vasilevsky planned to 'fix' the Japanese with a northern attack, while reserving his main effort for two pincer movements from either side. This would be supplemented by seaborne assaults. Vasilevsky didn't just depend on numbers; an element of surprise, the appropriate concentrations of resources and a rapid exploitation would give Stalin the quick victory he required.

In 1941, the Red Army had learnt the hard way that surprise could act as a force multiplier, so for this campaign they strove to disguise the imminence and direction of their attack. Elaborate precautions were taken to hide the build-up, but knowing the Japanese had to notice something, deceptions were planned. In the Maritime Provinces, Soviet troops dug fortifications where they could be seen, civilians near the frontier were not moved, normal leave was issued and troops were sent to help with the harvest. Even forward reconnaissance was strictly controlled – it was better attacking units should be ignorant of the enemy than *maskirovka*, the Soviet term for deception and surprise, be lost.

This should not have deceived the Japanese and, indeed, revised intelligence estimates warned of an attack in September. Soviet forces were not expected earlier, as summer is a period of seasonal rains over most of Manchuria. There was also an element of wishful thinking in this Japanese calculation, since they desperately needed Soviet mediation to enable them to negotiate peace with the U.S.A.

The Red Army also achieved surprise by attacking from an unexpected direction. The attack made by 36th Army down the railway towards Hailar was a feint designed to draw attention from Trans-Baikal Front's main thrust over the Great Hingan Mountains, which were considered impassable by the Japanese. Further south, the Soviet-Mongolian Cavalry Mechanized Group achieved surprise by advancing across the Gobi Desert. In the east 1st Far Eastern Front faced fortifications, wooded hills and numerous rivers, considered by the Japanese an unlikely direction for a major attack.

Even at the tactical level the Red Army strove to achieve surprise. On 9th August many initial advances took place without prior artillery fire and where artillery was used it was in a brief, 'hurricane' bombardment. Infantry advances were small group infiltrations, not the human waves typical of the Red Army earlier in the war.

Vasilevsky expected different types of advance from each of his three fronts. Trans-Baikal Front was the key mobile thrust and consequently it received a disproportionate allocation of tanks. Facing formidable river barriers, 2nd Far Eastern Front obtained the services of the powerful Amur River Flotilla. In the east 1st Far Eastern Front had its artillery component strengthened to enable it to deal with Japanese fortifications.

The spearhead of Malinovsky's Trans-Baikal Front was elite 6th Guards Tank Army, whose experience of mountain warfare in the Carpathians was put to good use as it led the

A Red Army mortar crew prepares to fire. The Soviets had massive artillery and mortar superiority over their Japanese opponents. First Far Eastern Front, which faced the stronger Japanese fortifications, had its artillery element strengthened. They achieved tactical surprise by either dispensing with any preliminary artillery preparation or else using a brief 'hurricane' bombardment.

Red Army self-propelled guns on the move. The Japanese had nothing capable of matching the powerful Soviet mechanized forces – neither their anti-tank guns or their tanks could effectively combat Soviet armoured units. It was logistics that held back the Soviet armoured thrust over the Great Hingan mountains, not the Japanese.

advance over the Great Hingan Mountains. Attacking on a narrow front, it enjoyed a 15:1 advantage in tanks, total control of the air and glorious sunny weather. Kravchenko's tanks advanced rapidly against feeble opposition, taking the Khorokhon Pass on the evening of 10th August and gaining access to the central Manchurian plain. Here the tanks ran out of fuel but, using the 400 planes of 453rd Aviation Battalion, Malinovsky resupplied the force and the advance resumed. Deploying a powerful forward detachment, Kravchenko was able to keep the bulk of the tank army in march formation, maximising its speed – in just eleven days it covered 900 kilometres.

To the south of Kravchenko's army, 17th Combined Arms Army (CAA) reached the coast with little opposition. The 53rd CAA provided the second echelon, advancing with relative ease behind 6th Guard Tank Army. Only the 39th CAA, of all the armies of the main thrust, encountered strong opposition: Japanese resistance in the Arshaan-Wuchakou area was fierce.

The thankless task of advancing down the route that the Japanese expected Soviet forces to take was given to 36th CAA. As it crossed the northern section of the Great Hingan, Japanese opposition was heavy. Although advancing less spectacularly than the rest of the Front, 36th CAA's achievement was in enabling other armies to advance relatively unopposed.

Pliev's Cavalry-Mechanized Group made the most exotic advance in crossing the Gobi Desert. Careful logistical support enabled it to advance up to ninety kilometres a day and the only real resistance was met northwest of Kalgan. Crossing the Great Wall, Pliev met the Chinese Communist 8th Route Army and was preparing to enter Beijing when the campaign ended.

Meretskov's 1st Far Eastern Front faced Japanese fortifications in awkward terrain. Despite this his front penetrated up to 600 kilometres into Manchuria, and the southern 25th CAA reached northern Korea.

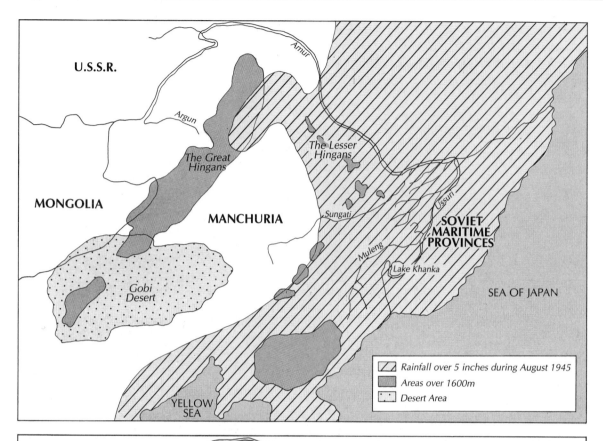

The Soviets sweep into Manchuria on 8th August, 1945, against the Japanese 1st, 3rd, 4th and Kwantung armies. Due to their superior weaponry, the tactical use of surprise and bold command, the Soviets achieve victory before the month is out.

Legend:
- Rainfall over 5 inches during August 1945
- Areas over 1600m
- Desert Area

Russian Advances

**2nd FAR EASTERN FRONT**
*Gen. Purkayev*
337,096 Men
1,280 Tanks and Sp. Guns
5,988 Guns and Mortars
1,260 Planes

**4 ARMY**
Lt Gen. Vemura Mikio

2ND CAA
• Aihun
• Sunwu

**FAR EASTERN COMMAND**
*Marshal Vasilevsky*

36TH CAA

• Hailar

15TH CAA

**TRANS-BAIKAL FRONT**
*Marshal Malinovsky*
654,000 Men
2,416 Tanks and Sp. Guns
9,668 Guns and Mortars
1,324 Aircraft

• Tsitsihar

• Arshaan
39TH CAA

53RD CAA
6TH GUARDS TANK

17TH CAA
CAV. MECH.GRP

**1ST AREA ARMY**
*Gen. Kita Seiichi*

• Harbin

**KWANTUNG ARMY**
Gen. Yamada Seiichi

**1st FAR EASTERN FRONT**
*Marshal Meretskov*
586,589 Men
1,860 Tanks and Sp. Guns
11,430 Guns and Mortars
1,387 Planes

35TH CAA
1ST CAA

**3RD ARMY**
Gen. Ushikoru Jun

Mukankiang •

5TH CAA
25TH CAA

**CHINESE EXPEDITIONARY FORCE**

• Mukden

(Chongjin) Seishin

• Kalgan

• Beijing

SEA OF JAPAN

YELLOW SEA

**34 ARMY**

**SOVIET COMMANDERS**
Cav. Mech. Col. Gen. Pliev
17th CAA Lt Gen. Danilov
6th Guards Tank Col. Gen. Kravchenko
53rd CAA Col. Gen. Managarov
39th CAA Col. Gen. Lyudnikov
36th CAA Lt Gen. Luchinsky
2nd CAA (Red Banner Army) Lt Gen. Terekhin
15th CAA Lt Gen. Mamanov
35th CAA Lt Gen. Zakhvatayev
1st CAA (Red Banner Army) Col. Gen. Bebborodov
5th CAA Col. Gen. Krylov
25th CAA Col. Gen. Chistyakov

**Soviet cavalry on the move. The Manchurian campaign was the last major appearance of cavalry in modern warfare. Pliev's Cavalry-Mechanized group emulated the feats of the ancient Mongols in their dramatic advance across the Gobi Desert. Pliev's advance was made possible by the thorough logistical support of Trans-Baikal Front.**

A few months earlier 5th CAA had distinguished itself during fierce fighting in the awkward terrain of East Prussia, and now they were to assault in similar countryside north of Suifeno. Meretskov strengthened the artillery and tank components of the army, making them the key elements in the thrust towards Japanese 1st Area Army HQ at Mutankiang. Krylov decided to forego the advantages of bombardment, partly as he lacked information on enemy positions, and instead attacked in hilly country north of the easiest route of advance. The initial assault was lead by small groups of about a hundred men taken from first echelon rifle battalions. These units were balanced combat teams whose task was to infiltrate deep into Japanese defences. For the main thrust Krylov had 5.4 battalions, 218 guns or mortars and forty tanks or self-propelled guns (SP) per kilometre.

Attacking in heavy rain at 1.00am on 9th August, 5th CAA caught the Japanese by surprise. The assault groups recklessly penetrated deep into the Japanese defences, leaving points of resistance to be taken by the 2nd echelon. For example, the 'Camel' strongpoint was taken by infantry, supported by tanks and 152mm SP guns, later in the morning. By nightfall leading elements of the 5th CAA were fifteen to twenty-two kilometres into the Japanese rear. Having broken the initial Japanese defences, 5th CAA deployed a powerful forward detachment of a tank brigade, two battalions of infantry and a regiment of SP artillery; this force, reinforced when it faced serious opposition, enabled the

Facing page top: men of a Soviet anti-aircraft, who unit had little to do during the Manchurian campaign. The Japanese air force there was heavily outnumbered and consisted of inexperienced pilots in training planes. Wisely the Japanese high command ordered their planes out of the region on the second day of the campaign.

Facing page bottom; the 'Stalin' tank, a powerful armoured fighting vehicle with a 122mm gun and frontal armour roughly four inches thick. Despite its power it was a relatively fast, light vehicle capable of taking on the heaviest German tanks. Its power was wasted against the Japanese, who were equally impotent against the T-34.

Right: a reconnaissance plane of the Soviet air force. Accurate intelligence was only one of the benefits conferred by control of the air. Not only did the Soviet air force provide invaluable close tactical support, thereby facilitating the advance, but they also kept 6th Guards Tank moving by supplying their petrol by air.

bulk of the army to move forward rapidly in march formation. Defeating two Japanese infantry divisions, 5th CAA, supported by the 1st Red Banner Army, entered Mutankiang on 16th August.

At the southern end of the Front, Chistyakov's 25th CAA demonstrated the value of amphibious operations, while the rapid land advance was also supplemented by several airborne assaults. The biggest landing was at Seishin, the second largest city in northern Korea. Three separate landings – on 13th, 14th and 15th August – secured the city for the advancing 393rd Infantry Division. An infantry division, a marine brigade and two maritime battalions held out until 16th August when 393rd Division arrived. Had the campaign lasted longer, it would have been evident that 1st Far Eastern Front had ruined Japanese hopes of a defence based on northern Korea and precluded any chance of the Kwantung Army receiving reinforcements.

The least spectacular role in the campaign was given to 2nd Far Eastern Front commanded by Purkayev. He concentrated his forces for an advance on three axis, ignoring most of the 2130-kilometre frontage. The Front's job was to 'fix' Japanese forces in the north while the two Soviet pincers joined in central Manchuria.

A distinctive feature of Purkayev's campaign is the use made of the powerful Amur River flotilla. The 15th CAA crossed the Amur helped by the flotilla, which then supported a 700-kilometre advance down the Sungari River into Harbin. The 2nd Red Banner Army was the only Soviet army unable to achieve surprise on 9th August. Held up in the Aihun-Sunwu fortified region until 20th August, they still managed to push elements of the army over the Lesser Hingan Mountains to Tsitsihar by the end of the campaign.

Purkayev was also responsible for operations against southern Sakhalin. Here, once again, the Soviets combined an overland advance

A Red Army artillery man loading his weapon. Soviet combat troops deservedly acquired a reputation for dogged defence, but in the Manchurian campaign they demonstrated their capacity for innovative and flexible offensive action. Anyone wishing to see the Red Army as a 'steamroller' would be surprised by the offensive panache displayed in Manchuria.

Facing page top: Red infantry take cover in light woodland prior to resuming the advance. In the First Far Eastern Front small groups of infantry spearheaded the advance, penetrating deeply into Japanese defences. Soviet infantry demonstrated that they had learned to create balanced combat teams with automatic weapons.

Facing page bottom: a Red Army nurse providing first aid on the front line. Soviet women played a much more prominent role in the fighting than their counterparts in the west. Fortunately, the skills of this particular 'angel of mercy' were rarely needed in the Manchurian campaign as Soviet losses were relatively light.

with a thirty-three-ship amphibious expedition. At the eastern extreme of the Front's extensive area, a division landed on Shumsu Island and, by 3rd September, Soviet forces had landed on all the Kuriles islands.

Japan's formal surrender on 14th August did not immediately stop the fighting in Manchuria. For a while it seemed that the Kwantung Army would continue fighting, but wiser councils prevailed and on 19th August Hata signed the surrender document at Vasilevsky's HQ. The Soviet advance continued; as the campaign ended ad-hoc airborne units occupied Manchuria's major cities.

The Kwantung Army had compounded an impossible task by responding ineptly to the Soviet threat. Despite basic weaknesses, such as lacking any air cover, (after two days combat Japanese planes were ordered out of Manchuria), the Red Army should not have won so quickly. The problems faced by 2nd Red Banner Army demonstrate that the Kwantung Army as a whole could have made things harder for the Soviets. Otuzu's plan for a fighting withdrawal was ruined by the disobedience of Ushikoru Jun, commander of 3rd Area Army, who failed to pull back from the frontier zone as ordered.

Nevertheless, the Soviet achievement should not be belittled because of the errors of their opponents; after all, the Red Army had worked hard to bring about these errors. The campaign was a virtuoso performance. It achieved surprise at all levels, created purpose-built forward detachments to maintain the momentum of the advance and displayed the capacity to take the initiative at lower levels of command. Only the precipitous end of the Asian War deprived the Red Army of recognition for an impressive victory. Nevertheless, Stalin's army had delivered the rapid triumph his political objectives required, thereby enabling him to underline the U.S.S.R.'s claim to great-power status in the Far East.

## 318 BIBLIOGRAPHY

L. ALLEN, *The Longest War* (London, 1984)

ANGELUCCI & MATRICIADI, *World Aircraft* (Sampson, Low and Mondaradi, 1977)

S. BADSEY, *Normandy 1944 - Allied Landings and Breakout* (London, 1989)

A.J. BARKER, *The March on Delhi* (London, 1963) *Dunkirk, The Great Escape* (Dent, 1977)

C. BARNETT, *The Desert Generals* (London, 1960)

J.H. BELOTE & M. WILLIAM, *Corregidor: The Saga of a Fortress* (New York, 1967)

G. BENNETT, *Battle of the River Plate* (Ian Allan Ltd., London, 1972)

*Naval Battles of World War II* (B.T. Batsford, London & Sydney, 1975)

B. BOND, *France and Belgium 1939-1940* (London)

P.M. BOWERS, *Boeing B-17 Flying Fortress* (Museum of Flight, 1985)

P. BRICKHILL, *The Dam Busters* (Evans Bros., 1951)

BROWN, SHORES & MACKSEY, *The Guinness History of Air Warfare* (Purnell, 1976)

H.C. BUTCHER, *Three Years With Eisenhower* (London, 1946)

P. CALVOCORESSI & G. WINT, *Total War* (London, 1972)

P. CARRELL, *Hitler's War on Russia: The Story of the German Defeat in the East* (London, 1964)

M. CARVER, *Alamein* (London, 1962)

W. S. CHURCHILL, *The Second World War* (Cassell)
Vol. I *The Gathering Storm* (1948)
Vol. II *Their Finest Hour* (1949)
Vol. III *The Grand Alliance* (1950)
Vol. IV *The Hinge of Fate* (1951)
Vol. V *Closing the Ring* (1952)
Vol. VI *Triumph and Tragedy* (1954)

M. CLARK, *Calculated Risk* (New York, 1950)

J.D. CLAYTON, *The Years of MacArthur* (New York, 1975)

T.M. COFFEY, *Decision Over Schweinfurt* (David McKay, 1977)

M.L. VAN CREVALD, *Supplying War: Logistics from Wallenstein to Patton* (Cambridge & New York, 1977)

J. D'ARCY DAWSON, *Tunisian Battle* (1943)

L. DEIGHTON, *Blitzkrieg* (London, 1979)

T. N. DUPUY, *Options of Command* (New York & London, 1984)

J. ELLIS, *Cassino, the Hollow Victory* (London, 1983)

J. ERICKSON, *Stalin's War on Germany* (Weidenfeld & Nicolson, London, 1983)

G. EVANS, *Slim as Military Commander* (London, 1969)

G. EVANS & A. BRETT-JAMES, *Imphal - A Flower on Lofty Heights* (London, 1964)

N.L.R. FRANKS, *Conflict Over the Bay* (William Kimber, London, 1986)

J. FROST, *A Drop Too Many* (London, 1982)

B.I. FUGATE, *Operation Barbarossa: Strategy and Tactics on the Eastern Front, 1941* (California, 1984)

M. GILBERT, *Finest Hour - Winston S. Churchill 1939-1941* (London, 1983)

C.V. GLINES, *Doolittle's Tokyo Raiders* (Van Nostrand, 1964)

L. GOURE, *The Siege of Leningrad* (Oxford & Stanford, 1962)

F. GROSSMITH, *Dunkirk - A Miracle of Deliverance* (London, 1978)

H. GUDERIAN, *Panzer Leader* (London, 1952)

N. HAMILTON, *Montgomery* (London, 1978)

J. HANLEY, *The Battle of the River Plate* (Picture Post Special)

J. HARRIS, *Dunkirk: The Storms of War* (London, 1980, 1988)

M. HASTINGS, *D-Day and the Battle for Normandy* (London, 1984)

INOGUCHI, NAKAJIMA & PINEAU, *The Divine Wind* (Hutchinson, 1959)

W. JACKSON, *The North African Campaign* (London, 1974)

G. JUKES, *The Clash of Armour* (London, 1968)
*Hitler's Stalingrad Decisions* (University of California Press, 1985)
*Stalingrad, The Turning Point* (Macdonald, London, 1968)

J. KEEGAN, *Six Armies in Normandy* (London & New York, 1982)

L. KENNEDY, *Pursuit - The Sinking of the Bismarck* (Collins/ Fontana, 1974/1975)

G. KENT, *Guadalcanal, Island Ordeal* (London, 1971)

A. KESSELRING, *Memoirs* (London, 1968)

J.D. LADD, *Assault from the Sea 1939-1945* (David & Charles, London & Vancouver, 1976)

V. LARINOV (et al.), World War II: Decisive Battles of the Soviet Army (Progress Publishers, Moscow, 1984)

B.A. LEACH, German Strategy Against Russia 1939-1941 (Oxford, 1973)

R. LEWIN, Rommel as Military Commander (London, 1968)
Slim, The Standardbearer (London, 1976)

B.H. LIDDELL HART, The Other Side of the Hill (London, 1983)

C.B. MACDONALD, The Battle of the Bulge (New York & London, 1984)

D. MACINTYRE, The Battle for the Mediterranean (B.T. Batsford, 1964; Pan Books, 1970)

K. MACKSEY, Crucible of Power, the Fight for Tunisia 1942-3 (London, 1969)

F. MAJDALANY, Cassino - Portrait of a Battle (London, 1963)

E. VON MANSTEIN, Lost Victories (Methuen, London, 1958)

J. MASEFIELD, The Nine Days Wonder (The Operation Dynamo) (Heinemann, 1941)

F.K. MASON, Battle Over Britain (McWhirter, 1989)

I. MATANLE, World War II (Colour Library Books, 1989)

T.G. MILLER, JR., The Cactus Air Force (New York, 1969)

B. MONTGOMERY, El Alamein to the River Sangro (London, 1952)

E. MORRIS, Corregidor, the Nightmare in the Philippines (London, 1982)

BARON B. VON MULLENHEIM-RECHBERG, Battleship Bismarck: A Survivor's Story (Grafton Books, London, 1982)

I. PAROTKIN (ed.), The Battle of Kursk (Moscow, 1974)

B. PERRETT, Tank Tracks to Rangoon - The Story of British Armour in Burma (London, 1978)

J. PIMLOTT, The Battle of the Bulge (London, 1983)

B. PITT (ed.), History of the Second World War (London, 1968)

I.S.O. PLAYFAIR & C.J.C. MOLONY, The Mediterranean and Middle East (HMSO, London, 1966)

K. POOLMAN, Ark Royal (William Kimber & Co. Ltd., London, 1956)

G.W. PRANGE, Miracle at Midway (McGraw Hill, 1982)

Q. REYNOLDS, The Amazing Mr. Doolittle (Cassell, 1954)

D. RICHARDS, The Royal Air Force 1939-1945 Vol. 1 The Fight at Odds (HMSO, 1953)
The Royal Air Force 1939-1945 Vol. 2 The Fight Avails (HMSO, 1953)

J. ROHWER AND G. HUMMELCHEN, Chronology of the War at Sea 1939-1945 (Ian Allen, Shepperton, 1972)

L. ROTUNDO, The Battle for Stalingrad (Pergamon-Brassey, London, 1989)

C. RYAN, A Bridge Too Far (London & New York, 1974)
The Longest Day - The D-Day Story (New York & London, 1982)

H.E. SALISBURY, The 900 Days: The Siege of Leningrad (London & New York, 1969)

H. ST. G. SAUNDERS, The Royal Air Force 1939-1945 Vol. 3 The Fight is Won (HMSO, 1954)

A. SEATON, The Russo-German War 1941-1945 (London & New York, 1971)

G.A. SHEPPERD, The Italian Campaign, 1943-1945 (London, 1968)

J. SIMS, Arnhem Spearhead (London, 1978)

P.C. SMITH, The Battle of Midway (New English Library, 1976)

J. SWEETMAN, Schweinfurt: Disaster in the Skies (Ballantine Books, 1971)

P. TOMPKINS, The Murder of Admiral Darlan (London, 1965)

R. URQUHART, Arnhem (London, 1958)

R. WARD, Fall of the Philippines (London, 1971)

R. WHEELER, A Special Valor: The U.S. Marines and the Pacific War (New York, 1983)

H.P. WILMOTT, The Great Crusade (London, 1989)

J. WINTON, War in the Pacific - Pearl Harbor to Tokyo Bay (Sidgwick & Jackson, London, 1978)

A. WYKES, The Siege of Leningrad: Epic of Survival (London, 1968)

F.E. ZIEMKE, Stalingrad to Berlin (Washington, 1968)

J.L. ZIMMERMAN, The Guadalcanal Campaign (New York, 1949)